CW01080866

# The Origins of Unfairness

# The Origins of Unfairness

*Social Categories and Cultural Evolution*

Cailin O'Connor

OXFORD
UNIVERSITY PRESS

# OXFORD
UNIVERSITY PRESS

Great Clarendon Street, Oxford, OX2 6DP,
United Kingdom

Oxford University Press is a department of the University of Oxford.
It furthers the University's objective of excellence in research, scholarship,
and education by publishing worldwide. Oxford is a registered trade mark of
Oxford University Press in the UK and in certain other countries

First Edition published in 2019

Impression: 1

Published in the United States of America by Oxford University Press
198 Madison Avenue, New York, NY 10016, United States of America

British Library Cataloguing in Publication Data

Data available

Library of Congress Control Number: 2018967875

ISBN 978-0-19-878997-0

Printed and bound by
CPI Group (UK) Ltd, Croydon, CR0 4YY

*To Jim*

# Contents

# Acknowledgments

So many people have contributed to the production of this book. Many thanks first to my colleagues Jeffrey Barrett, Jean-Paul Carvalho, John Duffy, Simon Huttegger, Louis Narens, Mike McBride, Brian Skyrms, Kyle Stanford, and James Weatherall for feedback at various stages of this project. Thanks also to the many graduate student researchers who worked on the project including Calvin Cochran, Emma Cushman, Travis LaCroix, Aydin Mohseni, Sarita Rosenstock, Hannah Rubin, and Mike Schneider. And thanks to other students at UC Irvine for feedback along the way, including Nikhil Addleman, Gerard Rothfus, Gregor Greslehner, and Ben Conover. Thanks to the Experimental Social Science Laboratory at UC Irvine, and those involved in running it, for facilitating experimental work on the cultural Red King effect.

Several visiting fellowships proved crucial in creating the space and time to write this book. Special thanks to the Pittsburgh Center for the Philosophy of Science, and to John Norton. Thanks to my fellow fellows and postdocs, especially Agnes Bolinska, for ideas and feedback. Thanks to the MCMP at LMU Munich, the London School of Economics, and Australia National University for visiting fellowship positions during the time I was writing this book. And thanks so much to the many people at each of these universities who listened to talks on the project, and gave comments and feedback.

Many thanks to both Ellen Clarke and Kevin Zollman for extensive comments on the manuscript, and thanks to Liam K. Bright and Remco Heesen for comments along the way. To all the other people who gave comments and feedback at talks but who I have forgotten about – thank you!

There were several collaborators whose work and insights were invaluable. These include Liam K. Bright, Justin Bruner, Calvin Cochran, Travis LaCroix, Aydin Mohseni, Hannah Rubin, and Mike Schneider. Special thanks to Justin Bruner, whose paper on the cultural Red King was the inspiration that eventually led to this book, and who collaborated with me on so many of the papers described here. And thanks to Nicole Bourbaki for ongoing support.

This material is based on work supported by the National Science Foundation under STS grant 1535139 "Social Dynamics and Diversity in Epistemic Communities". Many thanks to NSF for their support, and to Fred Kronz in particular.

So many thanks to my family and friends for putting up with me during the painful process of writing a first book. Maureen and James Weatherall, all my thanks for the extensive childcare and emotional support! Jim Weatherall, you are my rock. Eve and Vera, you are ridiculous.

# List of figures

# Introduction

Imagine you are in a group of ten people. In a minute, you will all be randomly paired with a partner. At the count of three, without a chance to talk or communicate in any way, you must dance the tango. If you both step forward, you'll collide. If you both step back, you'll look stupid. If one of you steps forward, and the other back, you'll do the dance successfully. This is an example of a coordination problem—a situation where actors have similar interests but nonetheless face difficulties in coordinating their action. Presumably neither you nor your partner really cares which one of you steps forward and which back, at least not as much as you care about executing complementary actions. In other words, what you really care about is coordination.

Now imagine a slightly different scenario. You are in a group of five men and five women who will each be paired with a partner of the opposite gender. And again, at the count of three, you dance the tango. This is another example of a coordination problem, related to the first, but with an extra element, which is that the group is divided into two observably different types.

One thing that is immediately obvious about these coordination problems is that one is easier to solve than the other. In the second case, just a small amount of information (something like one person shouting "women step back"!) would be enough to get the entire group coordinating effectively. If a group can be easily divided into types, and can agree ahead of time that certain types take certain actions, this eliminates the need for extensive planning later.

Likewise, one could imagine a scenario where instead of a group of men and women one was in a group with people of two different races, or observably different religions, or redheads and brunettes, or tall and short people, elderly and young people, goths and band geeks. In any of these cases the coordination problem is easier to solve because there are visible traits that the actors can take advantage of when coordinating their action.

Now imagine a slightly different scenario. You are in a room with ten really hungry people and five pizzas. Everyone is going to split a pizza with a random partner. There are many ways to divide the pizza—you could get one slice and your partner five, or you could each eat three slices, or you could even decide that one partner will get all the pizza—and in order to have a peaceful, happy lunch each pair is going to have to choose a division. This sort of situation is usually referred to as a bargaining problem, but notice that it too demands a sort of social coordination. No one wants to leave pizza behind, or to argue over the pizza.

One way to avoid squabbles is to decide ahead of time on some division that everyone will follow. Probably the one that sounds most natural to you is the 50–50 split. This sounds attractive, of course, because it's fair. Everyone gets the same amount of pizza. But there is something else attractive about this split. Suppose the group instead agrees that everyone should divide their pizza 80–20. Once random pairing happens, there then must be further deliberation over who gets 20% and who 80%. This is because the 80–20 split, unlike the 50–50 one, is asymmetric. In fact, 50–50 is the only symmetric division of pizza available to the group (assuming they want to eat the whole pizza), and thus the only one that completely solves the lunch problem ahead of time.

Now once again imagine the same set-up but with five women and five men, each pair of whom will go on a date. In this case, the group can solve their problem by agreeing on the 50–50 split, but they can also solve their problem by agreeing that each woman gets 80% and each man 20% of the pizza once pairings are made. The addition of gender here means that one single decision is enough to coordinate on an inequitable division in a way that wasn't possible for a uniform group.

$\bullet \quad \bullet \quad \bullet$

Humans continually face real coordination problems. Consider, for example, division of labor. Dividing labor in an organized way is crucial to the success of human groups. Households where everyone cleans and no one cooks are unsuccessful, as are societies where everyone is a soldier and no one is a farmer. Just like the silly dancing problem described above, in these real problems members of a group have to take complementary social roles to be successful.

Dividing resources is also a ubiquitous part of human interaction. In the workforce, coworkers must decide who will obtain the benefits, in terms of salary, bonuses, time off, etc., of their joint action and who will do the work to produce these goods. In the household, partners must decide who does how much of the work (dividing the resource of free time) and who receives which economic goods produced.

The central aim of this book will be to explore the ways in which social categories—especially gender, but also categories like race and religion—interact with and contribute to social solutions to problems of coordination and resource division. In particular, this book uses formal frameworks—game theory and evolutionary game theory—to explore the evolution of norms and conventions that piggyback on seemingly irrelevant factors like gender and race to solve these problems. As we will see, these frameworks elucidate a variety of topics from the innateness of gender differences, to collaboration in academia, to household bargaining, to minority disadvantage, to homophily. In particular, these frameworks help show how inequity can emerge from simple processes of cultural change. In groups with gender and racial categories, the process of learning conventions of coordination and resource division is such that in a wide array of situations some groups will tend to get more and others less. Clark and Blake (1994) wrote that: "... explanation of the origins of institutionalized social inequality and political privilege must resolve the central paradox of political life—why people cooperate with their own subordination and exploitation in non-coercive circumstances" (17). The answer to this paradox on the framework here will be that even if everyone learns to do what is best for themselves at every stage of cultural evolution, the group will still tend to end up in situations where people of one sort take advantage of people of another sort. No one is behaving irrationally in this story, and at every point everyone is making the most of their social environment. Once we look through a cultural evolutionary lens, there is no paradox—inequity is the expected outcome of basic cultural evolutionary processes.

According to Smith and Choi (2007), "In the history of social thought, accounts of the rise of inequality tend to sort into two categories: those that emphasize the benefits that hierarchy brings to all ... and those that emphasize exploitation or coercion by one segment of society" (118). This book is divided into two parts. Part I can be loosely understood as modeling the first sort of inequity, and Part II the second. Another way to think about this is as follows: Part I shows why social categories can play a useful social function, despite leading to some inequity. Part II shows why social categories facilitate processes that lead to inequity with no beneficial function.

In the first half of the book I focus on the role social categories can play as symmetry breakers in certain types of coordination problems. I start by introducing coordination games—simple models that can represent and inform real coordination problems. I use these games to show how groups that use categories like gender to coordinate behavior can be more efficient and more successful, in many cases, than those that do not. The result, however, is a differentiation of roles that, while mutually beneficial, are often inegalitarian. As I argue, the success of these social patterns means that we should expect groups, via social learning or cultural evolution, to adopt social categories for just this purpose. In the case of gender, groups take advantage of existing biological sex differences to create gender roles and conventions.

In the second half of the book, I shift focus to analyze the emergence of more pernicious inequity between social groups. I introduce bargaining games, intended to represent situations of resource division. Once categories have been adopted, the cultural dynamics that lead to bargaining norms are radically changed. New norms that are inequitable, but not especially efficient, arise. And once they do, they can be self-perpetuating. In other words, the development of types sets the stage for serious inequity to spontaneously emerge and to persist between social groups. I analyze, in particular, the conditions under which one social group will tend to gain an advantage in terms of bargaining and resource division.

One theme that runs through both halves of the book is that surprisingly minimal conditions are needed to robustly produce phenomena related to inequity that we usually think of as psychologically complex. It takes very little to generate a situation in which social categories (such as gender) are almost guaranteed to emerge. The preconditions under which models move toward outcomes that look like discrimination, inequity, and distributional injustice are, again, very minimal. Once inequity emerges in these models, it takes very little for it to persist indefinitely.

Of course, in the real world, gender and inequity are psychologically complex—in-group preference, stereotyping, and biases are clearly part of the story. Demonstrating that you don't need these factors to generate inequity, though, is important for a number of reasons. The models we will consider show us that even if we eliminate psychological biases, this will not solve the problem of inequity. They indicate that we need to think of inequity as part of an ever-evolving process. It is not something we can expect to fix and be done with.

Along these lines, at the end of the book, I use concepts from evolutionary game theory to address social change. As I argue, a cultural evolutionary framework can provide sometimes surprising insights into shifting inequitable norms of resource division. Even when moral education seems to have little effect on existing inequitable norms, it can nonetheless change the underlying strategic situation in ways that erode the stability of these norms, allowing for change later. Alternatively, existing fair norms can be eroded in ways that make them unstable, even though observable behavior has not changed. In general, as just described, the ultimate picture I present is one where those concerned with social justice must remain vigilant against the dynamic forces that push toward inequity.

This book also demonstrates how useful in principle tools from game theory and evolutionary game theory can be in elucidating causes of and potential solutions to inequity. And, in particular, it develops a general framework that can be used to further explore questions related to social categories like gender, race, caste, and class, and the inequities that emerge between these categories. I hope the tools developed here prove fruitful to others in philosophy and the social sciences who are interested in the emergence of inequity.

## 0.1 Overview

The body of the book, as mentioned, is divided into two parts. Part I, which includes Chapters 1 through 4, focuses on coordination, and, in particular, the case of gendered division of labor. Part II, including Chapters 5 through 7, shifts gears to focus on inequitable divisions of resources between social groups more generally. In Chapters 8 and 9, I draw together insights from both halves of the book.

In Chapter 1, I start by introducing a case that will be used to illustrate the role social categories can play in coordination—that of gendered division of labor. I then begin to build the evolutionary modeling framework used throughout the book by introducing coordination problems and coordination games. As I point out, once one builds models of coordination problems it is easy to see that different ones provide different sorts of challenges to groups. Some problems can be solved when an entire group arrives at a convention for a single, universal behavior. This will not work for problems where actors must engage in different behaviors to succeed. This distinction sets the stage for the rest of Part I, where I show how social categories can facilitate coordination in the latter kinds of problem.

In Chapter 2, I introduce the notion of type-conditioning, or differential treatment of interactive partners based on irrelevant social types (often referred to as "tags" in the literature). What does this sort of behavior entail in the real world? How does it function in a model? As I will show, once type-conditioning is possible in coordination games, it allows for populations to reach outcomes that can provide a benefit in terms of group efficiency, and often in terms of individual payoff, but that may be inegalitarian in character. In the case of gendered division of labor, groups use gender to divide roles efficiently, but in a way that sometimes advantages one side. Chapter 3 extends this discussion by showing how the presence of types and type-conditioning in a model radically alters cultural evolutionary processes. In particular, I demonstrate that groups engaging in coordination problems with types reach the beneficial, but inegalitarian, outcomes just described.

Chapter 4 fleshes out the upshot of these evolutionary models to the case of gender. First, I show how we can understand conventionality as coming in degrees, and how this should inform our understanding of the innateness of gender roles. The second main argument from this chapter is that from a completely undifferentiated society, the behaviors associated with gender, and perhaps what we would even want to call gender itself, can emerge endogenously as part of a solution to coordination problems.

Part II begins with Chapter 5 where I present an analysis of the role of power in the emergence of bargaining conventions. As I show, small power asymmetries, like those that emerge in Part I of the book, can translate to advantages for a powerful group. Furthermore, these advantages can persist in conditions where winning one bargaining contest impacts the power of a social group and improves their chances of winning future bargaining contests. In other words, they can compound. In Chapter 6, I focus on asymmetries in learning environments (rather than power) and the role they play in the emergence of inequity. I show how minority status in particular can lead to disadvantage as a result of the different learning environments that minority and majority members tend to inhabit. In addition, at the end of this chapter, I consider the role of power and learning asymmetries in intersectional populations. Throughout, I highlight how little is needed to generate inequity of a pernicious sort between social groups.

Chapter 7 extends this analysis to ask: what happens once inequitable bargaining conventions arise in a social group? In particular, does discrimination lead the oppressed to avoid their oppressors? To address this question, I look at network models, which explicitly represent interactive structures between individuals. As will become clear, discrimination can lead to segregation. Those who suffer discrimination from out-group members tend to choose in-group members to interact with instead. Though, as I will illustrate, when one group has advantages with respect to resources and power, a disadvantaged group will sometimes tolerate discrimination to gain access to those resources.

Chapter 8 models in greater depth a particular case of interest to economists and sociologists—the emergence of household division of labor and household bargaining. The models address how inequity can emerge in the household, and also why certain patterns of coordination are likely to arise. In doing this, I draw on both parts of the book, and show how the different sorts of inequity addressed in Part I and Part II can interrelate. This exploration leads into the final chapter where I focus on changing inequitable social patterns of bargaining. In particular, I use the cultural evolutionary framework developed in the book to ground a discussion of the conditions that facilitate or hinder norm change. As I point out, social dynamical patterns may mean that we are thinking about such change in the wrong way. Instead of conceptualizing inequity as a social ill to solve, a more fruitful approach will treat inequity as a continuing process, requiring continuing effort to counteract it.

## 0.2 Explanation and Models of Cultural Evolution

Before continuing to Part I of the book, I'd like to say a word about the methodology used.

This book attempts to understand deep mathematical regularities in some of the social dynamical patterns that arise around gender and inequity. For the most part, this work is highly abstract and highly idealized. In almost every case, I provide the models discussed with interpretations—matching up elements of the models to elements of real-world situations and, where appropriate, arguing that this match is a good one. I also use empirical work, when possible, to assess whether the models discussed are, in fact, providing insight into the phenomena under discussion. Because the book addresses many related phenomena these discussions necessarily vary in levels of carefulness. Some of the models presented are tied to the relevant phenomena quite tightly. Others are suggestive of the phenomena, but the details are not filled in as meticulously. This means that the explanatory role of the models will differ from case to case.

In some cases, the models discussed can be thought of as providing "how-possibly" information. If something can evolve in an evolutionary model under basic conditions, we come to believe that these conditions are enough to possibly support the evolution of that behavior in the real world. In other cases, I take the models to have deeper explanatory power, giving us insight into how some patterns of behavior may have *potentially* emerged. The difference here is not in the models, but in the epistemic role they play. In the "how-potentially" cases, the models are intended to increase our confidence in the potential of a process to have really occurred.[1] In particular, many of the examples of how-potentially modeling in the book will involve what Weisberg (2007, 2012) describes as minimalist idealization, where the model pares away causally irrelevant factors to reveal candidates for the underlying causal variables responsible for a phenomenon.[2] In still other cases, I will argue that

---

[1] These models can be especially important in directing us toward future empirical research (Rosenstock et al., 2017).

[2] Along these lines, Potochnik (2007) presents a picture of why evolutionary models that appeal to payoffs while abstracting away from the details of the mechanistic interactions that

the models discussed play an important epistemic role by outlining the minimal conditions for certain social patterns—especially inequitable ones—to arise, regardless of how these patterns were actually generated in the real world (O'Connor, 2017b). This kind of "how-minimally" modeling is especially useful in thinking about intervention. For instance, suppose we intervene on real groups via implicit bias training. If inequity emerges under minimal conditions that do not include biases, we should not expect this intervention to fully solve our problem.

Importantly, sometimes the same model will play multiple epistemic roles. For example, I provide models of the emergence of gender roles that I think potentially illuminate how these patterns emerged in the real world. At the same time, they demonstrate how such roles can possibly emerge from minimal preconditions. Altogether, the explanatory picture that emerges echoes Downes (2011), who emphasizes the wide set of explanatory roles that models can play.[3]

When it comes to cultural evolution, there are many modeling choices to employ. Sometimes the debates about the efficacy of these modeling frameworks (or the efficacy of modeling cultural evolution at all) get quite hot.[4] Part of the problem is that cultural evolution is itself a varied and sometimes disunified phenomenon. There is no reason to think that humans, with our big brains and our cornucopia of cultural practices, should undergo cultural change of the same sort in every case. In fact, there is room for many different modeling practices to successfully represent cultural evolution, with the appropriateness of the practice varying from case to case. (This said, for interested readers Mesoudi et al. (2006) gives an influential unifying account of cultural evolution, and Henrich (2015) gives an extensive overview of the varied processes of cultural evolution and gene-culture co-evolution.)

Of course, any one modeler will have to choose a framework to elucidate the phenomena they hope to represent. The sorts of behaviors

---

actually drive evolution are still useful. These models capture what we might describe as core causes of evolutionary progress.

[3] See also, for example, Nersessian (1999); O'Connor and Weatherall (2016).

[4] Cultural attraction theorists accuse those using population biology-type models of trying to fit the square peg of cultural evolution into the round hole of biological evolution. In response, cultural attraction theory is accused of circular reasoning. Evolutionary game theorists are criticized for over-simplification, while accusing others of building models that lack causal transparency.

this book focuses on include things like gendered division of labor, racial bias, and norm emergence in the workforce. These behaviors are the result of many processes. They are shaped by (at least) rational (and not so rational) decision-making, individual learning as a result of past events, social learning from successful or prominent social models, parent-to-offspring cultural transmission, and peer-to-peer transmission. In other words, the real processes shaping these behaviors are massively complex, and essentially unmodelable in their full detail. Rather than trying to pull these processes apart, I will focus on a simple change process that captures some of what happens—especially adaptive changes—in many of these individual processes. It will not be a perfect representation, but it can provide understanding while doing well enough. This method reflects a choice to elevate causal transparency, simplicity, and tractable explanation over complexity and accuracy. Philosophers of modeling have argued that models must always trade off desiderata, and this work is no different (Weisberg, 2012).

One might ask: why use models at all? Why not stick to empirical data in exploring these issues? Stewart (2010), in a paper modeling the emergence of racial inequity, compellingly justifies the use of models in this sort of case. Gender norms and norms of inequity emerge in the context of dynamical, human interaction. Empirical results gathered at a single time will fail to capture these interactions. Even if we wanted to gather dynamical data on the emergence of broad social conventions and norms, this data is often removed from us in time. Also, it often involves countless interactions across many, many social actors. In short, it is not practical to gain a full understanding of the dynamics of the emergence of conventions and norms in human society via empirical means. Models can fill the gap. There is something more to say, applying specifically to cases where social interventions are called for (as in the topics studied here). Social interventions are costly in terms of time and effort. They also pose a risk when they impact the lives of those involved. Models present a way to study counterfactual dependencies in the social realm with minimal risk, and relatively little cost. They can then be used to direct further empirical study that is well grounded in theoretical prediction.[5]

---

[5] Thanks to Liam K. Bright for pulling out this role for the models in this book.

# PART I

# The Evolution of Inequity Through Social Coordination

# 1

# Gender, Coordination Problems, and Coordination Games

Women in the Ashante tribe of West Africa make pottery to be used day to day for cooking and storing food. Men, on the other hand, are responsible for woodworking. In the Hadza tribe, men tend to hunt meat, while women focus on the acquisition of vegetables. In the United States during the 1960s, women were primarily responsible for preparing breakfast, while men did the lawn care.

These patterns are part of what is referred to in humans as the gendered division of labor. Across all observed societies, it is the case that men and women have, at least to some degree, divided labor between them. This creates an explanandum for social scientists—why do we see such patterns? It isn't as if human groups had to arrange themselves in such a way. Labor could have been divided by individual preferences or strengths. Or labor could be undivided, so that each individual does a bit of whatever job needs doing. This has led to questions like: do men and women have different innate preferences that cause them to naturally choose different jobs? Is there a cultural function fulfilled by this division of labor?

Part I of this book will illustrate (among other things) how social categories, like gender, can break symmetry in certain sorts of coordination situations, and so allow groups with categories to coordinate better than groups without them. Because of this functionality, as I will argue, cultural evolution has taken advantage of social categories, shaping many of our conventions around them. In order to tell this story, I'm going to make use of gendered division of labor as a key case. This is, in part, because it is so well studied in the social sciences, and in part because it is a paradigm example of how irrelevant differences between individuals can nonetheless become completely central to social coordination. Crucially, previous authors have argued that gendered division of labor is the starting point for gender inequality (Okin, 1989; Ridgeway, 2011), and the cultural evolutionary framework I develop will help inform how natural processes of learning and cultural transmission might lead groups to inequitable norms and conventions of this sort. As we will see in Chapter 4, a cultural evolutionary framework can also shed light on some puzzling features of the gendered division of labor.

All this is not to say that gendered division of labor is the only interesting case where the framework developed here might apply. Both caste and class are social categories that seem to be part of solutions to coordination problems. Since these cases are very different in their details, though, it will be beyond the scope of this book to carefully illustrate how and where this framework applies more broadly. In Part II of the book, we will consider models that apply straightforwardly to a broader set of cases.

In the Introduction, I described two simple coordination scenarios—one where people want to coordinate their dance steps, and another where they need to decide on a division of pizza. Coordination in the broadest sense of the word is central to this book. In particular, coordination problems define the set of strategic, social scenarios where social categories end up mattering deeply to the evolution of conventions and norms. I'll start the chapter with a brief discussion of gender and gendered division of labor, drawing out the features most relevant to the framework developed here. Then I'll discuss generally what coordination problems are and introduce the models used to represent them—coordination games. I'll draw on previous work in economics to explain why division of labor is, itself, a coordination problem in the standard sense. (Along the way, we'll discuss the notions of convention and norm, and the use of game theoretic models to represent them.) As we'll see, not all coordination games are equal. While some can be solved by conventions and norms that are identical for everyone in a society, others, those that require people to take different, complementary actions, pose a special problem. Coordinating behavior in these sorts of games requires extra information to break symmetry between those who are interacting—who is the one who steps forward, and who back? Division of labor, as it turns out, is just such a problem. Actors have to decide who will do which of several complementary actions. This will set the stage for the next two chapters, which will explore how social categories like gender can provide a means of symmetry breaking in these sorts of cases.

## 1.1  Gender and Gendered Division of Labor

### 1.1.1  What is gender?

The answer to this question is not straightforward. Gender is not a simple concept, nor is it a unified one. Across academic disciplines different definitions of gender are employed for different reasons.[1] Since this book is not a work of gender theory, but a work of evolutionary game theory that addresses social categories, we will want to understand the aspects of gender that have the most to do with strategic social behavior. In particular, I will focus more here on the role gender plays in such strategic behavior, rather than, say, how gender shapes personal experience.

Sociologists Candace West and Don Zimmerman, in their seminal paper, "Doing Gender," point out that "[i]n Western societies, the accepted cultural perspective on gender views women and men as naturally and unequivocally defined categories of being ... Competent adult members of these societies see differences between the two as fundamental and enduring" (West and Zimmerman, 1987, 128). The claim is that we tend to think of men and women as inherently different, and as belonging to clear, distinct categories. These categories seem so natural that until relatively recently, there was little push to examine them. Money (Money et al., 1955) was the first academic to use the term "gender role" to refer to something that associates with biological sex, but is not identical to it. Theorists have subsequently endorsed the distinction between biological sex and gender, where, roughly, the former tracks inborn biological differences, and the latter constructed social categories. (Things are not actually so simple because, for example, cultural differences

---

[1] In philosophy, Haslanger (2000) provides a discussion of different types of definitions of gender, and introduces what she calls a pragmatic definition—one that is useful for positive social change.

shape the development of bodies (Butler, 2011a), but such consider-ations are beyond the scope of this exploration.[2] See also Haslanger (2015b) for an analysis of the ways culture influences our concept of "sex".)

A useful notion of gender for our purposes goes something like this. Based on innate biological sex differences, we can determine *sex categories*, or categories that neatly divide the human population into types based on sex (West and Zimmerman, 1987; Ridgeway and Smith-Lovin, 1999). These categories piggyback on biological sex differences, but are separate from them because, for example, intersex people tend to be assigned to one category or the other and trans people may switch sex categories (Money and Ehrhardt, 1972).[3] Using these sex categories, societies develop patterns of social behavior that constitute gender. These patterns are governed by normative expectations for a person's behavior across many behavioral arenas.

So what are these normatively governed patterns of behavior? There are several broad classes of patterned behavior related to gender that I will focus on here as especially useful for understanding the evolutionary models that will be developed, though these will not capture all gendered patterns of behavior. First, cross-culturally, gender, as a rule, is used to divide labor, but this division is often conventional. In the next section, this will be elaborated. Second, sex category and gender identity is usually signaled, often elaborately, through both appearance and behavior. In Chapter 2, I will further discuss this sort of signaling in service of a more general discussion of social categories and their instantiation in models. Third, gendered behaviors are reproduced in human populations via learning and punishment. In Chapter 3, we will come back to the relevance of this to evolutionary models of gender.

---

[2] Butler (2011a) argues that sex should be understood "no longer as a bodily given on which the construction of gender is artificially imposed, but as a cultural norm which governs the materialization of bodies" (xi).

[3] Additionally, in some societies, there are more than two sex categories. For example, some societies have a third category consisting of biological males who are socially like women, such as hijras in India and some Native American two-spirit people. Other African and Native American societies have third categories for biological females who behave like men by taking the social responsibilities of fathers and husbands (Martin and Voorhies, 1975; Blackwood, 1984; Williams, 1992; Thomas et al., 1997).

## 1.1.2  Gendered division of labor

As mentioned, every culture divides labor by gender.[4] This is true even though human societies have taken on radically different modes of organization cross-culturally and over the course of history ranging, for example, from traditional foraging societies, to agricultural societies, to industrial, and to post industrial, societies (Basow, 1992). Within each of these categories are countless structural differences related to political organization, social structures, marriage rules, etc.

There are two sorts of ways in which labor is divided, the first relating to who does which tasks and the second to the overall amount of work done (Blood and Wolfe, 1960). Under the title "division of labor," I will be concerned with division of complementary jobs. The division of overall amount of labor will fall under "division of resources" and "household bargaining" in particular, and will be discussed at length later in the book, especially in Chapter 8.

Although every society divides labor by gender, this division takes on very different forms (Murdock and Provost, 1973; Dahlberg, 1981; Costin, 2001; Marlowe, 2010). Murdock and Provost (1973), in a classic article look at fifty "technological" activities in 185 societies including things like food collection, production, and preparation, material abstraction/processing, and manufacturing of articles. They coded these based on whether the activities were performed exclusively by men, predominantly by men, by both sexes equally, predominantly by women, or exclusively by women. They found that some activities, like hunting large game, metal and woodworking, mining, and (puzzlingly) making musical instruments, were performed almost exclusively by men across cultures.[5] Other activities—such as spinning, laundering, cooking (especially vegetable food), and dairying—tended to be performed by women. A larger range of activities, to varying degrees, were performed by one gender in some societies and the other in others. These included activities like making rope, planting crops, carrying burdens, caring for small animals, house-building, etc. Some activities were performed by both genders in

---

[4] Evidence discussed in Gibbons (2011) also suggests that this division of labor by gender in humans is ancient.

[5] Even activities like big game hunting, though, are sometimes performed by women cross-culturally (Bird and Codding, 2015).

some societies, though it has been subsequently pointed out that many of these activities, when more carefully parsed, consist of sub-activities that *are* divided by gender.[6] Subsequent research reports similar findings. Costin (2001), for example, looks at the manufacture of crafts for trade and sale and finds a substantial division of labor by gender though great variety cross-culturally in who makes what. The key observation here is that for a wide swath of activities, while each group divides them by gender, there is variability across groups as to which gender does the job.

In modern societies, like more traditional ones, household labor also tends to be divided by gender (Blood and Wolfe, 1960; Thrall, 1978; Pinch and Storey, 1992; Bott and Spillius, 2014). In a classic study Blood and Wolfe (1960) surveyed families and asked who performed which of eight household tasks. They found a significant division of household labor with some tasks usually performed by the husband (repairs, lawn care, shoveling snow) and some usually performed by the wife (cooking breakfast, cleaning the living room, and doing dishes), and a few that were performed by either gender (paying bills and buying groceries). Thrall (1978), in looking at household division of labor that included children as well as adults, found that only 20% of the tasks they considered did not fall largely to one gender or another.

Some have attempted to explain these divisions via appeal to innate sex differences in humans (as we will discuss in Chapter 4), though the massive cross-cultural variation in patterns of division of labor presses against such an explanation. A more promising line of explanation in game theory appeals to strategic aspects of coordination (Becker, 1981). The framework I will now begin to develop is in line with this second sort of explanation, though it takes a bigger-picture approach to the role of social categories and coordination, and emphasizes the importance of cultural evolution to understanding these phenomena. Let's get started by delving into the sort of strategic situation where social categories like gender can improve outcomes—coordination problems.

---

[6] Costin (2001) gives a few examples. "Among the Ashante in west Africa, women produced utilitarian domestic pottery for sale in the marketplace, while men produced ritual ceramic vessels on order for elite patrons" (2). Here pottery-making would count as one technological activity, but we can see that classifying this culture as one where men and women both make pottery misses an important division of labor.

## 1.2 Coordination Problems

What are the basic features of a coordination problem? Informally, we can boil them down to two. First, actors in a coordination problem usually have some level of *common interest* in that they want to coordinate. For example, in the tango problem described in the Introduction, actors want to end up at the same sorts of outcomes (where one steps forward and the other back). Second, coordination problems are *problems* because despite the common interest of the actors, it is nontrivial for them to coordinate their actions to meet these interests. This is usually the case because there are multiple ways for coordination to happen, and successfully coordinating involves settling on one of them. Schelling (1960) oriented game theorists' attention to this sort of problem. When actors must choose between many equally, or nearly equally, good possible joint coordination outcomes, how do they pick?

We can distinguish two classes of coordination problems. The first I will call a *correlative* coordination problem. In this sort of problem, actors in a social sphere need to coordinate action by making the same choice, or correlating what they do. A classic example is choosing what side of the road to drive on. In any society, everyone would like all members to drive on one side of the road, but it doesn't really matter which. To give another example, most societies have standard working hours and this standard allows for all sorts of further coordination (when restaurants are open, when trains run a heavier schedule, when people schedule meetings, when child care is available, etc.) In the US those hours are 8–5 and in Spain they are 9–2 and 4–8. It matters more that these happen at the same time than that they happen at any particular time. Another example relates to language. In each society, members would like to agree on which word means what, but the actual word itself doesn't matter (again, within reason).

There are also correlative coordination problems that do not need to involve broad societal choices, but more interpersonal ones. For example, a family might wish to do something together, and must somehow all decide what that will be. Perhaps the group could go to the movies, or to the beach, or to the fair, and while members may have preferences about which, their main preference is that they all do the same thing. The same sort of problem can arise for a couple on a date, or friends trying to spend time together, or work colleagues who schedule regular meetings but must decide where and when.

The second class of coordination problems I will call *complementary coordination problems*. In these cases, actors need to coordinate action, but they have to do so by using different strategies, or complementing each other, rather than by all doing the same thing. The tango problem introduced at the beginning of the book is a good example of a complementary coordination problem. People coordinate by taking complementary roles, stepping forward and back, rather than by both stepping forward or both stepping back. There are many coordination problems that have this complementary character. Consider things like getting on and off an elevator or stopped subway car. The people on the inside and the outside need to coordinate by doing different things, one group moving while the other waits. Or suppose two people want to order at McDonald's. Who goes first? What if two people arrive at a doorway at the same time—who enters and who waits (or holds it open)?

Division of labor falls squarely into this type of coordination problem (which will be further elaborated later in the chapter). Consider division of labor within a modern household. A single household needs a person to clean the bathroom, take out the trash, do the grocery shopping, etc.[7] However, there are many jobs to keep a household running, and it makes sense to divide them among various members. In this case, everyone wants to coordinate who does what, but often by *not* doing the same thing. (As I will elaborate later, this sort of division of labor is most important for jobs that require some skill. For entirely skill-less jobs everyone can more easily do a bit of everything.) In the same way, a village needs a police officer, a bank clerk, a grocer, etc., and ideally just one person (or a small number) doing each of these.

Another sort of complementary coordination problem relates to leadership. Human groups often need to coordinate flexibly, by responding to changes around them. Coordinated group action is facilitated by having one individual, or a small number, making decisions. For instance, a military without a strict hierarchy of leaders would be utterly useless. Even in romantic relationships, friend pairings, or small tribes, it is often easier to have a decision-maker than having to always make decisions by committee. In all these cases, actors can coordinate more effectively by taking different roles—leader and follower—rather than by taking the

---

[7] A similar point can be made about traditional households and groups if we substitute these jobs for gathering, hunting, toolmaking, etc.

same role. Now, though, these roles specify not a particular behavior, but a pattern of behavior (i.e. making the decisions, rather than driving on the left side of the road).[8,9]

One last category of complementary coordination problem we'll address, which will become particularly important in Part II of the book, involves the division of resources. Whenever humans jointly produce resources, or whenever they otherwise obtain sharable resources, they must decide who will get what. These problems have a complementary coordination character because in order to successfully divide resources, actors must have compatible expectations or demands for what they receive. We cannot both take home 60% of a carrot harvest. If our company earns fifty thousand dollars in surplus this year, we cannot each take home 30k. When two actors form a household, if they jointly take too much free time (arguably a precious resource) the outcome will be credit card debt and a pile of dirty dishes. Traditionally, these sorts of resource division cases have fallen under the heading of "bargaining" rather than that of "coordination," and they are usually represented by a bargaining game. I will wait until Chapter 5 to introduce models that specifically represent this sort of complementary coordination.

Lewis (1969), in his famous work on convention, calls the differences between correlative and complementary coordination problems "spurious" (10). As he points out, by redefining behaviors in a coordination game, one can go from one type of problem to the other. For instance, Lewis describes a real-world coordination problem he encountered while living in Oberlin, Ohio. All phone calls in the town were automatically cut off after three minutes. The coordination problem here was to determine which party would call back. This, on first glance, looks

---

[8] Notice that in the tango, the two partners must both know who will perform which of the two basic versions of the steps (the one that starts by going forward or the one that starts by going back). They also must select one partner to *lead*. Since there is no preset choreography for the entire dance, if both dancers try to lead, they will fail to coordinate, and ditto if they both try to follow. Both sorts of divisions are crucial for coordination in human groups.

[9] Millikan (2005) distinguishes what she calls "leader–follower" conventions from other sorts of conventions. These are conventions where one actor observably takes the leadership part of an established convention, and the other actor is then able to take up the follower role and coordinate. These are distinct from the types of problems just described, because they involve rigid, or semi-rigid behaviors that actors simply figure out how to divide via a leader–follower distinction. I refer here to flexible behaviors where the problem is to determine who will be the leader in general.

like a complementary problem—one actor must call and the other must not in order to be successful. As Lewis argues, though, one can instead think of the possible actions here not as "call back" and "wait," but as "call back if one is the original caller" and "call back if one is not the original caller." On this rebranding, a solution to the problem entails everyone taking the same action. As will become clear, this redescription of the problem is only available if there is some way to break symmetry between the two actors—some extra information available to determine who does what. (In his case, that asymmetry is provided by the fact that one person must always be the caller and the other receive the call.) For this reason, Lewis is overlooking a key difference between these sorts of problems. The restatement is only possible in some cases, and how to make a complementary problem a correlative one is a thorny topic in its own right.

## 1.3  Coordination, Convention, and Norm

In human groups coordination problems tend to be solved by conventions. When it comes to driving, the convention in the US is to go right, and the convention in India is to go left. As discussed, conventional working hours differ in Spain and America. In my childhood family, the convention is to go for a long walk after dinner, instead of playing Scrabble. My husband does the cooking, and I do the laundry, whereas we might have gone the other way.

Lewis (1969) was one of the first philosophers to bring game theory to bear on social conventions.[10] Indeed, he *starts* with coordination games in order to define what conventions themselves are. On Lewis's account conventions are behavioral regularities in groups of actors faced with repeated coordination problems. His definition is quite detailed, but, approximately, for such regularities to constitute conventions it is necessary that members of the group mostly conform to them, they expect others to conform to the same patterns, and they have generally similar preferences over outcomes in the problem (78). In addition, Lewis

---

[10] Though discussion of social convention by philosophers goes much farther back. Hume, in *The Treatise on Human Nature,* describes a convention with a coordination character. "Two men who pull at the oars of a boat, do it by an agreement or convention, tho' they have never given promises to each other"(Hume, 1888, Bk III, Pt II, Sec II).

stipulates a requirement of common knowledge, which is approximately that each actor involved knows that the things just listed hold true, and that the others know this, etc. If these conditions obtain, actors should be expected to continue to conform to their conventional solution to whatever coordination problem it is they face. Each expects that changing behavior will detriment them, and so continues to make the same choices. And, jointly, the actors continue to successfully solve their problem.[11]

On this definition, only groups of actors with high levels of rationality—really only groups of humans—can have conventions. Since Lewis's *Convention*, though, a body of work has emerged in philosophy showing that solutions to coordination problems can emerge endogenously through processes of learning or biological evolution, both for simple and for more complex actors. Skyrms (2010), for example, investigates how signaling conventions can emerge in evolutionary models as solutions to signaling games, which are a branch of coordination problem (and which Lewis uses to explain linguistic convention). The striking thing about these sorts of models is that they have served as successful representations of incredibly diverse sorts of populations—bacteria, vervet monkeys, humans, businesses looking to hire, etc. This diversity of explanatory success raises a question: are the solutions to these problems in human groups importantly different from the solutions elsewhere? In other words, is there an important difference between Lewisean conventions in human societies, and, say, alarm calls in animals? What about sex roles in plants?[12]

In this book, I employ evolutionary models with low to medium rationality requirements. I think it is useful to conceive of the solutions that arise in these as conventional, even when they do not involve expectations or common knowledge, or any of the human-level rationality requirements of Lewis. Conventions in this sense should be thought of as behavioral regularities across groups that solve coordination problems

---

[11] Schelling (1960), in his seminal work on coordination, has something similar in mind as the typical solution to a coordination problem—that actors have mutual expectations, and expectations about each others' expectations, driving them to a solution.

[12] Cao (2012), in a discussion of whether signaling games can represent neuronal signaling, makes a point relevant to distinguishing between these sorts of conventions. As she observes, if we look at different cases where signals "might have been otherwise" (the usual bare requirement for conventionality), some of these are easy to change now (like language), and others very hard (like bacterial signals). The sense of "could have been otherwise" in the latter cases appeals to deep evolutionary counterfactuals.

broadly defined. This is not a careful definition, but the goal of this book is not to provide an analysis of convention. The claim here, note, is not that *every* convention is a solution to a coordination problem. We will simply focus on a particular set of conventions that are.[13]

I would like to draw a few distinctions that will be useful later. The first distinction is between solutions to coordination problems that consist in behavioral regularities, on the one hand, and such solutions that have obtained normative force. Conventions, on the definition here, need not carry normative force. If bacteria have evolved a chemical signal that solves a coordination problem, this constitutes a convention. It should be obvious that if some bacterium fails to send this signal, the other bacteria will not shun or punish the dissenter, and there will be no expectations that something different *should* have happened. In human groups, on the other hand, conventional solutions to coordination problems often also constitute norms in the sense that members of the population feel that they themselves and others *ought* to act in a particular way.[14]

Arguably, most human conventions acquire some sort of normative force, and previous authors have argued that this is *always* the case. Gilbert (1992), for example, argues that conventions are norms because they consist in joint acceptance that a group ought to behave in a certain way. On the definition from Lewis (1969, 97) conventions are norms because one will be going against one's best interest by switching behavior, and so others will believe one ought to conform to the conventional behavior. Furthermore, others will respond badly to a failure to conform since it matters to their payoffs.[15] Weber (2009) defines convention as a

---

[13] The notion that every convention solves a coordination problem has been successfully challenged. Gilbert (1992) offers a thorough critique of Lewis's account of convention where she gives examples of social conventions that cannot be represented by Lewis's proper coordination equilibria. Millikan (2005), likewise, points out that conventions like saying "Damn" when you stub your toe are not well represented as solutions to coordination problems. Binmore (2008) argues against Lewis's common knowledge requirement for conventions, using an evolutionary game theoretic perspective.

[14] Although it is slightly orthogonal to this discussion, readers might be interested in Anderson (2000), who discusses several approaches to understanding social norms, including rational-choice and evolutionary-based approaches.

[15] Sugden (2000) outlines in detail why Lewisian conventions obtain normative force via an analysis of mutual expectations. And Guala (2013) uses an experiment to show that it is very easy for conventions in the Lewis sense to gain normative force, though he argues that they gain an intrinsic normativity rather than a "should" based on a consideration of others' payoffs as described by Lewis.

"binding" custom, where failure to meet it will lead to "sanctions of dis-approval" (127), implying that normative force is attached to conventions by definition.

This running together of conventions and norms in the human case obscures the fact that there is a continuum along which conventions hold normative force. For example, it is a convention that people wear formal attire to a wedding. Failing to do so will annoy and clearly is in violation of a social norm, but not to an extreme degree. Failing to drive on the correct side of the road, however, is an egregious norm violation and will tend to create quite a lot of consternation. Furthermore, there exist human conventions which meet the definition here, and even which meet Lewis's requirements, but almost entirely lack normative force.[16] Millikan (2005), who defines conventions as patterns of behavior that are reproduced, where part of this reproduction depends on the force of precedent, agrees that a distinction should be made between conventions and norms because many conventions are not typically followed (and thus are missing the "should").[17] An analysis from Bicchieri (2005) is perhaps most useful here. She distinguishes between conventions—behavioral regularities which actors wish to follow if they expect others to follow them because of the strategic structure of the interaction—and social norms, which actors wish to follow if others expect them to or will punish them for deviance. As she points out, stable conventions can become this sort of social norm over time, though this does not necessarily happen. She points out that this is especially likely when breaking a convention will lead to "negative externalities."[18]

Throughout the book, I will distinguish between conventions and norms, though, as mentioned, I think these are best understood as existing on a continuum. Because the work of the book consists in

---

[16] My husband and I have a convention of watching "The Office" together at the end of the day, but there is no sense in which either of us feels that we ought to do this. (Probably we ought to get to work on the laundry and dishes.) Failure to abide by this convention would lead to absolutely zero disapproval or censure by the other party.

[17] She gives an example of handing out cigars after having a child. This is not a convention of the sort I am concerned with here because it does not solve a coordination problem.

[18] Arguably, by definition, breaking a convention that solves a coordination problem will lead to a negative externality since it will lower a partner's payoff from what is expected. There are degrees to which this can happen, though. I might disappoint my husband by deciding not to watch The Office, but if I decide not to follow driving rules I might kill someone.

using evolutionary models to understand the emergence of behavioral regularities, I will focus on conventions to a much greater degree.

A second distinction has to do with the type of underlying coordination problem. Lewis (1969) claims that conventions are arbitrary, in the sense that they could have been otherwise. This arbitrariness is a key aspect of all accounts of convention. In her extensive critique of Lewis's account, though, Gilbert (1992) points out that there are coordination problems, in his sense, where "one of the two proper coordination equilibria gives each player a payoff vastly superior to the other, while the other gives each player a payoff little better than zero" (342). In other words, one way of coordinating will be strongly preferred by both players. For such problems, she claims, solutions will not be arbitrary in the right sense for them to be conventions. The tension in this critique can be resolved by pointing out that there is a continuum along which conventions are more or less arbitrary (as well as a continuum along which they are more or less normative). For some problems, there are multiple possible outcomes that might be equally good solutions. The left and the right sides of the road fall under this heading. In other sorts of problems, there are multiple solutions, but they vary with respect to goodness. For example, I cited working hours as a solution to a social coordination problem, but it is not the case that *any* hours will work. If working hours were from midnight until 8 am, people would be unhappy and unwell.[19] For still other problems, there might be one solution that is very clearly better than the others—in a pair of friends learning to rock climb, having the one with experience do the lead climb is clearly better than having the inexperienced climber do it, though the complementary roles could potentially be filled by either member. Coordination problems can be thought of as existing on a spectrum from those where there are many equally good solutions, and those where some solutions are more attractive (Simons and Zollman, 2018). I will call solutions on the former end of the spectrum more conventional and those on the latter end less conventional (and sometimes more functional). In Chapter 4, I will return to this theme to give a simple formal measure intended to capture where on this spectrum a coordination problem lies. As we will see, this understanding of conventions as having varying degrees of arbitrariness will help elucidate the conventionality of patterns of gendered division

[19] See, for example, Davis et al. (2001).

of labor. Let's now turn to game theory to start building models of coordination problems.

## 1.4 Coordination Games

Game theory was developed as a framework for modeling strategic interactions among humans. By "strategic," I mean any interaction that involves multiple actors who choose how to behave, where these actors care about what their partners do.[20] Coordination problems obviously fall under this heading—each person involved wants to make a choice based on what their partner does. If you step forward, I want to step back, and vice versa. Game theory attempts to explain and understand behavior by simplifying such interactions, modeling them, and then using a relatively bare set of assumptions about human choice to predict or explain strategic outcomes.

In game theoretic models of coordination problems—*coordination games*—actors have to coordinate strategies to be successful, and there are multiple ways to do so. In the last section, I sometimes described coordination problems with multiple actors. (In the military, for example, the coordination problem is solved when many actors align in a proper hierarchy that facilitates flexible action.) In this section, and throughout the book, I will focus on problems with only two actors. This is not because some of the interactions I will address cannot be fruitfully represented by more complex models, but because the goal here is to provide explanatory clarity, sometimes at the expense of more fine-grained representation. Furthermore, small games have been found, in many cases, to provide deep insight into behavioral interactions despite their simplicity (Sigmund et al., 2001).

### 1.4.1 Correlative coordination games

A game involves three things: *actors*, *strategies*, and *payoffs*.[21] Actors in a game are those involved in the strategic interaction. Strategies define what each actor can do (step forward or back in the tango, for example).

---

[20] Note that this definition does not require that these interactions involve conflict (as is sometimes assumed about game theory).

[21] Usually games also define *information* for the actors, or what each actor knows about the interaction. In this book, this element will be downplayed, since it is less relevant to emerging or evolving behaviors than it is to rationality-based analyses.

|  | Player 2 | |
|--|--|--|
|  | A | B |
| Player 1  A | 1, 1 | 0, 0 |
| B | 0, 0 | 1, 1 |

Figure 1.1  Payoff table for a simple, correlative coordination game

Payoffs determine outcomes for each actor given the set of strategies they have chosen.

Figure 1.1 shows what is called a *payoff table* for the simplest type of correlative coordination game—one with two players, where both coordination outcomes are equally preferred. The actors are player 1 and player 2, who each have two strategies—A or B. A could be "drive on the right side of the road" and B could be "drive on the left," and for this reason I will sometimes call this the driving game. Rows in the table correspond to possible strategies for player 1 and columns to possible strategies for player 2. Entries to the table represent payoffs to the two players for any combination of strategies, with player 1's payoff listed first. So if both players choose A, they each get 1. Ditto if they both choose B. If they choose A and B, they get nothing. They succeed only by correlating action.

What, in this figure, do the payoff numbers correspond to? The answer given by game theorists is *utility*, an abstract representation of whatever it is a player prefers or likes. Most game theoretic analysis proceeds by assuming that actors try to maximize their utility by choosing the strategy that is expected to provide the best payoff as determined by a calculation involving beliefs about the strategic situation. Sometimes it is easy to say what the best strategy will be. Other times, there may be multiple reasonable strategies to choose from. In many cases, expected behavior in games accords to what is called a *Nash equilibrium* (Nash, 1951). This is a set of strategies where no actor can deviate and improve her payoff. For this reason, these sets of strategies are thought of as stable and likely to arise in the real world.[22]

---

[22] Evidence from experimental economics indicates that, indeed, humans often learn to play Nash equilibria in the lab, though not always. (See Smith (1994) for examples of cases where experimental play does and does not conform to Nash equilibrium predictions.) Besides the Nash equilibrium concept, there are a host of other solution concepts developed by game theorists to predict and explain strategic behavior. A discussion of these concepts is beyond the scope of this book.

In any particular game, the absolute numbers are in some ways less important than the comparisons between the numbers for each player (though they still matter for plenty of things). Here it matters that player 1 prefers 1 to 0 and player 2 likewise, but this strategic scenario could also be represented by a game where the entries had 100 and 0, or 2 and -50 for the coordination and non-coordination outcomes. If these changes were made, the ordering would still capture the idea that each player prefers the coordination outcomes, and does not prefer one of these over the other. Once we use these games in evolutionary models, the significance of these numbers will shift, though, as will the method of analyzing the model. Instead of representing utility the numbers will instead determine how evolutionary change happens, and the details of payoffs will often be very significant. More on this in Chapter 3.

The game in Figure 1.1 has two Nash equilibria.[23] In fact, this is a general property of coordination games—that there be at least two plausible outcomes actors might end up at. The Nash equilibria here are the strategy pairings where both actors choose A or both choose B. In either of these pairings, neither actor can switch strategies and improve her payoff. (If either switches, she goes from getting a 1 to getting a 0.) Also note that, in this case, neither player prefers one Nash equilibrium over the other because both players get the same payoff (1) for either equilibrium. This means that they are both happy to coordinate in whatever way.

Correlative coordination games do not always have this character. Consider the games presented in Figure 1.2. In both of these games, there are two coordination equilibria, and they are the same as for the game in Figure 1.1 (A vs. A, and B vs. B). In both of these cases, though, there is a difference between the two equilibria. In (a), one coordination outcome is better than the other for both actors. While both players prefer to coordinate over not coordinating, they also both prefer B vs. B to A vs. A. This game represents scenarios where, for example, the less preferred outcome could represent working hours from midnight to 8 instead of 8 to 5. Note that this game moves slightly away from a pure

---

[23] To be more precise, the game has two *pure strategy Nash equilibria*. These are Nash equilibria where both actors play *pure strategies*, or choose the same action all the time. One can also consider *mixed strategies*, where actors make two choices probabilistically, but for now I will ignore these. For the most part, mixed strategies will only be discussed in this book when they are significant from an evolutionary point of view, and this will not be often.

|       |   | Player 2 | |
|-------|---|----------|--------|
| (a)   |   | A        | B      |
| Player 1 | A | 1, 1  | 0, 0   |
|          | B | 0, 0  | 2, 2   |

|       |   | Player 2 | |
|-------|---|----------|--------|
| (b)   |   | A        | B      |
| Player 1 | A | 2, 1  | 0, 0   |
|          | B | 0, 0  | 1, 2   |

**Figure 1.2** Payoff tables for two simple, correlative coordination games. (a) shows one where outcome B vs. B is preferred to A vs. A by both actors. (b) shows one where actors have different preferences over the two outcomes

convention character and toward a functional character, as discussed in the last section, for this reason.

In the game presented in (b), the actors now no longer have interests that perfectly line up. In each previous example, they preferred the same outcomes. Now, each actor prefers to coordinate, but player 1 prefers that both play A and player 2 prefers B. This game has traditionally been referred to (suggestively) as the battle of the sexes. The story is that a man and a woman would like to go out together, but she prefers the opera and he prefers the baseball game. Osborne and Rubinstein (1994) uses a non-gender normative story where two friends want to go to the opera, but one prefers Bach and the other Stravinsky. I'll refer to it as the Bach–Stravinsky game. Note that this game has a strongly conventional character, despite the modification to create conflict of interest. Here, as in the driving game, there is not an outcome that is obviously better. (At least from a general point of view. Players 1 and 2, of course, have views about which outcome is better.)

The Bach–Stravinsky game may be called a *conflictual* coordination game, indicating that while the coordination character holds, there is now some conflict of interest between the actors. Games are sometimes referred to as either conflict of interest or common interest games, but, in fact, many of the most interesting games in game theory are both. For zero-sum games, one player's gain is another's loss, for complete common interest games one player's gain is the other's gain. Bach–Stravinsky is a perfect example of something in the middle. Schelling (1960) refers to this sort of game as a "mixed-motive" game because it represents a "mixture of mutual dependence and conflict, of partnership and competition" (89).[24]

### 1.4.2 Complementary coordination games

In this section, I'll introduce the games that we'll spend the most attention on throughout the book, and, as we will see, that best represent gendered division of labor—complementary coordination games.[25]

Figure 1.3 shows the simplest example of a complementary coordination game. This two-person game is identical to that in Figure 1.1, but now the actors only receive payoffs when they choose complementary actions. The two Nash equilibria of this game are A vs. B and B vs. A. In these strategy pairings, if either party switches actions she goes from getting 1 to getting 0. For simplicity's sake, throughout the book, I'll call this game the dancing game, because in this game A could represent "step forward" and B "step back." A and B could likewise be "cook" and "clean," in a household. Or "lead" and "follow" in a management situation. Or "make pottery" and "make wood crafts."

As with the simplest correlative coordination game, actors playing the dancing game do not care which equilibrium they arrive at. They simply care about coordination. In other words, there is no conflict of interest in this game. Again, though, as with correlative coordination games, there are variations on this complementary coordination game that change the

|  | Player 2 | |
| --- | --- | --- |
|  | A | B |
| Player 1 A | 0, 0 | 1, 1 |
| Player 1 B | 1, 1 | 0, 0 |

**Figure 1.3** Payoff table for the dancing game

---

[24] He describes the following way of determining whether actors in a game have common interests, conflicts of interest, or something in between. Make a chart where the x-axis represents player 1's payoffs and the y-axis represents player 2's payoffs. Mark down a point representing each possible outcome. If the slope of lines between these points is always negative, the game is a conflict-of-interest game, and vice versa for common interest. A game in the middle will have both positive and negative slopes between outcomes.

[25] It is typical to call these "anti-coordination" games. There are a few reasons I do not use this label here. First, it seems to imply that actors do not wish to coordinate, which is the opposite of the truth. Second, they are sometimes referred to as "discoordination" games, and I have seen *both* of these labels applied to games where one actors attempts coordination and the other prefers to avoid it, like matching pennies. So I start with fresh terminology.

(a)

|  | | Player 2 | |
| --- | --- | --- | --- |
|  |  | A | B |
| Player 1 | A | 0, 0 | 2, 2 |
|  | B | 1, 1 | 0, 0 |

(b)

|  | | Player 2 | |
| --- | --- | --- | --- |
|  |  | A | B |
| Player 1 | A | 0, 0 | 1, 2 |
|  | B | 2, 1 | 0, 0 |

**Figure 1.4** Payoff tables for two simple, complementary coordination games. In (a) actors both prefer one coordination outcome to the other. In (b) actors have conflicting preferences over the two coordination outcomes

strategic character of the situation. Consider the games in Figure 1.4. They are complementary versions of those introduced in Figure 1.2.

In the game in (a), the two actors coordinate by taking complementary actions, but the overall payoff is better for both if they choose one particular pairing. This game could represent a scenario where, for example, one of the partners is better suited to one of the two complementary social roles. Perhaps one spouse really likes doing laundry and the other likes doing dishes. Obviously both will prefer the division of household labor that accords with these preferences. Or suppose that one person likes sitting down and thinking all day while another likes being outside walking around and talking to people. It is obvious which of these two should be a bank clerk and which a police officer. Throughout the book, I will call this the MFEO (made for each other) game since it represents scenarios where individuals fit well into complementary social roles. This game, like its corollary in the previous section, has a more functional character and less of a conventional one, since there is a preferable outcome for both players.

The game in (b) represents scenarios where actors need to take complementary actions, but one is preferable to both. For example, perhaps all members of a company would like to be the CEO, rather than the lowly clerk. When getting drinks at Peet's, everyone would like to order first, rather than second. In dividing labor, perhaps everyone prefers a job that gives them direct control over food resources. I will call this game the leader–follower game for scenarios like the first one mentioned here— where both actors would like to play a social role that has higher status or benefits. This is the first complementary coordination game we are considering that has a conflictual character. As will become clear later, these games are of special interest when it comes to inequity.

At this point, I have introduced quite a few coordination games, each corresponding to slightly different types of coordination problems. At the risk of overwhelming readers, I will discuss one further game that has a coordination character, but is less purely a coordination game. This is because actors have preferences about what happens when they do not coordinate, and these preferences can influence outcomes in this strategic scenario.[26]

Hawk–dove is shown in Figure 1.5. This is a game where two players have the choice to be aggressive or passive. If two aggressive types (Hawks) meet, they fight, to their detriment. If an aggressive type meets a passive type (Dove), the aggressive type takes advantage of the situation and extracts extra resources or benefits. If two Doves meet they both act passively and neither benefits at the other's expense.[27]

This game can also be interpreted as having to do with division of resources. Under this interpretation, the two parties will divide a resource of predetermined size (in Figure 1.5, this size is 4), unless they are both aggressive types. If both bargain passively, they divide the resource equally. If one is aggressive, they take home a greater portion of the resource. This could represent a situation, for example, where members

Player 2

|  |  | Hawk | Dove |
|---|---|---|---|
| Player 1 | Hawk | 0, 0 | 3, 1 |
|  | Dove | 1, 3 | 2, 2 |

Figure 1.5 Payoff table for hawk–dove

[26] I am being a bit imprecise here. A payoff of 0 in a game—which has been the payoff for non-coordination outcomes in the games so far—actually does correspond to a preference. Zero is better than −3 and worse than 3, for example. It is more precise to say that actors have preferences over which of the two non-coordination outcomes they arrive at.

[27] This game is sometimes called "chicken," and is interpreted in the following way. Two drag racers decide to play chicken. Both hurtle toward each other and have the choice to either swerve aside, or drive straight onward. If both drive straight (choose Hawk), they crash, which is obviously bad for both. If both turn, they do not crash, which is better, but neither improves their reputation as tough. If one drives straight and the other turns, the one who chose straight looks cool, while the other looks like a loser.

of a household are each incentivized to monopolize resources under the risk that their partner will instead.

Hawk–dove has two Nash equilibria—Hawk vs. Dove and Dove vs. Hawk. Again, these equilibria have a complementary coordination character. Both parties take complementary roles in equilibrium. However, those playing Dove would actually prefer that their opponents play Dove as well. In other words, they would like to be in a more egalitarian arrangement, even though this arrangement is not an equilibrium.[28]

Now that these games are on the table I will say something more general about when a game is a complementary coordination game. Figure 1.6 shows a payoff table, but with variables instead of numbers as entries. The usual requirements for a (two-player, two-strategy) game to be a complementary coordination game are that $e > a$, $c > g$, $d > b$, and $f > h$. These conditions hold for all of the complementary coordination games introduced so far. They mean that the Nash equilibria of the game will always be the complementary strategies B vs. A and A vs. B.

I have now introduced the games that will be employed in the first half of the book—a representation of resource division called the Nash demand game will be the primary focus of the second half, and I'll introduce it there. As mentioned, complementary coordination games will be of particular interest, and will be the main games employed to represent the sorts of situations in which social categories can facilitate coordination.

### 1.4.3 Why division of labor is a coordination game

In introducing coordination problems, I claimed that division of labor is a classic case of a complementary coordination game, but this claim

|  | Player 2 | |
|---|---|---|
|  | A | B |
| Player 1 — A | a, b | c, d |
| Player 1 — B | e, f | g, h |

Figure 1.6 A general payoff table for a two–person, two-strategy game

---

[28] The equilibria in hawk–dove do not meet the Lewis (1969) definition of a coordination equilibrium which is, "a combination in which no one would have been better off had *any one* agent acted otherwise, either himself or someone else" (14, emphasis his). Sugden (2000) calls these *mutual benefit equilibria*.

needs a bit more filling in. In particular, we need to explore why there is some coordination benefit to actors taking complementary roles in jointly beneficial labor.

Blood and Wolfe (1960) point out that "To a considerable extent, the idea of shared work is incompatible with the most efficient division of labor. Much of the progress of our modern economy rests upon the increasing specialization of its division of labor. A specialist is able to develop his particular skills in a way a jack-of-all-trades never can" (48). In fact, the complementary coordination games we have been looking at, when applied to the case of division of labor, implicitly make the assumption that Blood and Wolfe pull out here. There is no "jack-of-all-trades" strategy in these games. Actors can succeed only by choosing complementary strategies.[29]

We could consider instead, though, a coordination game with three options——two division-of-labor choices and one "jack-of-all-trades" choice where actors both perform some of each available task. Figure 1.7 shows such a game. Here we can see that actors get good payoffs (3) when they perform complementary tasks. When actors do not specialize, they get a less preferable payoff, 2, and when jack-of-all-trades types meet specialists, they each get a payoff of 1 since the various jobs are all being performed, but not at the right levels.

If tasks are particularly difficult to learn, as many traditional skills are, the payoff for the jack-of-all-trades equilibrium of this game will be very low compared to that for the coordination equilibria. In these cases, the model in Figure 1.7 will look increasingly like the dancing game. For

Player 2

|  | | A | B | A-B |
|---|---|---|---|---|
| | A | 0, 0 | 3, 3 | 1, 1 |
| Player 1 | B | 3, 3 | 0, 0 | 1, 1 |
| | A-B | 1, 1 | 1, 1 | 2, 2 |

Figure 1.7 A division-of-labor game with an egalitarian, but less efficient, option

[29] Notably, there is some empirical data suggesting that in traditional societies, failure to appropriately divide labor often leads to marital dissolution (Betzig, 1989). Furthermore, Gurven et al. (2009) find that among the Tsimane forager-horticulturalists of Bolivia, spouses choose partners in part based on their working abilities, spouses divide labor, and this division provides benefits to both members of the pairing, though the benefits may not be equal. They also find that higher-productivity pairs have more offspring. This data underscores the importance of complementary coordination to the success of a household.

this reason—that most human labor requires learned specialization—complementary coordination games effectively represent many sorts of gendered interactions. In game theoretic models from economics of the gendered division of labor, as we will see, complementary coordination games are a central paradigm for this reason.[30]

So, division of labor is a complementary coordination game, but this does not tell us what this has to do with gender. In the next section, I will make clear why correlative and complementary coordination problems pose different sorts of challenges to coordinating groups, and why this creates a role for social categories to play.

## 1.5 Pairs and Populations

How do coordination problems like those represented by the games above get solved? There are many answers to this question. When it comes to one-on-one human interactions, though, one obvious way to solve such problems is through communication, or else the development of a convention via individual learning.

Imagine that you and I are in a situation well-modeled by an MFEO game. Perhaps we are researchers synthesizing a new drug. You like pipetting, while I prefer working the centrifuge. I communicate to you which role I prefer to play, you communicate that you prefer the other, and the problem is solved. This sort of verbal negotiation is obviously more complicated in situations where our preferences do not line up so neatly. Suppose we are spouses and while one of us likes the movies, the other prefers a long walk. This scenario can be well modeled by the Bach–Stravinsky game. Despite the conflict of interest, it does not make sense to argue every evening about what we will do. Instead, we might develop a convention. Maybe we always go to the movies, or the reverse. An equitable solution is also available—switch movies and walks every other day, or week, or month—though this solution is less simple in that it requires us to remember what we did last, and suffer mild inconveniences from changing behaviors.

---

[30] Relatedly, Nakahashi and Feldman (2014) find that division of labor evolves in human groups when the benefits of acquiring skills are steeper, meaning that the situation more closely accords to a complementary coordination game.

One thing to note is that when solving coordination problems one on one, there is no real difference in solving a complementary problem from solving a correlative problem. Indeed, as mentioned earlier in the chapter, Lewis calls the difference between them "spurious." In either case, explicit discussion or the emergence of a private convention can solve the problem. One way to think about this is that in such cases there is always a piece of information that actors can use to break symmetry and choose roles—I am me and you are you. What I will point out now is that this is not the case when one considers many interacting individuals, all solving the same coordination problem.

Imagine a group where members periodically engage in two-person coordination games, but with different partners. For example, individuals might live with multiple partners over the course of their lives and have to divide labor with all of them. People regularly conduct business interactions with strangers and must decide whether to behave aggressively or passively during these interactions. And, in more mundane cases, group members engage in paired coordination problems such as choosing who will go first through a subway door, who will order their coffee first, which side of the sidewalk to walk down, etc.

What happens when a group of people play correlative coordination problems (ones, remember, where they must take the same actions)? This sort of problem can be solved when all group members adopt the same strategy in response to the problem—all choosing A, or all choosing B. (All driving on the left, or on the right.) If they do so, whenever any group members meet they will play a Nash equilibrium. Indeed, in real societies, these are the sorts of conventional solutions we tend to see emerging to solve these problems. We would be very surprised to see a country where some people drive on the left side of the road and some on the right, or a tight-knit community where people all speak mutually unintelligible languages.

The nice thing about correlative coordination problems is that they *can* be solved this way—with a single, broad convention that every member of a society should follow. In cases that are well represented by the Bach–Stravinsky game, where actors prefer to coordinate, but have different preferences about how to do so, some members of the society will be less happy with the social convention than others, but nonetheless in every case people will manage to coordinate, and benefit from doing so, as long as they follow the rule.

In complementary coordination problems, things are not so simple. Suppose every member of a group decided to take the same action by stepping forward in the dancing game. No one would ever be happy, because in each pairing actors would mis-coordinate. Likewise, if everyone in a society took the cooking role in a household, and no one the cleaning role, every household would have too much food and be completely filthy. Or imagine if everyone decided to play the role of the CEO of the company, or if everyone was socially aggressive, and never took a more passive or deferential role, or everyone tried to follow in all social interactions and never to lead. It is clear that there is no way for everyone to take the same role and do well, but there is something more to be said. For complementary coordination problems, there is no profile of strategies that a group can adopt that ensures the group always succeeds in coordinating. To see this, imagine a group that has at least two people playing strategy A—whenever they meet they fail to coordinate. Now imagine a group with at least two people playing strategy B. Again, they fail to coordinate whenever they meet. So, any group with more than two people (i.e., more than one person playing A and one playing B) is guaranteed to have pairings that fail to coordinate.

The distinction between these two sorts of situations can be illustrated by an example. Consider greetings in various societies. These are conventional, and take the form of handshakes, cheek kisses, multiple cheek kisses, waves, hugs, bows, and the like. All these behaviors are ones that both parties can perform identically upon meeting and successfully coordinate. In contrast, consider a greeting that is asymmetric, so that the two parties have to perform different roles to successfully carry it out. Perhaps one party must wave while the other bows, or the two parties shake right hand and left hand. It is perhaps noteworthy that standard greetings do not tend to take these forms. We see societies adopting conventions that simultaneously *create* the right sort of coordination problem (correlative) and solve it. Exceptions are greetings performed between actors of two observably different types. One example is the greeting where a lady puts out her hand and a gentleman kisses it. Or consider the convention of bowing in Japan. The lower-status actor must bow lower than the high-status actor.

A central observation of this book is that because populations cannot solve complementary coordination problems by adopting one conventional role, there is a function that social categories can play in these cases. In particular, actors can use social categories to identify what sort of role each actor should play in social interaction. This is not to say that categories provide the only sorts of solution to population-wide coordination problems; but they do provide a solution, and one that seems to crop up regularly in many real-world populations. In particular, we can conceptualize categories as providing an asymmetry necessary to redescribe a complementary game as a correlative game, a la Lewis. In the dancing problem one could relabel the possible choices as "step forward if you are a woman and back if you are a man" and "step forward if you are a man and back if you are a woman." Then the problem is solved when the group settles on one of these compound choices.

• • •

In this chapter, we introduced the central case that this half of the book will work around—that of gendered division of labor. As we saw, gendered division of labor raises an explanandum: why is there such regularity across cultures in the sense that humans always divide labor by gender? (And why is there such irregularity in the sense that these divisions vary widely from society to society?)

In order to start addressing this explanandum, we began to build a set of game theoretic models. I argued that division of labor is a coordination problem, and, in particular, a complementary coordination problem, or one where actors must take complementary roles to solve it. As we saw, this particular sort of coordination problem poses a special challenge to populations of actors. How do those engaged in it break symmetry and decide who will take what role? As we will see in the next chapter, social categories, such as gender, can provide solutions to this sort of problem by creating asymmetries between actors who are men and women, or black and white, or young and old, or brahmin and dalit. These asymmetries can improve group coordination, even when there is nothing relevantly different about members of the particular categories at hand. In the case of gendered division of labor, as we will see, gender provides just such a symmetry breaker.

# 2

# Social Categories, Coordination, and Inequity

In cultures where agriculture is mostly plough-based, men tend to have more power, and greater economic stability. In cultures where agricultural practices depend on hoes or digging sticks, not so (Alesina et al., 2013). The reason? Because ploughing requires great upper body strength, and is generally incompatible with child care, men tend to control crop production in societies that use ploughs. And as a result, these societies tend to be patriarchal.

The end of the last chapter introduced a special challenge for coordination—how can groups of people deal with complementary coordination problems when any profile of strategies adopted by the group will lead to instances of mis-coordination? (Or, alternatively, how can groups redefine a complementary coordination problem as a correlative one?) In this chapter we'll start to see why social categories provide ways to solve such problems. Men can step forward and women can step back. Or old people can go through the door first, and young people second. In other words, a group with types will be able to achieve a level of efficiency unavailable to a group without them.

As we'll see though, there is a catch. The efficiency gained by adding social categories to a group often comes at the expense of egalitarianism. In the Introduction, I introduced two sorts of inequity described by Smith and Choi (2007). Groups that use social categories to solve coordination problems often display inequity of the first sort—joint action with unequal roles can lead to unequal benefits for those involved. In the case of gendered division of labor, when men take certain jobs and women others, then only one gender will receive the benefits associated with whatever jobs they do. When there are clear advantages to certain jobs—such as control over a family's food supply—whichever gender does that job is the one that reaps the rewards.

We'll start the chapter by considering, in general, what it means for a group to have social categories, focusing on gender in particular. Then I'll describe how social categories can be represented in game theoretic models via types and type-conditioning. After that, we'll look at what sorts of coordination can be achieved by populations with and without types, noting, in particular, how efficiency can be improved by typing. At the end of the chapter, I'll explore the tension just described—that improved social coordination comes at a cost to egalitarianism.

## 2.1 Social Categories in Human Groups

In the models I'll introduce, two things have to be in place for groups to use social categories in coordination problems. First, members of the group have to jointly be able to identify these categories, or *types*, and to place other group members into them. Second, everyone must be able to condition their strategies on that membership. In other words, individuals must be able to treat people differently based on what social category they are part of, or *type-condition*. I'll define these terms from a modeling standpoint in the next section. For now, let's look at the evidence that these features are, in fact, present in real human groups.

The minimal group paradigm for experimentation in the social sciences nicely demonstrates how easily social categorization comes to human groups. A typical experiment of this sort first arbitrarily divides experimental subjects into groups, using meaningless criteria (a coin flip, for example). Subjects are then given an opportunity to perform a task, like dividing a resource between the other subjects. Experimental results show that subjects tend to favor those in their own group despite the arbitrariness of this membership. The division into groups alone is enough to cause type-conditioning of a special sort in these cases (Tajfel, 1970, 1978; Haslam, 2004).

In the real world, people often use external markers—either alterable or unalterable ones—to distinguish categories of people. Alterable markers are things such as clothing, hair style, piercings, tattoos, etc. Unalterable markers involve things such as biological sex differences, skin color, and body or facial appearance, including age or visible physical disability.[1] In particular, these sorts of markers can induce type-conditioning, especially out-group discrimination, much in the way minimal groups can.[2]

Of course, not all observable markers are used to identify in- and out-groups, or to type-condition. For example, there are no deep social patterns of behavior that depend on ear size, even though ear size is observable. Ridgeway (2011) uses the term *primary categories* to identify the groupings that societies rely on most heavily for coordination purposes. These are the sort of categories that, as Bicchieri (2005) puts it, "people tend to perceive...as natural kinds having high inductive potential and stability" (89). Cross-culturally gender and age seem to always be employed as primary categories. In some cultures, race, caste, and/or class also serve as primary categories (Ridgeway, 2011). In a meta-analysis, Kinzler et al. (2010) identify gender, age, and race as the most important social categories cross-culturally. There are reasons why these categories (and not ones based on ear size) are the ones we use. Gender is important to differentiate behaviorally for reproduction. Furthermore, heterosexual household formation means that it is a division that will be salient and present in many day-to-day interactions between household members. In particular, it means that dyads with a woman and a man are often the locus of joint production, and so benefit from categories that allow them to coordinate labor (Ridgeway, 2011). Age is also relevant when it comes to reproductive behaviors, and other behaviors where developmental stage is important.[3]

---

[1] Obviously to some degree sex and even skin color can be altered, but there is a huge divide between markers like clothing which can easily be donned and removed, and markers that take extreme medical measures to change. (Markers like tattoos occupy a middle ground, easy to get, difficult to remove.)

[2] Some theorists believe this is a result of out-group bias that was evolutionarily functional for early human groups (Cosmides et al., 2003). In other words, differentiating between those people who are kith and kin, and those who might be a threat, was important, as was reacting differently to these categories of people in some settings. Current evidence suggests that humans see out-group members as more homogenous than in-group members (Quattrone and Jones, 1980), and tend to dislike and discriminate against out-group types (Brewer, 1999). Modelers have shown how in-group preference can emerge in populations with types (Axelrod and Hammond, 2003; Hartshorn et al., 2013).

[3] Cudd (2006) argues that in explaining oppression, it is essential to look at social categories of this sort. The argument in this book will go further—as we will see, the bare fact that social categories exist is often sufficient to generate significant inequity.

As mentioned above, for these sorts of categories to play a role in social coordination, they must be recognizable. When it comes to gender, biological sex differences provide grounds for this sort of recognition in humans, but, in addition, people amplify the signal through dress, ornamentation, and indicative behaviors. As West and Zimmerman (1987) point out, "Neither initial sex assignment... nor the actual existence of essential criteria for that assignment (possession of a clitoris and vagina or penis and testicles) has much—if anything—to do with the identification of sex category in everyday life" (132). As mentioned in Chapter 1, one central aspect of gendered behavior, besides division of labor, is that humans adopt signals and displays to communicate their gender identity (Goffman, 1976; Lorber, 1994).[4]

What do signals of sex category or gender look like? Chances are that you can easily think of examples, though, as Lorber (1994) points out, "Gender signs and signals are so ubiquitous that we usually fail to note them—unless they are missing or ambiguous" (14). In modern Western society there are different standards of dress and ornamentation for men and women—women rarely wear three-piece suits, and men rarely wear lipstick, for example. In other cultures, likewise, it is very typical to see differences in dress and ornamentation for men and women. In Kerala (southern India), men wear a lungi (or mundu), which is a long cloth wrapped around the waist. Women typically add a blouse to this. Traditional Korean dress, or hanbok, consists of a long skirt for women and pants for men.[5] There are also behavioral signals of gender identity where the behaviors are not themselves strategically important, but nonetheless telegraph type membership. "Man-spreading" is a phenomenon recently much documented on the Internet, where people post pictures of men on the subway who spread their legs to take up too much space. Notably, no one is worrying about "woman-spreading," because this is a body position that women essentially never take.

---

[4] There might seem to be some circularity here—to efficiently divide labor by gender groups need gender signals, but these signals emerge to facilitate the division of labor by gender. As I will point out later, it is usually the case that a bundle of social features must be in place for gendered division of labor to work. While I do not develop a full account of how these features could emerge in concert, a plausible story involves some bootstrapping as both gender signals and full gendered division of labor slowly develop.

[5] The suggestion here is not that the only role of gendered dress is to successfully convey sex category, but that this is one functional role it plays.

What does it look like when members of a society recognize categories and use them to condition behavior? This can be observed when we see members of a society acting differently towards those in different primary categories under the same circumstances. Such behaviors are not limited to forms of in-group favoritism. Instead, there can be many ways in which actors type-condition, including favoritism for other types. Ridgeway (2011) argues that innate out-group bias primes the recognition of different types in human groups. Once we categorize people into types, this can set the stage for other sorts of type-conditional behavior to emerge.

Here is a short list of examples of research performed in the US finding type-conditioning. Of course, as noted, type-conditioning need not involve discrimination. These studies tend to focus on discriminatory behavior, though, because much identifiable type-conditioning is discriminatory, and discrimination is of obvious research interest. Researchers have found that when sending otherwise identical resumes out for jobs, those with male names and "white" names are more likely to receive job offers, and more likely to be offered higher pay for jobs (Steinpreis et al., 1999; Bertrand and Mullainathan, 2003; Moss-Racusin et al., 2012). Similar findings have been garnered for job applications where the candidate reveals that he or she is LGBTQ (Tilcsik, 2011). Black house-hunters are not given access to the same housing opportunities as whites (Yinger, 1986; Hernandez, 2009). Women, but not men, often receive negative backlash for assertive behavior in bargaining scenarios (Bowles et al., 2007; Tinsley et al., 2009). Black and female patients are less likely to be recommended for heart catheterizations than white males (Schulman et al., 1999). In bargaining for cars, female and black customers receive higher starting offers, and meet more resistance in bargaining prices down (Ayres and Siegelman, 1995). Employers treat Hispanic and white job seekers differently (Cross, 1990). This list could be extended ad nauseam, and to include other categories such as age and disability, as well as alterable markers. The point is hopefully made.

It must be noted that there are many cases where type-conditioning is necessary for a group to function well and social categorization sometimes allows for this. It is arguably a *good* thing to make a distinction between elderly and young bus passengers and to treat them differently by giving your seat to one type but not the other. It is a good thing for doctors to recognize that male and female patients, or patients of different racial backgrounds, may have different needs and to treat them appropriately.

## 2.2 Social Categories in Models

How do we go about capturing social categorization in a model? Throughout much of the literature, these are referred to as models with "tags," where a tag is a marker observable by other actors. Axtell et al. (2000) describe tags as having "no *inherent* social or economic significance—they are merely distinguishing features, such as dark or light skin, or brown or blue eyes. Over time, however, they can acquire social significance due to path dependency effects" (2).[6] In fact, in their models Axtell et al. refer to tagged groups by colors (i.e., "blues" and "reds") to make clear that these markers do not carry the significance that real social categories do. In this book, I use the term *type* rather than "tag" because I want to capture the way that types tend to be stable, persistent, and general identities in human groups.

*Type-conditioning* occurs when actors use these tags to differentiate their behaviors toward different types. As discussed in the last section, type-conditioning behaviors in the real world are often associated with psychological phenomena like out-group bias. In the models we will discuss, though, type-conditioning will be a thinner phenomenon. It will simply involve the possibility that actors develop different strategies when interacting with in- and out-group members. (Though in some places, I will introduce out-group biases to see how they influence outcomes.) This choice is part of the general strategy discussed in the Introduction of exploring the minimal conditions necessary to generate inequity. As it turns out, type-conditioning in this thinner sense will be enough, in many cases, to generate persistently inequitable social patterns.

Note that even with this stripped-down understanding of types and type-conditioning, the models have the capacity to represent situations where actors suffer distributional injustice, or discrimination. For example, we will see many models where groups of actors have evolved conventions such that members of one type receive fewer resources than members of another. Even without positing internal biases to explain how such a convention is maintained, we can say that the convention itself is inequitable.

---

[6] For examples of models with tags, see Holland (1995); Epstein and Axtell (1996); Axelrod (1997); Axtell et al. (2000); Bruner (2015). Many authors have focused on the role tags can play in facilitating cooperation (Hales, 2000; Alkemade et al., 2005).

## 2.2.1   Types and signals

There is an interesting connection between typing models and another widely used concept in game theory and evolutionary game theory—preplay signaling. In models with preplay signals, before actors play a game, they have the option to send a signal to the other player, and condition play based on any signal received. One way to conceive of types is as signals between agents that transfer information and, as a result, allow for conditioning behavior. First, player 1 signals that she is a woman, and player 2 that he is a man, then they play the dancing game.[7] In signaling models, though, an important part of what makes signals signals is that they themselves evolve. In a cultural evolutionary model, actors have the option to adopt a new signal if the current one is not working for them. Obviously when it comes to social categories, this is not so easy. This is why I use "types" here instead of directly importing the signaling paradigm. I am mostly unconcerned with how types themselves evolve for strategic purposes, and much more concerned with cultural evolution of other behaviors in populations with types that are essentially fixed. (Though, Bowles and Naidu (2006); Hwang et al. (2014) look at relevant models of class inequality where actors can change classes.) Furthermore, we will be interested, in Chapter 4 and in the second half of the book, in models where types encounter asymmetric interactive roles, and in these cases "types" cannot be treated as pre-play signals because such signals do not capture the asymmetric features of the multiple subgroups in a population.[8]

Note that the models discussed in this book do not represent cases where "types" consist in strategies in a game. For example, the types in a population cannot be those who drive on the left side of the road and those who drive the right side of the road.[9] Conditioning on an observable

---

[7] Relatedly, Skyrms (2004, 78) explores signaling models that are much like type models, where he sees the evolution of coordination in the dancing game.

[8] Of course, types can be amplified or diminished through dress, style, and behavior. This means that there are ways in which individuals can strategically change their type, at least to some degree, which would better correspond to a preplay signaling model. As mentioned, though, the goal here is to focus more on what happens to other strategies when types are held fixed. Thanks to Kevin Zollman for this point.

[9] In the literature on the evolution of cooperation, it is common to look at models where actors are able to recognize whether other agents will or will not engage in certain behaviors (whether they take certain strategies or not). For a few examples, see Frank (1988); Frank et al. (1993); O'Connor (2016).

strategy by an opponent moves away from tags as having "no inherent social or economic significance."

## 2.3 Social Categories as Solutions to Coordination Problems

As I have said, complementary and correlative coordination problems are different. Correlative problems do not pose a particular challenge to groups where members interact pairwise with many others. Complementary problems, on the other hand, do pose such a challenge. Suppose once more that we have a homogenous group of people playing the dancing game—who will step forward and who will step back? We should expect a lot of people stepping on one another's toes. Now we'll use game theoretic models to say, in greater detail, how types can solve this problem.

In order to do so, I must first introduce the concept of *expected payoff*. An expected payoff for an actor is a number representing what they should expect to receive as payoff in a situation where outcomes are probabilistic. For example, suppose we have a population of actors where 60% of them play A in the driving game and 40% play B. For an actor playing A, we can say that her expected payoff when she goes out driving is the chance that she meets another A player times the payoff she receives should she do so plus the chance that she meets a B player times that payoff. If we assume that she meets other players randomly, this comes out to $.6 * 1 + .4 * 0$, or $.6$.

I also must introduce the concept of a *population equilibrium* (as opposed to a Nash equilibrium in a game between two individuals). This is a set of strategies for an entire *population* such that no individual wants to change what they are doing. In a correlative coordination game, these consist in every person doing the same thing. (If everyone is driving on the right side of the road, no one wants to change to the left.) These equilibria, as we will see in the next chapter, are very important from a cultural evolutionary point of view, because they tend to be the endpoints of evolutionary processes. For now, we need this concept to compare how well people do in terms of expected payoff in groups with and without types that are at population level equilibria.

Let's start with our homogenous group playing the dancing game. As discussed, the group does very poorly if everyone adopts the same strategy. The best this population can do is for 50% of people to always step forward and 50% to always step back, and, indeed, this is an equilibrium. (If anyone switches what they are doing, their expected payoff will be slightly worse.) At this mix, when two random people meet there is a .25 chance they collide, a .25 chance they both step back, and a .5 chance they choose complementary actions. This means that, on average, the population will achieve coordination (a payoff of 1) half the time and fail to coordinate (a payoff of 0) the other half. This yields an average expected payoff of .5. We can immediately see that this isn't particularly good. In the very best-case scenario, everyone coordinates only half the time.

Now suppose that we add types to the model—half of the dancers are now men, and half are women, and everybody is able to recognize the two categories and condition their behavior on this. The best-case scenario is that men dance with women, and women with men, and everybody adopts one of two strategies. Either all the men step forward and all the women back, or all the women step forward and all the men back. (And, again, these are the equilibria of the population.) At these sets of strategies, coordination will be perfect in every case, so that the average expected payoff will be 1. The intuition here is that by recognizing types actors gain extra information that allows them to coordinate by picking one of the two equilibria of the game. When a man and woman meet, they can use the gender difference as an asymmetry to create expectations for who takes which role. When members of the same gender meet, this is not possible.

So, the addition of types to a model, in this case, can double successful coordination, and, as a result, double the payoff members of the group expect to receive. But, something extra was actually sneaked into the scenario just described, which is that men only met women, and women only met men to play the coordination game. We can also imagine a scenario where a group has two categories, but every pair of individuals sometimes engage in coordination problems. This sort of case occurs, for example, when deciding who will walk through a public door first. There are no restrictions on which members of a group will engage in this problem. Men and women and people of all races and classes approach doors at the same time and must decide who goes first. I will call this a *two-type mixing* model, in contrast to a model where everyone only meets their out-group, which I will call *perfectly divided*. For those familiar with evolutionary game theory, the perfect division corresponds to traditional two-population models.[10] Note that in both sorts of model the group is partitioned into two types, and everyone knows the type of everyone else. The difference lies in who meets whom.

Even in two-type mixing groups, where everybody can meet, types can still help with coordination. Suppose our group encounters the coordination problem where pairings of people have to decide who will hold the door and who will walk through. The best possible scenario for coordination is that when men and women play this game, they use their types to coordinate—women always hold the door for men, or vice versa. Whenever someone meets their own type half of people go to open the door, and the other half walk forward. In such a scenario, half the time coordination will be perfect because people have types to coordinate with (meaning a payoff of 1). In the other half of interactions, there will be a 50% chance of coordination (meaning an expected payoff of .5). This makes the expected payoff of the whole group .75, which is better than for a homogenous group, even though there is still some mis-coordination.

To get a more general sense of this phenomenon, consider Figure 2.1. (Readers who are less interested in technicalia may wish to skip to the next section.) This is a general, symmetric two-player game. A game is a complementary coordination game, remember, whenever $b > a$ and $c > d$. Let us further restrict our attention to games where $a + a$ and $d + d$ are $\leq b + c$. This means that actors at coordination equilibria cannot jointly do better by switching to a non-equilibrium outcome. Note that all the games we have looked at meet this requirement.[11]

Consider the possible payoffs for a homogenous group playing this game. Let $p$ be the proportion of the population playing 1 and $(1 - p)$ the

---

[10] In actuality, one can imagine a spectrum of situations where types interact with higher or lower levels of correlation. On one extreme are situations where actors only ever interact with their own types. These models are identical to models with no types at all, since they boil down to two individual, homogenous groups. On the other extreme are situations where actors meet only the other type (perfectly divided populations). Directly in the middle are the two-type mixing populations where interaction is not based on type at all. Henrich and Boyd (2008) consider two-population models that vary along this continuum. They find that when actors can learn from the other population, the level of homophily can impact how likely inequitable conventions are to arise. Because I consider models where actors learn from their own type only, we see similar between-group outcomes for all levels of homophily.

[11] We can make a version of hawk–dove where this would not be the case, though. Suppose that the Dove vs. Dove payoffs are 2.5 and 2.5, while the payoffs when hawks and doves meet are 3 and 1. The joint payoff for doves is 5, and the joint payoff at equilibrium is only 4.

Player 2

|  | | 1 | 2 |
|---|---|---|---|
| Player 1 | 1 | a, a | c, b |
|  | 2 | b, c | d, d |

**Figure 2.1** A general payoff table for a symmetric two-person, two-strategy game

proportion playing 2. Then the average population payoff will be $p^2 * a + p(1 - p) * c + p(1 - p) * b + (1 - p)(1 - p) * d$. This equation weights the probabilities that each of the two types meet by the payoffs they receive in meeting. (For example, because $p$ of the population play 1, they meet with probability $p * p$ and receive a payoff of $a$ when they do so.) The best this population can do is to divide so that $p = .5$, or each strategy is played by half the population. This maximizes the weight on the better coordination outcomes compared to the non-equilibrium outcomes. The best average payoff is $.25a + .25c + .25b + .25d$.[12]

Now suppose we have a perfectly divided population where one side plays strategy 1 and the other strategy 2. Half of this population will always receive the payoff of $c$ and the other half will always receive $b$. The average payoff will be $.5c + .5b$. Notice that this second equation will always be greater than the first. Why? Because $b > a$, $.5b > .25a + .25b$, and because $c > d$, $.5c > .25c + .25d$. A two-type mixing population (where everyone encounters everyone, but they all recognize both types) will always have an intermediate payoff between the perfectly divided and single populations, so their payoff will be greater than that of the single population as well.

### 2.3.1 Types all the way down

We have just seen how a group with two social categories can get better payoffs than a homogenous group. In many real-world populations, though, there are multiple primary social categories that actors use to condition behavior. What happens in populations with multiple kinds of types?

Consider a group with both men and women and young and old people. Furthermore, assume that these types intersect one another so

---

[12] Note that is will not always be a population equilibrium, but it will maximize payoff, so that if the equilibrium is $p = x$ where $x \neq .5$, the payoff will not be greater than at this point.

that there are young men, young women, old women, and old men. Forget about perfectly divided populations for now—in perfectly divided populations the group coordination problem is completely solved with two types. In two-type mixing groups, where everyone meets everyone else, however, there are still failures to coordinate when people meet their own type, which happens 1/2 the time. In *four*-type mixing groups, it will be less likely that this ever happens, because each person is a member of a relatively small subgroup and so meets their own type only 1/4 of the time. Whenever they meet another type, they can use the asymmetry between them to coordinate. In the dancing game, this means that their average expected payoff is $.25 * .5 + .75 * 1 = .875$. This is higher than the .75 that actors in the two-type group get.

This same argument can be given for more and more type divisions. (These need not be created as intersections of base types. What matters is simply to have shared divisions that all agents are able to recognize and use as symmetry breakers.) People interact inefficiently in these games only when they meet their own type. If the size of each type is smaller, this is less likely to happen, and so there is always a benefit of adding more type divisions.[13] Of course, at some point the benefits gained from further type divisions will be outweighed by the impracticality of identifying and remembering how one interacts with all these different types. It has been observed many times that humans are only boundedly rational, and that cognitive limitations will prevent some sorts of optimal strategies, from a game or decision theoretic perspective, from emerging.[14] Suggestively, Brewer (1988) argues that owing to cognitive limitations human groups typically employ only three or four primary social categories. Hoffmann (2006), in a model where actors use types to coordinate play of hawk–dove, finds that groups improve their payoff only by adding up to three type divisions. After that, as he says, "...the trait diversity of the population rises more rapidly than the sophistication of agent discrimination" (244).[15]

---

[13] This continued benefit of types is very similar to the continued benefit of extra pre-play signals that Skyrms (2004, 79–80) describes for a dancing game.

[14] For a compelling defense of bounded rationality in modeling human cultural evolution see Alexander (2007, 1–8). For empirical discussion of bounded rationality see Gigerenzer and Selten (2002).

[15] This result occurs in part because Hoffmann's agents apply their experiences to all the social identities of their opponents, rather than thinking of combinations of types as separate

### 2.3.2  Gradient markers

There is another way to use tags to solve complementary coordination problems in a group. Suppose we have a population with tags where the tags do not form categories or types, but instead have gradient values. In the model, this might look like a population of agents with tags that take values between 0 and 1—.012, .566, .78, etc. In the real world, this might represent a group where actors display different levels of femininity and masculinity, or engage in displays of social class to different levels, or have finely different skin color, or are of different ages. In this case, the solution to the coordination problem can be a unified rule such as "if my tag is of higher value choose step forward, if of lower value step back." This sort of tag can allow for perfect coordination in every interaction, assuming that actors' tags are finely varied enough that they never meet others with the same value.

## 2.4  Coordination and Discrimination

To this point, it might sound as if social categories are an unequivocally good thing. When we add them to our groups, we improve coordination, and everybody benefits. One of the messages of Part I of this book is that, indeed, social categories have the capability to do something for us. They can play a functional social role. But, as we will now discuss, this functional role opens the door to the possibility of inequity.

Before beginning this discussion, let's introduce some basic terminology from work on distributive justice—or the study of the ideal distribution of goods in a society. There are different norms one might want a social distribution of resources to meet. *Equality* refers to a norm where individuals ought to receive equal amounts of resources. *Equity*, on the other hand, is the principle that individuals ought to receive equal amounts of resource given something like equal contributions. Skyrms (2004) identifies the equity norm thus: "If the position of the recipients is symmetric, then the distribution should be symmetric. That is to say, it does not vary when we switch the recipients" (18). In the following, we will discuss unequal outcomes, which also can be interpreted

---

types of their own, but the general idea is that the benefit of breaking into further types grows smaller and smaller.

as inequitable in many cases—although actors in division of labor cases end up doing asymmetric things, there is no reason to think their contributions are deserving of less. When members of one gender control agricultural production, they benefit not because they are working harder, but because the type of work they are doing garners better direct payoffs.[16]

In the dancing game, the homogenous group gets an expected payoff of .5. When types are added, everyone gets a bump up to 1. In other words, types benefit everybody equally. But this is not so for all games. Recall the leader-follower game from Figure 1.4. In this game, remember, everyone would prefer to play B (be the CEO, not the clerk) where they get a payoff of 2, rather than A where they get a payoff of 1, even though everyone prefers coordination over mis-coordination.

At equilibrium, a homogenous group playing this game will be 1/3 followers and 2/3 leaders. (While a 50–50 profile would make the average payoff better, some followers would do better to switch and be leaders, meaning that it isn't an equilibrium.) When the group takes these strategies, everyone gets an expected payoff of 2/3.[17] Once we add types, however, at equilibrium we see different payoffs for the two types. If men play B and women A, then men get a payoff of 2 and women a payoff of 1. (In the two-type mixing group, where all meet one another, women get 5/6 and men get 4/3.) The reason this payoff difference is possible is that no one can switch types—if they could, they would until payoffs were the same and equilibrium was reached. Social categories provide the extra information needed to facilitate coordination, but they also block people from taking certain social roles, and, in doing so, create the possibility of unequal outcomes. In fact, one of the things that make social categories so effective at solving coordination problems is that people can't switch categories—they are stuck in their complementary roles.

Outcomes where members of one type play B and the other A are unequal, potentially inequitable, and furthermore can represent discrim-

---

[16] It is beyond the purview of this book to discuss implications of the modeling work here for theories of distributive justice. Okin (1989) argues compellingly that because of the sort of type-based inequities modeled here, any such theory must take gender into account.

[17] Followers meet leaders 2/3 of the time, and when they do they get a payoff of 1. Leaders meet followers 1/3 of the time and when they do they get a payoff of 2. $2/3 * 1 = 1/3 * 2 = 2/3$.

inatory conventions.[18] People treat those in different social categories differently, and as a result one sort gets poorer outcomes, on average, than the other. This could represent a situation where because women work at home they have less freedom and control over their lives, or where members of a lower caste do a job that yields fewer material benefits.

So now the story is more complicated—types allow for coordination, but they also allow for inequality. There is another kink though. For many complementary coordination problems, even though type–conditioning creates inequalities, it is still better for *both* types. To see what I mean by this, consider the last case just described. Men do better than women (2 versus 1). But they *both* do better than the homogenous group where everyone gets 2/3. From a payoff point of view, the discriminatory outcome with coordination is better for everyone than the egalitarian outcome without it. The type that ends up discriminated against should still choose a state of unequal coordination over one of equal disarray.

This last observation isn't necessarily true for games where actors care about what happens when they do not manage to coordinate. In hawk-dove, a homogenous group can get an average payoff of 1.5.[19] If a group is perfectly divided, hawks expect to receive a payoff of 3, because they always meet doves, and doves expect a payoff of 1. In other words, doves receive a *lower* payoff than they would expect in the homogenous group.

One might well ask—how common are these different sorts of scenarios in human populations? Which of these games represent real-world interactions? Understanding this may help us understand whether typing actually hurts people as opposed to creating an unequal situation that nonetheless benefits all involved. The answer to this question must necessarily be a very complicated one, and different for different groups. As discussed in Chapter 1, there are many, many complementary coordination problems that groups of people solve. These will be best modeled by various of the games that I have presented. One thing that I will elaborate on in Chapter 5 is that advantage will tend to accrue for

---

[18] For previous authors who have used this sort of outcome to represent discrimination see Axtell et al. (2000); López-Paredes et al. (2004); Phan et al. (2005); Stewart (2010); Poza et al. (2011); Bruner (2017); Bruner and O'Connor (2015); O'Connor and Bruner (2017).

[19] Doves meet doves half the time and get a payoff of 2. They meet hawks the other half of the time and get a payoff of 1. These outcomes average to 1.5. Hawks meet doves half the time and get a payoff of 3, and receive 0 the rest of the time upon meeting hawks. Again this leads to an expected payoff of 1.5.

members of the same types across situations. This exacerbates concerns about inequity. Ultimately, types can emerge to play a role in mutually beneficial coordination (the first sort of inequity) but come to facilitate the second sort of inequity, which entails advantages to only one group, and fails to fulfill any beneficial social function. On this picture, even when there is sometimes a benefit gained for the first sort of inequity, the overall result is a disadvantage to one type.[20]

## 2.5  Other Solution Concepts for Complementary Coordination

As I've hinted at, breaking groups into social categories isn't the only way to solve complementary coordination problems. In particular, there are a few solution concepts that bear some relationship to type-based solutions. The first is from Aumann (1974, 1987), who describes what he calls *correlated equilibria*. These are equilibria where actors use some external correlating device to determine which equilibrium to choose when confronted with games with multiple equilibria. For an example, consider hawk–dove, but let us consider the "chicken" interpretation— you and another actor are both deciding whether to swerve or drive straight in a game of chicken.[21] Suppose that you and the other player really don't want to crash and you secretly decide to use a nearby traffic light to avoid this worst-case scenario. If it is green, you will be the one who swerves. If it is red, your opponent will swerve. In this way, you use further information from the world—the state of the traffic light— to choose an equilibrium.[22]

---

[20] Notice that, of course, this entire discussion centers around payoffs. One might point out that there are ways this framework will fail to capture relevant aspects of inequity inherent in gender roles, such as restrictions on personal freedom. Okin (1989), for example, points out that a Rawlsian should require the abolition of gender, since restriction to gender roles based on irrelevant types is inconsistent with his notions of political justice.

[21] Because you are apparently in a 1950's greaser gang?

[22] For work in philosophy arguing for the importance of correlated equilibrium type concepts see Vanderschraaf (1995). For an example from biology, consider organisms that broadcast their gametes. This usually occurs in the ocean, and can pose a problem because gametes are tiny, and each faces the challenging task of finding another gamete of the right type to combine with in order to mate. To do this, they must coordinate spatially, and also temporally. This is a correlative coordination problem, then. There are many possible times available for gamete release and individuals do best to release all at once. If females broadcast their eggs three days after males broadcast their sperm so much for all of them.

Skyrms (2014) discusses the evolution of correlating devices to solve the coordination problem in hawk–dove. He points out that strategies incorporating an external correlating device take over populations without such strategies. Where do such correlational devices come from, though? (We can't use traffic lights for everything.) In complementary coordination games, another way to think about the role types and type-conditioning can play in coordination is as a correlating device. The observable difference between players takes the role of the traffic light in providing the extra information necessary for equilibrium selection.

The second concept, arguably more relevant to that of types and type-conditioning in coordination games, is that of uncorrelated asymmetry, from Maynard-Smith (1982) who addresses complementary coordination games in the biological realm. In these games, as he points out, actors can use extra bits of information unrelated to the game in question, or uncorrelated asymmetries, to break symmetry. These allow actors to figure out who plays which role and so turn complementary coordination games to correlative coordination games.

To see how this works, consider another example employing hawk–dove, but now where the players involve a property owner and an intruder on the property. In this problem, there is extra information, which is that one player is the owner and the other the intruder. A single convention such as "play hawk if owner and dove if intruder" can solve the population coordination problem (Maynard-Smith and Parker, 1976; Skyrms, 2014).

With types and type-conditioning, something very similar is happening. Actors are using observable types to turn the game into a correlative coordination game. Now the uncorrelated asymmetries are social categories, and the choices that the entire population arrives at are things like "play A if woman and B if man." There is a disanalogy, of course, because men and women have no chance to play the other role. This also means that they need not keep track of a conditional behavioral rule, (i.e., they don't need to know what to do when in the other situation).

Note both of these concepts can be phrased in terms of information. A correlating device gives extra information to the players which they

Moonlight can play the role of an external correlating device that allows actors to correlate their behavior (Kaniewska et al., 2015). In this case, the solution is both conventional—because there are multiple possible solutions—and functional, because moonlight itself correlates with the state of the tides, so there are better and worse levels of moonlight to use for coordination.

use to choose roles in a coordination game. An uncorrelated asymmetry builds extra information into the structure of the game. This, of course, ties into the idea of conceiving of types as signals to other players. Under this framework, types are literally a way of transferring information to the other opponent to allow for coordination.

• • •

Social categories are a solution for groups engaged in complementary coordination problems. They create asymmetries that answer the question, who should do what? In doing so, though, they also create a situation where a preferred role is always taken by members of one category—where men always plough and control livestock, for example. Thus we see a case where inequity is the result of features that play a social functional role. Now we'll fill out this picture further by adding the dynamics of social change. As we'll see, in cultural groups with social categories, cultural evolutionary patterns are radically shifted in ways that lead to norms where different groups play different complementary roles, and where inequity results.

# 3

# Cultural Evolution with Social Categories

Cultures that use the plough for agriculture are more patriarchal than those that use the hoe, but that is not the end of the story.

In communities descended from those that used plough-based agriculture, women tend to work outside the home less, and there is greater gender inequality (Alesina et al., 2013). In other words, these cultures have developed norms of gender inequality, which have staying power over cultural evolutionary time, even under new circumstances where there is no current ecological reason for men to be more powerful.

In the last chapter, I discussed type-conditioning, and described how type divisions can facilitate efficient outcomes in complementary coordination games that are unavailable to homogenous groups. In this chapter, I move on to explicitly evolutionary models. I follow authors like Young (1993a), Skyrms (1996), and Bicchieri (2005) in thinking of these models as capable of representing the emergence of conventions between actors in different social groups. What we will see is that from a starting point of uncoordinated behavior, groups move toward states where everyone follows unified patterns in a way that tends to lead to successful outcomes. Once groups have arrived at these coordinated behaviors they tend to remain there, so that the patterns of behavior persist over time.[1]

---

[1] Of course, there are mismatches between model and world. Actors in these models will uniformly adopt the same sorts of behavior, whereas real-world conventions and norms are followed to greater or lesser degrees, and almost never universally. These real patterns, though, involve what Young (2015) calls *compression*. The vast variety of human choices are compressed so that normative or conventional behaviors happen much more than would be expected if these patterns had not evolved culturally. The models capture this idea—that from an uncoordinated state emerges relative coordination.

As we will see, when a group develops norms and conventions, the addition of social categories radically changes the evolutionary process. Entirely different sets of norms are expected to emerge in a group with social categories from those emerging in a homogenous one. In particular, groups with categories reach the inequitable, but efficient, outcomes described in the last chapter. Thus we manage to answer the explanandum for social scientists regarding gendered division of labor. Why do all cultures divide labor by gender? In situations where groups encounter complementary coordination problems, gender improves efficiency by dint of breaking symmetry. This efficiency drives cultural evolutionary processes to select norms where gender plays this role, whether or not these norms are equitable.

I will begin by describing a different set of models entirely. In economics, the question of why gendered division of labor is so ubiquitous has also been addressed using models where actors must take complementary roles to succeed. As I argue, these models capture important insights about the strategic situation that generates gendered division of labor, but miss some crucial aspects of the process by which groups end up divided by gender. I will then describe and discuss the strategy used here to model cultural evolution, including some non-trivial modeling choices. We'll move on to look at what happens to groups in cultural evolutionary models who play complementary coordination games, noting, in particular, the differences between outcomes in groups with social categories. Although one might question some of the modeling choices used to generate these results, as we will see, the results are supported by a host of related models from across the social sciences. In other words, they are highly robust, supporting the claim that we should expect real cultural evolutionary processes to take advantage of social categories to solve coordination problems. I finish by showing how radically the addition of social categories changes the evolutionary process even when complementary coordination is not occurring—for models of correlative coordination and prosociality.

## 3.1 Rational Choice and Division of Labor

Economists, starting with Becker (1981), employ models of the marriage market to explain widespread household division of labor. As mentioned, these models are in some ways similar to the ones in this book, but are based in rational choice (rather than cultural evolutionary processes), and put weight on the idea that individuals choose to specialize in certain types of labor to impress potential mates. Here I will not survey this literature, but will discuss some representative work from it.[2]

Hadfield (1999) presents a model of a population with two types where these each form households with only the other type. It is assumed that actors invest in skills before marriage, and that they may choose between two types of skill sets—representing those appropriate for home and market labor. This investment translates into payoffs after marriage where those with strong skills in either area will generate better outcomes for the household. Lastly, actors choose partners based on whether they have complementary skills. As she shows, the only plausible equilibria of this model are those where all males specialize in one of the two forms of labor, and all females in the other form. This is because actors need to make choices about skill specialization well ahead of when the actual coordination interaction happens. The benefits of skill learning mean that households do best when each individual fully specializes. Gender acts as a symmetry breaker which allows all individuals in the population to successfully commit to a skill that they know will pair well with the skill their future partner has learned. In other words, benefits of coordination, along with a desire to cultivate skills that will attract a mate, can lead to complete division of labor even if the types are modeled as otherwise identical.

These models, much like those here, show that when specialization is beneficial, and when types meet for interaction, society-wide patterns of division of labor are stable equilibria. The difference from evolutionary models is that the story of how actors come to reach these equilibria is not particularly filled in, and when we try to fill it in using the assumptions of the model, things look implausible. In order to reach such an equilibrium, on a rational choice model, actors must decide whether to specialize based on expected returns. They must each predict what the other type will be learning, and so what the other type will prefer on the marriage market, in order to decide what they themselves should learn to do. Then they must

---

[2] For a non-exhaustive list of other work in this area see Francois et al. (1996); Danziger and Katz (1996); Echevarria and Merlo (1999); Peters and Siow (2002); Baker and Jacobsen (2007); Nosaka (2007).

choose a partner based on specializations in a way that maximizes output. And furthermore, these calculations must be performed generation after generation anew. Notably there is no reason, in these models, that from one generation to the next the genders should not switch which role they perform.

Evolutionary models put a lower burden of rationality on actors by supposing that social learning and individual learning are doing the work to drive populations toward division of labor equilibria. Furthermore, the assumption that individuals are choosing spouses primarily based on their marketable skills, and developing their own skills in anticipation of this is dropped. This is to say that the preconditions in these models for the emergence of division of labor by type are similar, but the processes by which this division of labor is attained are very different. Evolutionary models offer a more natural representation for how this division arises, as it is clear that social learning is an important factor when it comes to gender socialization and division of labor. They also explain why we see stable patterns for the division of labor emerging in a society and persisting across generations. (In the case of the plough, this is exactly what we see—social transmission maintains a norm over the course of several generations.) And lastly, as we will see in the next chapter, evolutionary models can tell us something about why some patterns of division of labor seem to be highly conventional (basket-making) others not very conventional (big-game hunting), and others in between.

## 3.2 Cultural Evolution and Dynamics

As mentioned, the goal of this chapter is to look at what strategies evolve in populations with types playing complementary coordination (and some other) games. To answer this question with respect to human societies we must ask: how do cultural evolutionary processes happen? And: how should we model them? I will start by describing the approach that evolutionary game theory takes in general, and then fill in the details of how this approach will be used here to represent cultural change.

### 3.2.1 The evolutionary game theoretic approach

The game theoretic approach to understanding and predicting behavior, described in Chapter 1, can be contrasted to the evolutionary game theoretic approach. In evolutionary game theory it is assumed that actors slowly develop strategies over time, usually in the context of an interacting population or group.[3]

This methodology was developed in biology, starting with Maynard-Smith and Price (1973), to represent the evolution of strategic behavior in animals.[4] It was subsequently adopted by social scientists, and eventually philosophers, to model the cultural evolution of human behavior. Actors in biological models leave behind more offspring when they are strategically successful. Actors in cultural models update strategies based on whether they do or do not work in practice. There are various ways this is done. One common method is to assume that actors imitate successful or influential peers. (More on this shortly.) Another way is to assume actors simply repeat what has worked for them in the past. It should be noted that cultural evolution, here, simply refers to change over time in behaviors of human actors. We do not need to invoke memes, or any cultural analog of genes, nor do we need to answer thorny questions about information transfer to suppose that human cultures change in regular ways based on the successes of various behavioral choices.

In evolutionary game theory, all these types of change are modeled by applying what are called *dynamics* to games. Dynamics are rules for how strategies are updated based on their past success (and sometimes other factors). Below I will describe the *replicator dynamics*—the most commonly used model of change in evolutionary game theory, and the main process I will use to model cultural change.

It is important to keep distinct game theoretic and evolutionary game theoretic models. Of course, evolutionary game theory is grounded in, and deeply related to, game theory. This connection can at times be misleading, however. Games, in the two contexts, are formally similar, but often need to be interpreted in different ways. In particular, under the game theoretic interpretation, as discussed, payoff in a game represents utility. When games are employed in an evolutionary model, however, payoffs simply specify, based on the dynamics, how evolution happens. For example, payoffs determine whose strategies are most imitated by

---

[3] For a more in-depth treatment of this paradigm, see Weibull (1997), Gintis (2009), or Sandholm (2010).

[4] Well before this development game theorists were starting to think in terms of dynamic solutions to games, rather than static ones (Brown, 1951; Robinson, 1951).

group members, or who has what number of children, or, for some of the models in this book, they determine how quickly actors learn.

The disanalogy means that there are two ways to interpret evolutionary models. The first continues to associate payoff with success, or preference, or happiness, and further assumes that cultural evolution also tracks these things. We learn to do things that made us, and others, happy or well in the past. The second sort of interpretation pulls apart evolution and preference. For instance, the sorts of behaviors that make one a successful business person lead to prominence in an institution and increased social imitation as a result. But this prominence need not be associated with happiness or pleasure for a "successful" actor. In this case, utility and evolvability pull apart, and an evolutionary model should generally be thought of as tracking the latter.[5] Throughout the book, I generally use the first interpretation for cultural evolutionary models—that actors are learning to do things that benefit them and/or that they prefer.

Predictions and explanations from evolutionary game theoretic models often differ dramatically from those provided by standard game theory. Although evolutionary models are used for myriad explanatory purposes, there are a few particularly salient roles they have played in the literature. First, they have often been used to explain seemingly irrational human behaviors. Many theorists have used evolutionary game theoretic models to explain the prevalence of altruism in the biological and social realms, for example, despite the irrationality of altruism.[6] Another way evolutionary models have been successfully employed is to solve what are called 'equilibrium selection problems'. Sometimes rational choice models predict a set of possible equilibrium behaviors, while evolutionary models show that only one of these is likely to arise in an evolutionary context. Young (1993b), for example, predicts the emergence of fair bargaining equilibria, rather than inequitable ones, in an evolutionary model. Evolutionary models can also give deep insights into the conditions

---

[5] An excellent real-world example comes from the advent of agriculture. Early agriculturists seem to have been generally miserable. They suffered from poor nutrition, worked harder, and were less healthy than the hunter/gatherers that directly preceded them. Agriculture spread rapidly through human groups nonetheless in part because it increased the number of children humans could raise (Armelagos and Cohen, 1984; Armelagos et al., 1991; Steckel and Rose, 2002).

[6] This literature is truly massive, but for a few examples, see Nowak (2006); Alexander (2007).

under which behaviors can emerge in a way that is often not possible using rational choice models Alexander (2007), for example, shows how social interaction with neighbors can promote the emergence of prosocial behaviors in models (like the stag hunt) with multiple equilibria.

The evolutionary models in this book will especially play the last sort of epistemic role. As we will see in Chapter 4, knowing something about how likely various equilibria are to arise in coordination games will help inform gendered division of labor. In Part II of the book, the evolutionary framework will help us analyze the conditions under which equitable and inequitable outcomes are more or less likely to arise. In Chapter 9, the evolutionary perspective will be crucial to understanding how to intervene on inequitable conventions.

### 3.2.2 Modeling cultural evolution

As I elaborated in the Introduction, cultural change happens via a number of processes—social learning from peers, parents, and other teachers, individual learning as a result of experience in the social sphere, and rational choice, at very least. Furthermore, each of these processes may happen in different ways. Individual learning, for example, is itself a process that is updated over the course of a human lifetime. There are many versions of each sort of social imitation, and these, too, may be updated by agents who learn to learn better.

I will mostly abstract away from these complex processes by using a few simple models of evolutionary change to represent cultural evolution. Most of the models I will discuss involve change via the replicator dynamics, mentioned above. These dynamics assume that within a population better strategies will proliferate and poorer strategies will die out. Furthermore, strategies proliferate, under these dynamics, in proportion to how much they benefit those who employ them. This type of change can be thought of as underlying many evolutionary processes—behaviors that do well continue to exist and expand in number, behaviors that do not fail. Weibull (1997) shows that the replicator dynamics can be explicitly used to model cultural change via differential imitation of successful group members, a process that regularly occurs in human societies (Lancy, 1996; Fiske, 1999; Henrich and Gil-White, 2001; Henrich and Henrich, 2007; Richerson and Boyd, 2008). And Börgers and Sarin (1997) and Hopkins (2002) show that the replicator dynamics can act as a successful model of individual reinforcement learning, which has also been observed to guide the dynamics of human behavioral change (Thorndike, 1898;

Herrnstein, 1970; Roth and Erev, 1995).[7] Many previous authors have used the replicator dynamics to represent cultural change, often with explanatory success. The Appendix describes the equations that govern these dynamics.

The replicator dynamics, in their basic form, represent a purely *adaptive* process. The reason populations shift in their composition is that some traits are more successful than others, and there is a process by which success translates into prevalence. This is obviously an idealization away from real cultural processes which are sometimes driven by non-adaptive processes such as prestige bias, where actors copy prestigious group members regardless of the success of their behaviors, conformity bias, where actors simply copy popular behaviors, and similarity bias, where actors copy those they judge similar to themselves (Henrich and McElreath, 2003; Boyd and Richerson, 2004). In addition, these dynamics will miss "attraction" effects, where because of psychological biases or ecological conditions populations will tend to progressively move toward particular cultural variants regardless of adaptiveness (Sperber and Sperber, 1996; Claidière and Sperber, 2007; Claidière et al., 2014). Furthermore, because the replicator dynamics are purely adaptive, their simplest form does not include any representation of stochastic effects on cultural evolution. Of course, real populations are messy and random. Perfectly good behavioral variants may die out for no good reason, and poorer variants may become prevalent along the same lines.

Should all these idealizations be concerning? The modeling strategy here is to represent a generic selection process in a large population. This should capture the underlying, general direction of many of the processes of learning/cultural evolution mentioned above, while avoiding the sticky problem of how to accurately represent these various, interacting processes. It seems quite likely that for some cases, this generic process will not be a good representation of the cultural evolutionary path of a real population as a result. In other cases, it will be a good representation, and the simplicity of the models will allow us to gain explanatory clarity when it comes to the emergence of conventions related to gender and other social categories. Furthermore, even in cases where

---

[7] For both these dynamics, the replicator dynamics are the *mean field dynamics*, meaning that they track expected change in these models if the stochastic elements of change are averaged out.

the details of a real population do not match the models well, the models can help us understand the underlying selective pressures that such populations undergo, if simultaneously ignoring other sorts of change. And lastly, in order to ameliorate worries about the modeling choices, I employ "robustness checks" throughout the book. This is a technique that involves altering various factors of models to ensure that the key insights still emerge even under different assumptions. (More on this shortly.)

### 3.2.3   Learning from those like us

There is one more issue to tackle regarding modeling choices. In the models I will present shortly, one assumption is that everyone imitates those in their own social category, rather than other social categories.[8] As we will see, this assumption is not necessary to generate the main results, but it is still worth asking, is this realistic? To answer this question, I will describe the last set of empirical results related to gender—those on same-gendered cultural transmission.

When it comes to gender it is clear that separate modes of learning are happening. If they weren't, we wouldn't see such significant behavioral differences between men and women. (We know these differences cannot be completely innate, since there is significant cross-cultural variation.) Children are socialized into gendered behavior very early. Usually by age 2 or 3, they can say which gender they belong to, and shortly there-after begin the long process of learning behaviors appropriate to their gender (Thrall, 1978; Bem, 1983; Basow, 1992; Wood and Eagly, 2002; Lippa, 2005; Kinzler et al., 2010; Kamei, 2010). Both adults and peers involve themselves in gender socialization, with adults directly teaching children proper gendered behavior, children using same gender models for imitative learning, and peers encouraging proper gendered behavior and discouraging inappropriate behavior. (See Wood and Eagly (2012) for an excellent review.) Henrich (2015) reviews a broad range of studies that have found social imitation of same gender types for many behaviors. Losin et al. (2012) find that own-gender imitation, but not other-gender imitation, of irrelevant gestures activates reward circuitry in the brain.

---

[8] Relatedly, Tilly (1998) identifies emulation, by which he means the copying of estab-lished behaviors, as a key mechanism leading to the emergence of inequity between social categories.

Henrich and Henrich (2007) point out that selective processes should favor copying those of the same gender and same ethnicity, for the very reason that doing so improves uptake of appropriate social roles and behaviors.

Proper gendered behavior, in all the arenas discussed, is subsequently enforced via gossip, ostracism, open criticism, and sometimes more serious forms of punishment (West and Zimmerman, 1987; Butler, 1988; Lorber, 1994). Fagot (1977) finds, for example, that among school-aged children peer criticism is harsh for cross-gender behavior. Glick and Fiske (2001) find that experimental subjects hold approving beliefs about women who conform to gender stereotypes and hostile beliefs about those who do not. The adoption of signals of gender membership in humans is also normatively regulated in many cultures. Men and women who adopt the wrong signals are subjected to social sanction (Garfinkel, 1967; West and Zimmerman, 1987).[9] (See Wood and Eagly (2012) for an extensive overview of the literature on social sanctions and gender.) All these sorts of social punishment should enforce same-gender learning, and increase the relevance of social models that involve same-gender imitation.

There is a worry here, which is that same-gender imitation, and other mechanisms for enforcing proper-gendered learning, are surely at least in part a response to the existence of gender roles and norms. In other words, while the models assume this sort of learning in order to get gendered division of labor, perhaps that is putting the cart before the horse. As I will point out at the end of Chapter 4, there is actually a bundle of social features that must be in place to get gendered division of labor (including own-gender learning). A full account of how groups manage to get all these features in place at once is beyond this book, but I will say a bit more there about this chicken and egg issue.

---

[9] To share a personal anecdote—when I took my twin girls for their three-month doctor appointment, I dressed one of them in a blue-striped onesie. The doctor's receptionist exclaimed, "He's so cute! Oh, but look, on his chart it says he's a *girl.*" When I explained that my daughter was a girl she apologized for my mistake, saying, "When dads dress them, they just put anything on." In this case, she took the gender signaling so seriously that she trusted it over a medical chart. And upon discovering that I had failed to perform the correct gender signaling act, she felt the need to diffuse my expected embarrassment by trying to foist my lapse in normative duties onto my husband!

## 3.3 Evolving to Solve Complementary Coordination Problems

Lewis (1969) describes situations where precedent and repeated interaction lead to joint expectations between actors for solving coordination problems. Schelling (1960), meanwhile, points out that with respect to such solutions, "[t]he fundamental psychic and intellectual process is that of participating in the creation of *traditions*" (106, emphasis his). Although both thinkers were focused on a rational choice perspective, the processes they describe are essentially dynamic.

What happens when homogenous, two-type mixing, and perfectly divided populations evolve while the actors in them play complementary coordination games? In each case, the outcome is very different. I will start by discussing evolution in homogenous populations, and then move on to perfectly divided ones. The two-type mixing population results are a sort of combination of the other two, so I will save those for last.

### 3.3.1 *Homogenous groups*

Let us imagine a homogenous group where individuals randomly meet one another and engage in coordination problems. Over time people imitate those who seem to be doing well vis a vis coordination, and repeat behaviors that have worked for themselves in the past. Slowly, individuals develop patterns that tend to work for them.

For reference, Figure 3.1 shows the dancing game. As discussed, a homogenous group playing this game does very poorly if all members play either of the available strategies. When a group playing this game is evolved using the replicator dynamics, for this reason, they end up with a mix of strategies. In particular, regardless of what individuals start doing, a group playing this game under the replicator dynamics will end up with half of its actors playing A and half B.

Figure 3.2 shows what is called a *phase diagram* for a single population playing the dancing game and evolving according to the replicator

|  | Player 2 | |
|---|---|---|
|  | A | B |
| A | 0, 0 | 1, 1 |
| B | 1, 1 | 0, 0 |

Player 1 (label for rows A and B)

Figure 3.1 A dancing game

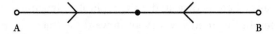

**Figure 3.2** The phase diagram for a single population playing the dancing game

dynamics. The line in this diagram represents all the possible states of this population, from every member playing A (on the far left) to every member playing B (on the far right). Each other point on the line represents a unique population proportion—.37 play A and .63 play B, for example. There are three dots on this line, and each represents what is called a *rest point* for the replicator dynamics. At these points, the population will stop evolving. The two rest points on the ends represent all A and all B. At these points, the population does not change because it is assumed that there is no cultural model to copy from of the other sort. (Or in the genetic case that no genes of the other sort exist to spread in the population.) These rest points are unstable, though, in the following sense. If the population is perturbed from them, even a tiny bit, it will be carried away from the rest point. (A "perturbation" of this sort might occur when individuals experiment with other strategies, or err, or in a biological population perturbations might be the result of mutation.) This is what the arrows on the line represent—the direction of change for the population at states represented by that area of the phase diagram. To the right of all A, the population moves toward a state with more Bs. To the left of all B, the population moves toward a state with more As.

The central rest point, represented by a filled-in dot, is stable in the sense that if a population is perturbed, it will return to this state. Imagine, for example, moving a population away from this rest point a bit to the right. The direction of change carries it right back. This particular point is *asymptotically stable*, meaning that for some set of other population states, the dynamics will move the population toward this state and then remain there.[10] For the models we will look at (though not every possible evolutionary game theoretic model) the rest points we will be interested in are the asymptotically stable ones. These represent the outcomes that we expect real evolving populations to end up at.

[10] This particular rest point is actually *globally asymptotically stable*—not only do other population states evolve to this one, but every other possible population state (except the other rest points) evolves to this one.

The take away here is that, under the replicator dynamics, in every case the group in this model will evolve toward the state where half of all actors play A and half play B. (Note that this outcome corresponds to the population level equilibria described in the last chapter.) This sort of population state, where some actors use one strategy and some another, is called a *polymorphism*.[11] For a game with different payoffs, like the leader–follower game, the actual proportion of As and Bs will be different, but in general any complementary coordination game will end up with a mix of the two available strategies. As Henrich and Boyd (2008) point out, if we use this model to represent division of labor, this could correspond to a case where everyone does some of each available job, rather than splitting jobs between actors.

One natural question is whether polymorphic outcomes of this sort really occur in the biological and social world. There are many documented cases of real-world polymorphisms in the biological world.[12] When it comes to coordination, though, human populations usually seem to to find better solutions than polymorphic population states. We tend to make use of the sorts of solutions identified by Aumann and Maynard-Smith, and, of course, of types and type-conditioning to improve coordination

### 3.3.2 *Perfectly divided groups*

Now imagine a group with both men and women playing a dancing game. They only meet each other for interaction, and over time women imitate the successful actions of other women and men of other men.[13] Slowly they adopt strategies that work for them.

Perhaps unsurprisingly, the efficient population equilibria described in the last chapter are what evolve in this case. One type always learns to play

[11] Alternatively, we can interpret this outcome as one where every actor plays the same strategy, which is to mix between both possible actions, taking each 50% of the time. For our purposes the interpretory difference will not matter.

[12] For example, Sinervo et al. (1996) describe populations of side-blotched lizards where males display one of three throat colors, each associated with a different mating strategy. These strategy/color pairings persist side by side analogously to the three strategies in the evolutionary game theoretic version of rock-paper-scissors. See also Morgan (1980); Kaitala and Getz (1995).

[13] As discussed, social learning often involves own-gender imitation, but this is by no means a hard and fast rule. In section 3.4 I show how a model that makes different structural assumptions, but does not involve own-gender imitation, yields similar results to those here.

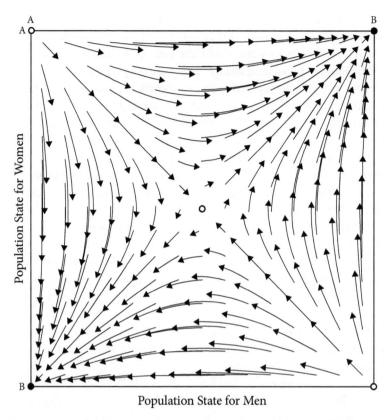

Figure 3.3 A phase diagram for the dancing game evolved with the two-population replicator dynamics

one strategy, and the other the other. Figure 3.3 shows a phase diagram for the dancing game under the *two-population replicator dynamics* (see the Appendix).[14] Obviously this figure is a bit different from the one pictured in Figure 3.2. This space represents *all* the possible population states for each of the two types in such a model. The x-axis represents proportions from 0 to 1 of actors of the first type (men, say) playing A and B. The y-axis represents the same thing for actors of the second type (women)

---

[14] This figure, and others like it throughout the book, were made using the program Dynamo developed by Sandholm et al. (2012). The dynamics are the continuous time version of the two-population replicator dynamics.

playing A and B. Each point in the diagram, then, represents one joint population state (for example, the first type is .25 A and .75 B, the second type is .55 A and .45 B). For each of these points, the diagram also shows the direction of population change. These arrows play the same role as the ones in the single-population phase diagram, but now instead of just pointing right or left, they can point in any direction in the plane. Look, for example, at the lower-right hand corner. This corner represents the state where both populations all play B. There is an arrow pointing up and to the left, which indicates that from this point, the replicator dynamics carry the populations away from this point, and toward a state where more actors in both groups play A. The lengths of the arrows tell us how quickly the population is evolving at any particular spot.

In this figure one can see that the arrows successively point to the lower left-and upper right-hand corners. In fact, from any starting point, the population will go to one of these two rest points. These represent the states just described. (Men engage in woodworking, and women practical pottery. Men mow the lawn, and women clean the dishes.) Notice here that we expect these outcomes to emerge, even though the two types are completely symmetric. They face the same strategic situation. They have the same preferences and abilities. But nonetheless, we expect them to end up at asymmetric outcomes.

We can identify what are called *basins of attraction* for each of these rest points. The basin of attraction, for a rest point, refers to the collection of states that eventually evolve to that rest point.[15] For the upper right rest point, here, the basin of attraction is the upper right triangle of the diagram, and for the lower left rest point, it is, likewise, the lower left triangle. Note that these basins of attraction are the same size. What this means is that for this model either type is equally likely to end up playing either strategy, assuming we don't know where the population starts.

There are also three unstable rest points, two at the other corners of the phase diagram and one right in the middle. Again, these are not evolutionarily significant because populations that are slightly perturbed from them will tend to move toward the stable rest points. Notice, though, that the rest point in the middle corresponds to a population where half

---

[15] For the homogenous populations, I did not bother identifying the basins of attraction. Since there is one globally asymptotically stable rest point, the basin of attraction for it is the entire state space (minus the two unstable rest points).

of all individuals take strategy A and half B. In other words, it is exactly the population that was the *only* stable rest point in the homogenous group. This is just to drive home how drastically the introduction of types changes the evolution here—the rest point which was guaranteed to evolve is now guaranteed not to.

As in homogenous groups, changing payoffs of the game will change the location of the interior rest point in these evolving populations, but will not change the general shape of the phase diagram. Figure 3.4 shows the phase diagram for the leader–follower game introduced in Chapter 1. In this figure, the interior rest point has shifted, but the stable rest points and their basins of attraction are the same. It is worth noting that as long as we assume complete symmetry between the two types—same strategies,

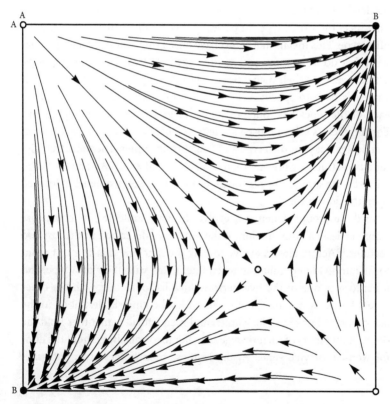

**Figure 3.4** A phase diagram for the leader–follower game evolved with the two-population replicator dynamics

same payoffs, same dynamics—we will also find that the types are equally likely to end up at either outcome. In the case of gendered division of labor, this symmetry means strong conventionality as to gender roles. Later in the book I will look at models where these assumptions are dropped.

### 3.3.3 *Two-type mixing groups*

Last imagine a population where individuals have to decide whether to open doors for each other, or whether to walk through. The population is divided into women and men. As they interact women imitate other women who seem to be doing well, and men other men.

This is a slightly different evolutionary situation from either of the previous ones described. In either homogenous or perfectly divided models, actors meet only one other type. In homogenous groups, actors only meet their own type. In perfectly divided ones, they meet only the other type. This means that actors have only a single strategy that specifies what they do when they meet another agent. In two-type mixing groups, actors meet both their own type *and* the other type. This means that their strategies have to specify what happens for each interaction, meaning each of the types has four possible strategies for a two-strategy game. For simplicity's sake, I'll list a strategy as a pair $<X,Y>$, where X is what you do against your own type and Y against the other. The four strategies for a two-strategy game are then $<A,A>$, $<A,B>$, $<B,A>$, and $<B,B>$, representing something like "open the door for other women, but let men open the door for me".

In these groups, when you evolve the four strategies, outcomes are (more or less) a combination of the outcomes described in the last two sections.[16] Actors always evolve to play the outcome that is a rest point for the undivided population when interacting with their own type, and learn to play one of the two perfectly divided outcomes with the other type. (These, again, are the population level equilibria described in the last chapter.) For example, women and men will all sometimes hold the door for members of their own gender, but men will always hold the door for women, or vice versa. Again, in these models these two outcomes

---

[16] See the Appendix for the dynamics governing this process.

against the other group will happen equally often as long as the game is symmetric. Unfortunately, it is not possible to show a phase diagram for this evolving population because it has too many strategies.

The main take away should be that in the class of games we are largely concerned with here, all three of the sorts of groups we are looking at evolve in dependable ways. Homogenous groups evolve to a mixture of both strategies (with different proportions based on payoffs), perfectly divided groups evolve so that each type takes one strategy, and in two-type mixing populations each type evolves to play the polymorphic equilibrium against their own type, and a coordination equilibrium with the other type. So what we see is a case where social categories change the almost inevitable evolutionary outcome to a completely different (and more successful) one. On a cultural evolutionary picture, we expect groups of people to, in fact, end up taking advantage of social categories to improve coordination.

A more general note is that the simple addition of categories to these models dramatically alters cultural evolution. This observation tells us first that as a methodological point, cultural evolutionary predictions of behavior in human groups should take categories into account. It also provides deep explanation of the fact that social categories are so often associated with different social roles, and often attendant inequity (Tilly, 1998; Ridgeway, 2011).

## 3.4 Bounded Rationality, Evolution, and Robustness

The main claim on the table is that we should expect real human groups to culturally evolve such that social categories end up being important for coordination. In particular, as we saw in the last chapter, this will mean that some types should end up relatively disadvantaged by the processes that create more efficient groups. Women will end up with less, for example, because they, as a group, do not control food production. But to this point, these claims are grounded in one set of highly simplified, idealized models. How do we grow a bit more confident in their ability to tell us about real groups?

Robustness analysis in modeling involves changing various features of a model to ensure that those features are not responsible for a result attributed to something else (Weisberg, 2006).[17] In other words, robustness can be checked by reinstantiating causal variables in a different structure and seeing whether they lead to the same outcome. In our case, the variables responsible for the outcome (groups developing sometimes inequitable conventions to solve coordination problems) are that 1) groups encounter complementary coordination problems, 2) groups learn to do what benefits them, and 3) groups have two types. Let's explore some models from the literature with these features to test the robustness of the emergence of inequity.

Young (1993b) presents some of the first results showing that class inequities can emerge endogenously in populations with types where actors play bargaining games, Axtell et al. (2000) reproduce these results in a computational framework.[18] Although we will not introduce bargaining games until Part II, all we need to know here is that they have a partially complementary coordination structure. Axtell et al. (2000) model finite populations (sized 10–100) where agents are either in a homogenous group or of two types (landowners and sharecroppers, say), and where they repeatedly interact with both their own and the opposite type. (This corresponds to the two-type mixing model.) These authors use a dynamics that is very different from those employed here, where agents update their behavior based on a string of past interactions. Each round, several agents are paired to play the game. Each agent remembers some short set of interactions they have had, say the last five. Based on this list, they play whatever strategy will yield the best payoff assuming that their recent interactions reflect the larger population. In other words, agents *best respond* to their memory. When the population has two types, actors remember and best respond to their interactions with the two types separately. With some small probability agents play another strategy instead of their best response. Note that this sort of dynamic involves actors that display *bounded rationality*. The actors do not have infinite

[17] Some philosophers of science think that robustness analysis is not effective for scientific confirmation (see Cartwright (1991); Orzack and Sober (1993); Odenbaugh and Alexandrova (2011)), while others argue that robust results are better confirmed (see Levins (1966); Weisberg (2006); Wimsatt (2012); Heesen et al. (2017)).

[18] As they also point out, short- and medium-run behavior in these models is very important in understanding real-world behavior. Mohseni (2017) demonstrates why short and medium-term behavior is important in this sort of model. Their results have been replicated computationally by López-Paredes et al. (2004); Phan et al. (2005); Poza et al. (2011).

memories, neither do they have higher-order expectations about what their opponents will do given their opponents' beliefs. On the other hand, they do not blindly copy cultural variants, but instead make some calculation as to what will benefit them. In groups with types, Axtell et al. (2000) find that, as in our replicator dynamics models, inequity can emerge that would not be possible for a homogenous group. Again, this is because the types break symmetry.

These models demonstrate a sort of "throw everything at it" robustness of the results described in this chapter. The models in Axtell et al. (2000) have finite groups, randomness, and a boundedly rational choice rule for strategy selection, as opposed to replicator dynamic models with an infinite population, non-random dynamics, and a selection-based strategy update. Furthermore, under the most common cultural interpretation of the replicator dynamics (imitation of successful group-mates), actors copy the successes of their own type, while in the Axtell et al. models they simply respond to what they encounter in the environment. (This is the sense in which own-gender imitation is not necessary to the main results of this chapter.) We might even say that the Axtell et al. models do not involve type-conditioning. Agents do have separate memories for the separate types, so they recognize type distinctions, but they use one general rule (best response) for deciding behavior in both cases.[19] Nonetheless, largely similar outcomes are seen. This can increase our confidence that these are the sorts of outcomes we expect in evolving populations with types playing complementary coordination games.

There are other results that support the robustness of these evolutionary results. Henrich and Boyd (2008), in an exploration of the emergence of social stratification and division of labor, consider models that are very similar to those discussed here, but that add several features.[20] In particular, they consider conditions where learning does not occur

[19] The Axtell et al. models can be thought of as representing the emergence of what Millikan (2005) calls "counterpart reproduction," where actors learn complementary roles using their opponents as templates, rather than using social imitation of others. She uses the example of reproducing a handshake to illustrate this sort of reproduction. I think this is an ineffective example of what she is trying to pick out, because actors might learn to shake hands by exactly replicating their partner's actions. In complementary coordination problems where actors learn a complementary role from their opponent, direct social imitation cannot lead to the perpetuation of the behavior.

[20] They look at models where two populations evolve under the replicator dynamics and play a complementary coordination game where one role is preferable to both types.

entirely from members of one's own type. Instead, actors learn from their own group with some probability, and from the other type the rest of the time. Importantly, they find that under a wide range of conditions the same outcome still emerges where the population uses type membership to divide labor. When mixing is very high, so that the groups are more like a homogenous group, this does not occur, but for low to moderate levels of mixing (depending on a few other factors), the benefits of typing and type-conditioning drive the population toward the relatively efficient, inequitable equilibrium.[21,22]

Additionally, Bowles (2004); Bowles and Naidu (2006); Hwang et al. (2014) look at game theoretic models that, like those presented by Young and co-authors, involve finite populations and best response dynamics, though they assume that actors observe the current state of the other population and best respond accordingly, rather than responding to some small set of memories. In addition, their actors tend to err toward conventions that will benefit them. In models where actors play a coordination game with an equitable and an inequitable equilibrium, these authors find that the stochastically stable equilibrium between groups will be one of these two Nash equilibria depending on other parameters of the model. (This equilibrium concept looks at where an evolving population spends its time as the likelihood of mutation goes to zero. See Foster and Young (1990).) They find similar results when actors are networked. In other words, again, their groups use types to improve coordination, sometimes to the detriment of one type. Hoffmann (2006) likewise presents agent-based models where actors play hawk–dove and have a number of social

---

[21] As I have argued for the case of gender, in many cases in-group learning is a good assumption, but surely this learning is not a solid rule. These results from Henrich and Boyd (2008) indicate that even in cases where actors sometimes learn from other types, we can see the sorts of outcomes described in this chapter.

[22] Nakahashi and Feldman (2014) provide another model of division of labor. While their model does not involve game theory, the set-up is one where actors can take advantage of two different sorts of resources via two different skill sets, and where they have some common interest as a result of resource sharing. They must decide how much effort to put into learning these skills, and then into exploiting the resources. Although their model does not assume a complementary coordination problem exactly (because actors can gather resources for themselves only and because they share as a group) there are suggestive similarities to the models here. They find that gendered division of labor emerges only when the genders have different innate skills, but this is because their models involve groups that share resources together, rather than situations where pairs of individuals have to figure out how to coordinate behavior.

identity markers which they use to generalize their expectations about opponent play. His actors best respond to their learned expectations. He finds that they use their identities to facilitate complementary coordination, as in the models here.

So in models with infinite and finite populations, in models on networks, in models with cultural imitation, and with boundedly rational response, in models where actors learn from their own and from other types, we see groups evolving so that social categories facilitate complementary coordination. This reflects a deep truth about efficiency outlined in the last chapter—social categories do something that homogenous populations do not. We shouldn't be entirely surprised that many sorts of cultural evolutionary processes are responsive to this efficiency.

## 3.5 Social Categories and Correlative Coordination

As we have seen, the addition of categories to a social evolutionary process drastically changes outcomes. In the case of complementary coordination, it does so in a way that allows for inequity, where previously only equitable outcomes were expected. But this is not the only way that social categories shape cultural evolution. In this section, we'll take a short detour to see how conventions and norms for correlative coordination turn out differently in groups with types, sometimes to the detriment of one type.[23] (Since this strays beyond the main narrative of the book, and introduces some games that will not be relevant elsewhere, readers can safely skip this section.)

### 3.5.1  Correlative coordination games

Suppose we have a homogenous group learning which side of the road to drive on. Unsurprisingly, what happens is that everyone evolves to do the same thing—drive on the right or the left. If we have a perfect division— men meeting only women and women only men, for example—again cultural evolution will drive everyone to solve the coordination problem by all doing the same thing.

---

[23] Thanks to Justin Bruner for inspiration here. He explores the evolution of the stag hunt in two-type mixing models in a previous version of Bruner (2017).

In these cases, we should not expect inequity unless there is a situation with something like a Bach–Stravinsky game (remember, this is where everyone wants to listen to music together, but some people prefer Bach and others Stravinsky) and where for some reason members of one social category generally have different preferences or needs from the other. Suppose that everyone faces a coordination problem in deciding how much parental leave to grant. The optimal level for men and women might differ owing to the physical demands of childbirth, and so a coordination outcome that is symmetric and equal might nonetheless yield higher payoffs for one type.

What happens in a two-type mixing population evolving to play correlative coordination games? Here things get interesting. Because there are two types, it is no longer the case that everyone will necessarily evolve to do only one thing. Instead, actors develop three separate conventions. The first governs what happens in the in-group of the first type, the second governs what happens in the in-group of the second type, and the third governs what happens between groups. For an example, in a Bach–Stravinsky game, it could be that women listen to Bach together, men listen to Stravinsky, and when men and women meet they listen to Bach.

Of particular interest here are games where one outcome is generally preferable to the other. Consider Figure 3.5, which shows the game presented in Figure 1.2. In this game, the B vs. B outcome is preferable to both players. But the other outcome will still be an end result of some evolutionary processes. While this may sound unintuitive, the worse equilibrium is still an equilibrium. (In fact, societies end up at suboptimal social equilibria all the time. Bicchieri (2005) gives a number of examples.) In two-type mixing populations, outcomes can occur where only one group learns the more beneficial equilibrium. Or where the poorer equilibrium arises only between groups. As a result, one group will have higher payoffs on average than the other. Although these outcomes

|  | Player 2 |  |
|---|---|---|
|  | A | B |
| Player 1 — A | 1, 1 | 0, 0 |
| Player 1 — B | 0, 0 | 2, 2 |

**Figure 3.5** Correlative coordination game with a preferable outcome for both players

are not as compelling as representations of discrimination as those we have been discussing, they still represent a case where the existence of social categories can lead to a sort of inequity, or at least different ultimate levels of payoff for different types.

### 3.5.1.1 THE STAG HUNT

The motivating story behind the stag hunt comes from Rousseau (1984, orig. 1754). Two hunters each have the choice to pursue a stag, or to hunt small game—hare. If both hunt stag, they are able to collectively take down the stag, and benefit accordingly. If either hunts hare, she catches the hare and gets a small payoff. If one hunts stag, and the other hunts hare, the stag-hunter is unable to succeed on her own and gets nothing. This game is represented in Figure 3.6. The payoff here is 2 for hare, 3 for successful stag hunting, and 0 for unsuccessful stag hunting.[24]

The stag hunt is usually thought of as a model of cooperation under risk, but it technically also fits into our definition of a correlative coordination game.[25] For this model, the two Nash equilibria are the two outcomes where actors correlate their behavior—Stag vs. Stag and Hare vs. Hare. Actors in this game have preferences about what happens when they do not coordinate—Hare always yields a dependable payoff—but coordination is expected. Unsurprisingly, when a homogenous group evolves to play this game, everyone plays Hare or else they all play Stag.

When two types evolve to play this game, sometimes only one type will learn to play stag, or else everyone will play stag only with their outgroup. As Justin Bruner has pointed out, when everyone cooperates with

|  |  | Player 2 | |
|---|---|---|---|
|  |  | Stag | Hare |
| Player 1 | Stag | 3, 3 | 0, 2 |
|  | Hare | 2, 0 | 2, 2 |

Figure 3.6 A stag hunt

[24] This game has been employed by philosophers as a model of cooperation in human groups (Skyrms, 2004; Alexander, 2007; Skyrms, 2014).
[25] We can see that if we take the analysis of what counts as a coordination game—the payoffs for the complementary coordination choices are higher than the alternative payoffs given the other actor's choice—it will apply here as well. 3 is greater than 2, and 2 is greater than 0.

their in-group, but not the out-group, the convention looks like a kind of discrimination against the out-group. These sorts of outcomes have combined basins of attraction that make up about 38 percent of the state space in these models—a significant portion of outcomes. In outcomes where types cooperate between each other, but one type learns not to cooperate with their in-group, the non-cooperative group will be worse off. These outcomes have basins of attraction that make up another 9% of the state space. Again, in this case, the mere presence of types creates unequal possibilities that wouldn't exist otherwise.

•   •   •

We have seen that groups with social categories evolve and develop conventions in very different ways from homogenous groups. In particular, evolution takes advantage of social categories to improve coordination, even when the resulting conventions are inequitable. In general, separate conventions can arise for those in different social categories, and sometimes this can mean inequality of a different sort.

The case we have been using to illustrate how social categories can act as a solution concept—gendered division of labor—is thus addressed. Gendered division of labor is what we should expect from cultural evolution given a set-up where labor takes specialized skills. Details about the skills and preferences of men and women, notice, have not played any role in the story so far. This is because it is the simple fact of symmetry breaking that makes social categories functional, not any features of the categories themselves. This also helps explain the conventional nature of gendered division of labor. Why do we see different jobs performed by men or by women cross-culturally? Because while it matters that labor be divided for coordination purposes, it does not particularly matter how. In the next chapter, we will complicate this story, and use evolutionary models to explain why, despite this conventionality, some jobs are primarily performed by men, some by women, and some by either gender cross-culturally.

Before continuing to the next chapter, where some of the ways this framework shines light on gender will be addressed at greater length, I'd like to drive home a point made in the Introduction. The models presented so far, I think, are how-potentially models, potentially representing the sorts of causal processes that, in the real world, occur in groups with social categories. They are also how-minimally models—showing that remarkably little is needed to generate inequity via cultural evolution. All we need is a group with two types, playing a complementary coordination game, and undergoing an adaptive process of cultural change. There is no bias in this model, no stereotype threat, not much psychology in general, but nonetheless we see group-level patterns that mimic inequitable conventions. We see something like stable norms where the men who control the plough continue to reap benefits over cultural evolutionary time.

# 4

# The Evolution of Gender

In almost every society men are responsible for hunting big game (as mentioned in Chapter 2). In almost every society, women provide the majority of the infant care. And when it comes to rope-making, while labor is usually divided by gender, there is no strong pattern determining which gender will do the job.

This chapter will do two things. The first is to use the evolutionary framework we have developed to explain this particular feature of the gendered division of labor—that some aspects of it seem conventional, and others less so. In Chapter 1, I argued that conventionality comes in shades of gray. Along these lines, we will see here that cultural evolutionary processes are more or less variable. Some coordination outcomes are almost guaranteed to emerge, while others are more truly conventional in the sense that they really could have been otherwise. Gendered division of labor is a case where we see the full range of conventionality—some jobs are almost guaranteed to end up performed by one gender or the other, and for others their assignment is better explained by appeal to chance. This discussion contributes to debates on the innateness of gender roles by showing that even when patterns of division of labor seem enduring and fixed, and even when these patterns show cross-cultural regularity, we should understand them as nonetheless conventional, at least to some degree.

The second thing I will do in this chapter is, again, address an explanandum for social science via evolutionary modeling. Chimpanzees do not have genders, so somewhere between our most recent common ancestor and now this categorical distinction emerged in human groups.[1]

---

[1] To be clear, chimpanzees have some sex differences in behavior, but they do not have culturally learned behaviors and roles for males and females.

Not only that, it has emerged in every human group. The question is—why? What is it about gender that makes its cultural emergence completely dependable? The answer can't simply be that gender is innate, again, because of massive cross-cultural variability. Some social scientists have argued not just that gender facilitates division of labor, but that gender itself *exists* in order to divide labor (Lorber, 1994). Could the efficiencies associated with using social categories to solve coordination problems themselves lead categories to evolve? We will look at a model that provides a how-possibly story for this sort of evolution.

I will start the chapter by describing a measure intended to capture conventionality. In particular, I'll illustrate how for any evolutionary model we can generate a number that represents how conventional the outcomes of that model are. This will give us a way to grasp the difference between coordination problems where one outcome is highly likely, and those where things are more uncertain, and, in doing so, develop a representation of what is happening in different cases of gendered division of labor. We'll then move on to the second part of the chapter and look at how the efficiencies of dividing labor might lead to something like gender itself evolving. As we'll see, this process again occurs dependably under relatively bare preconditions. For any group faced with a complementary coordination problem, and where there is some underlying visible tag to attach a category to, categories can emerge spontaneously.

## 4.1 Conventionality and Basins of Attraction

A basin of attraction for an evolutionary model, remember, is the set of population states that end up at some particular equilibrium. In the last chapter, we saw that for a group with two types playing the dancing game, there were two basins of attraction—one for the equilibrium where women stepped forward, and the other for the equilibrium where men stepped forward—and these were of equal size.

Now, let's use this concept to return to a topic raised in Chapter 1—how to measure which sorts of coordination problems have a more conventional character. According to Skyrms (2004), "A convention is typically an equilibrium in an interaction which admits many different equilibria. That is what makes conventions conventional. An alternative equilibrium might have done as well" (51). As discussed, this is a typical requirement for conventionality—things could have been otherwise. But there are many games where it is the case that there exist multiple equilibria, and any of them might do, but some of these will do *better* than the others. Conventions do not come in black and white, but in shades of gray between those that are more arbitrary and those that are less arbitrary (or more and less conventional). In recent work focusing on linguistic conventions, Simons and Zollman (2018) make a similar point. They use game theoretic models to show that some conventions will be less arbitrary in that they provide better payoffs, are harder to disrupt, or are more likely to emerge in the first place.

I will here use the sizes of basins of attraction for a model to create a measure for conventionality based on this last idea. In some games, as mentioned, basins of attraction for different outcomes will be of more or less identical size, meaning that in evolutionary settings, with no information about a population starting place, it is equally likely that either outcome arises. In such a case, it seems appropriate to think of the outcomes as highly conventional. There aren't reasons, besides differences in initial conditions, or vagaries of chance, for one outcome versus the other to arise. For this reason, a successful explanation of the emergence of such a solution will often draw on chance occurrences. We always listen to Bach instead of Stravinsky because that is what was playing when we first met. Or my mother gave me Settlers of Catan for Christmas ten years back, and that is why we always play Settlers on Sundays.

In other models, the basin of attraction for one outcome will be significantly larger than that for the other(s). In such a case, outcomes of the evolutionary process often seem more functional in the sense that one can typically give a functional explanation for their emergence based on the underlying scenario. Jim does the cooking and Cailin does the cleaning because Jim never "remembers" to clean anything and Cailin mostly cooks root vegetables.

One might further wish to say that in cases where there are many possible outcomes for an evolutionary process, the outcomes of the model are more conventional than for one with just a few outcomes. (Though it is perhaps stranger to say that the outcomes in a model with fewer equilibria are more "functional".)[2] Millikan (2005), for example,

---

[2] Thanks to Mike Schneider and Hannah Rubin for this point.

describes conventions as patterns of behavior that would be unlikely to emerge a second time. In cases with many equilibria, the preponderance of possibilities may mean that the outcome is less predictable and depends more on chance differences or initial conditions. To illustrate this, compare the coordination problem of which side of the road to drive on with the problem of what word to use to refer to a fork. These are both classic examples of conventional solutions to coordination problems. In the first case, though, there are only two possible solutions, while in the second the number of solutions is extremely large.

One possible way to measure conventionality versus functionality, capturing both the differences between games with many and fewer equilibria, and the differences between games with basins of attraction of different sizes, is to use the Shannon entropy measure (Shannon, 2001). This formula calculates, for a channel transmitting information and a receiver, the expected value of information contained in a message. The equation for Shannon entropy is:

$$H(x) = \sum_i P(x_i)I(x_i) \tag{1}$$

$H(x)$ is entropy. It is equal to the sum, over all possible messages, $i$, that might arrive via a channel, of the probabilities of each message ($P(x_i)$) multiplied by the information contained in the message ($I(x_i)$). $I(x_i)$ is calculated as $-log_2 P(x_i)$ meaning that information from an observed message is very high if the probability of the message is low, and reaches 0 as the probability of the message reaches 1. We can think of the amount of information in a message as corresponding to how surprised one would be to receive it. Holding other aspects fixed, this measure will be larger if there are more possible messages and if they are closer to equiprobable.

This may seem like a strange measure to use in our case, but here conventionality can be thought of as measuring the level of how unsure one is about what the outcome of an evolutionary process will be (absent other information), and so the amount of information one expects to receive upon learning what the outcome is. Conventional problems are ones where there is more uncertainty about what will happen—where things might really be otherwise. To be clear, the entries to the entropy formula indexed by $i$ are now basins of attraction for a model and $P(x_i)$ refers to the size of the basin of attraction (how likely this outcome is).[3] Holding other aspects fixed, coordination problems with more possible outcomes will be more conventional on this scale, as will problems where the basins of attraction are more equal in size. Of course, this measure can be applied to any evolutionary model where there are multiple basins of attraction. Perhaps for some of these it might be strange to call them conventional at all. I do not claim that any possible application of this measure will make sense, but rather that for coordination games it is a good way to capture the level of conventionality.

One might point out that even in conventional type models, there will be situations where we know quite a lot about the initial conditions of a situation. In explaining outcomes, then, one will appeal not to chance, but to pre-existing features of a population—it contains a lot of bigots, or people here mostly drove on the left side of the road before, or this population evolved from one that already had this feature.

For a good example, consider the emergence of coordination behavior in a small company that employs both men and women, where interactions are well modeled by hawk–dove. We expect that the group evolves to a convention so that when men and women meet, either women get more, or men get more. We also know that the members of this company come from a larger population where, say, 80 percent of people adhere to a general convention where women get more. As a result, we expect that this group of people is likely to come to adhere to this norm as well. But, of course, there is some probability that each of them does not and so we aren't sure how they will establish their own conventions. In calculating the conventionality of solutions to this problem, one might want to use chances of the initial starting place of the population's being in each basin of attraction as inputs to the measure described above, rather than the objective sizes of the basins of attraction. If you think there is a 90% chance that the population is in one basin and 10% that it is in the other, the measure yields a value of .469, in contrast to a value of 1 for two basins

---

[3] There are some strange features of this measurement. Consider a model where the basins of attraction measure 99% and 1% of the state space. Now imagine breaking the 1% area into ever smaller divisions. This process will make the conventionality of a model arbitrarily high, though it is still very likely that the 99% equilibrium will emerge. Thanks to Nikhil Addleman for pointing out this case. Justin Bruner suggests that in a stag hunt with many stag options there could be a high level of conventionality despite a large basin of attraction for the arguably unconventional hare hunting outcome. And thanks to Agnes Bolinska for inspiring this entire discussion.

of attraction of size .5. In general, we can add a probability distribution over potential population starting points to tackle cases like these.

In the next section, we will put this measure to work for the case of gendered division of labor.

## 4.2  Asymmetry and Division of Labor

Part of the story that our evolutionary models tell us is that division of labor by gender is conventional. This means that a good answer to the question, "why do men, but not women, weave nets in this society?", may not involve anything about innate differences between men and women, or about special ecological circumstances. Instead the story may have to appeal to chance. Remember, though, that data on the division of labor by gender reveals a range of patterns from what looks like complete conventionality (cross-culturally men and women are equally likely to perform a particular job) to complete functionality (men almost always perform a particular job cross-culturally, or else women do).

As I will argue, we can appeal to the understanding of conventionality just elaborated to better understand these patterns. For some jobs, there is little functional advantage in having either men or women perform them (though there is still advantage to be gained from dividing the job). For some jobs, there is great functional advantage for one gender because of sexual dimorphism. For many other jobs, there is a moderate advantage for one gender to perform them. In evolutionary models, these cases range from strongly to less strongly conventional. In other words, our explanations for patterns of division of labor can incorporate facts about innate sex differences without losing conventionality. Although there are sometimes reasons for particular gendered divisions of labor, this does not mean that they could not have been otherwise.

Consider the game in Figure 4.1. This is a version of the MFEO (made for each other) game introduced in Chapter 1. It is identical to the dancing

Player 2

|  |  | A | B |
|---|---|---|---|
| Player 1 | A | 0, 0 | 1, 1 |
|  | B | $1+\alpha$, $1+\beta$ | 0, 0 |

**Figure 4.1** Payoff table for an MFEO game where $\alpha$ and $\beta$ determine the benefits to the two actors for reaching the preferable equilibrium

game except that both actors get an extra benefit ($\alpha$ for player 1 and $\beta$ for player 2) for one combination of roles but not the other. The idea is that one of the coordination equilibria is better, in some way, than the other.

This is an asymmetric game whenever either $\alpha$ or $\beta$ is not equal to 0, because the two players have inherently different roles. In our evolutionary models of symmetric complementary coordination games, it is always equally likely that either type takes either role. In this game that is no longer the case. To illustrate this, let's turn to computer simulations. In particular, imagine a population with two types given random strategies, so that the group starts at some random point in the phase diagram. Let them play the MFEO game over and over in the course of a simulation. At each stage they update what they are doing according to the replicator dynamics, and we see which equilibrium (A vs. B or B vs. A) they end up at. Figure 4.2 shows outcomes for 10,000 runs of simulation where actors played this MFEO game with $\alpha = \beta$ for a range of values. The x-axis tracks different values of $\alpha$ and $\beta$ and the y-axis shows how often the less desirable equilibrium is reached.

As $\alpha = \beta$ increases, the basin of attraction for the less preferable A vs. B equilibrium gets smaller and smaller. This should be no great

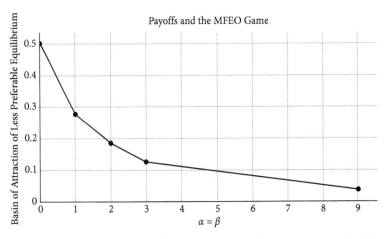

**Figure 4.2** Proportions of simulations that go to the jointly less preferable equilibrium for a perfectly divided population playing the MFEO game where $\alpha = \beta$

surprise. Cultural evolution is selecting the better equilibrium with higher probability the more attractive it is. We can get a better sense of what is going on by looking at the phase diagrams of this model in Figure 4.3 where $\alpha = \beta = 1$ and where $\alpha = \beta = 4$. These phase diagrams look similar to that for a dancing game, but now the central rest point (white dot) is shifted to one side, increasing the size of the basin of attraction for the better equilibrium (at the bottom left corner). In (b), where the payoff at the better equilibrium is higher than in (a), the dot is shifted further, making the sizes of the basins of attraction more disparate.

Exactly what is causing this shift? Under the replicator dynamics, strategies that do better than average expand. When one coordination strategy yields a significantly higher payoff, it will expand under the replicator dynamics as a result, even if it leads to lower levels of coordination initially. For example, suppose that for the game in Figure 4.1 women act as player 1 and men act as player 2. If 80% of men are playing B, women coordinate more often on average if they choose A. However, if $\alpha = 9$ the expected payoff of choosing A is $1 * .8 = .8$ and the expected payoff of choosing B is $10 * .1 = 1$. In other words, the Bs in the female population do better and proliferate even though they coordinate much less often. This drives a much larger percentage of populations toward the mutually preferable equilibrium. In cases where $\alpha \neq \beta$, note, we can see similar outcomes when even one of these payoffs gets larger. This change for one

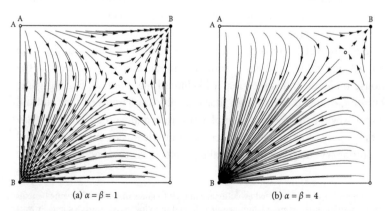

(a) $\alpha = \beta = 1$    (b) $\alpha = \beta = 4$

**Figure 4.3** Phase diagrams for perfectly divided populations playing MFEO games where $\alpha = \beta$ varies. As $\alpha = \beta$ increases, the size of the basin of attraction for the better equilibrium also increases

side will also increase the size of the basin of attraction for the better outcome.

Notice that in this model, we see a range of conventionality. When $\alpha = \beta = 0$, the two equilibria will have equal basins of attraction. Using our Shannon entropy measure, this yields a conventionality level of 1. If $\alpha = 9$, meaning that the preferable outcome arises more than 96% of the time, the conventionality of the model will be .24. We could increase $\alpha = \beta$ indefinitely, making the size of the basin of attraction for the worse equilibrium smaller and smaller. As we did, we would become increasingly certain that cultural evolution would select the better equilibrium, driving the measure closer and closer to 0.

We can use this particular set of models as a rough representation of what is going on when we see either strongly conventional, or very functional patterns for division of labor. Suppose that pair-bonded individuals producing children both have strong preferences for their family unit (or a larger extended family unit) to remain healthy, well-fed, and safe. In other words, the preferences of the parents strongly align toward measurable, visible positive outcomes for their loved ones. In such a case, the MFEO game can tell us why net-making is conventional cross-culturally, house-building tends to be performed by men, and big-game hunting almost always is. Consider our game above and for each type of labor suppose that actors engage in a strategic interaction where $A$ is "do job X" and $B$ is "do not do job X, spend your time contributing elsewhere". For each of these types of labor, all the benefits of division by gender hold. But for net-making, $\alpha$ and $\beta$ are low, meaning that in each culture either gender is likely to evolve to adopt that role. For house-building, $\alpha$ and $\beta$ take a moderate value, so there is some likelihood that women become the house-builders, and some greater likelihood that men do. For big-game hunting, $\alpha$ and $\beta$ are so high that it is almost guaranteed that cultural patterns will evolve where men play this role, and women evolve to play it only rarely.[4] Remember that there are multiple ways to interpret cultural evolutionary models. One is to take payoffs to correspond to objectively

---

[4] Of course, we do not need evolutionary models to guess that when everyone benefits from a particular division of labor, people will tend to follow it. As Murdock and Provost (1973) point out, without the help of mathematical models, "The probability that any activity will be assigned to males is increased to the extent that it has features which give males a definite advantage and/or females a definite disadvantage, in its performance, regardless of whether the distinction is innate or socio-cultural" (211).

successful outcomes—obtaining food, raising healthy children, etc.—and to assume that preferences track these. The explanation I provide here uses this sort of interpretation.

Of course, this is all overly simplistic. Particular ecological facts, and other facts about a culture, will influence all these processes. If it is the case that house-building materials near a group tend to be lighter and require less upper-body strength to deal with, the payoffs for women and men performing that job will be very different from those for a group where houses must be built with chopped lumber. For agriculture, as we have seen, the details of how crop production happens determine the likelihood that planting is done by men and women. In other words, there will be no set values for $\alpha$ and $\beta$ that hold for every human group, but there will be general patterns for these values, which means that overall certain outcomes are more likely than others cross-culturally. It is also the case that once certain jobs are adopted by one gender, this can change the conventionality of another, related coordination problem. It has been widely pointed out that child care and big-game hunting are largely incompatible, so that if child care has been adopted by women, the basin of attraction for women hunting big game is decreased and this becomes a more functional problem.

Another simplification is the assumption that we will have complete common interest between genders when it comes to the emergence of division of labor. Varying interests between genders can arise in situations where there are differences in what outcomes are desired by either side, such as cases where one job provides better control over desired resources and so is preferable to each gender. We can make small variations to the models to better track these cases.

Consider games where one equilibrium is preferable to one player, and the other to the other, but one equilibrium still provides a greater joint payoff. The simplest case of this sort is shown in Figure 4.4. This is like the leader–follower game but where one outcome is relatively more preferable for one of the players.

|  |  | Player 2 | |
|---|---|---|---|
|  |  | A | B |
| Player 1 | A | 0, 0 | 1, 1+β |
|  | B | 1+α, 1 | 0, 0 |

Figure 4.4 An asymmetric leader–follower game

In this case, if $\alpha > \beta$, the B vs. A equilibrium will have a larger basin of attraction and if $\beta > \alpha$ the opposite will be true. In other words, the type that derives the greater benefit from their preferred strategy will be more likely to evolve to it. For example, if $\alpha = 1$ and $\beta = 9$, the preferable outcome for player B is reached about 75% of the time, making this problem less conventional than if $\beta = 0$. So in cases with conflict of interest between genders as to which sort of division of labor is preferable, we can still see a range of conventionality. This might occur in a case, for example, where a particular job is dangerous, and so is not preferred, but facts of pregnancy and breastfeeding make it especially dangerous for women.

As I suggested in the last chapter, evolutionary models do a better job than rational choice models, in some ways, of explaining the gendered division of labor. In this last section, we saw a new reason to care about the evolutionary perspective—rational choice models of the marriage market analyze which population outcomes are equilibria, but this does not give us fine-grained predictions about which of these equilibria are more or less likely to emerge in an evolutionary process. As such, they tell us less about why there is a range of conventionality when it comes to gendered division of labor.

### 4.2.1 Convention and justification

Innate sex differences in humans are often taken to justify inflexible gender roles and gender status divisions (Lorber, 1994; Okruhlik, 1994). In particular, such arguments often take on a functional flair. Women are naturally better at nurturing, and men are naturally poor at it. Or else, women are less aggressive and so fail in competitive interactions, while men are more aggressive and so excel at competition. We see in these narratives an appeal to the innate skills of men and women to not just explain, but also justify, the role divisions that emerge. Even Becker (1981), whose early models of household division of labor do not depend on any innate differences between men and women, suggests that traditional divisions of labor result because "normal" boys and girls are oriented toward market and household work, respectively, while only "deviant" ones show the opposite preference. Part of the goal of feminist gender theorists has been to simultaneously explain the pervasiveness and seeming naturalness of gender roles and gender differences while still maintaining that inegalitarian gender roles cannot be justified by appeal to biological sex.

The analysis here suggests that justifying gender roles and status divisions by appeal to function will not always work. Many divisions of labor, even ones that are distinct and enduring in a society, are nonetheless highly conventional. In these cases, there is no actual function to appeal to in justifying gender roles, and any attempt to do so is simply ad hoc. For divisions of labor that are less conventional, a functional explanation can often be provided for the cultural pattern that appeals to sex differences in ability, as described. However, it is a further question whether this sort of explanation can also justify gender roles. Our analysis suggests that the appeal to abilities can be used in some cases to partially justify gender roles along the following lines: "Women have feature X, which men lack, therefore there are benefits to various parties from women taking job Y." However, our analysis tells us that such justifications *cannot* appeal to anything like the inevitability or innateness of gender roles, even in cases where there is strong cross-cultural regularity. Such roles still "could be otherwise" in a stable society. To some degree, at least, they are arbitrary. Furthermore, in modern societies, where many jobs tend to be intellectual rather than physical, the functionality of many such roles disappears.

Some theorists focus especially on supposedly innate differences in the preferences, rather than abilities, of men and women for different sorts of work in justifying gender roles. In particular, a debate has broken out between evolutionary psychologists and sociologists over this topic. The evolutionary psychologists involved claim that psychological sex differences in humans can be attributed to different evolutionary environments for human males and females (Buss and Schmitt, 2011). These different environments led to significantly different preferences for different sorts of labor. Social structure theory, on the other hand, posits that gender roles largely create sex differences in psychology (Eagly and Wood, 1999; Wood and Eagly, 2012). Gender roles emerge first on cultural evolutionary time scales, and then actors come to behave in ways that fit the roles they take, including preference differences. One accusation against this latter theory is that it claims that gender roles emerge arbitrarily. In other words, the worry is that social structure theory fails to provide an explanation of why we have particular gender roles at all, and so does not actually provide an alternative to accounts from evolutionary psychology. Wood and Eagly (2012), in response, point to the role of ecological conditions in determining which gender will take what roles.

The analysis here gives them, arguably, a much better response. In fact, arbitrariness *is* a part of the emergence of gender roles, and is a perfectly appropriate part of a cultural evolutionary explanation. When there are not significant functional differences between roles for genders, division of labor is still expected, and it is expected to be highly conventional. Even where there are significant functional differences, we should expect evolution to sometimes choose the less efficient outcome. (Wood and Eagly (2012) give examples of cultures where women have assumed traditional warrior roles, for example. Alternatively among the Aka tribe, men literally suckle infants (Hewlett and Lamb, 2005).) Far from being a worry for social structural theory, the arbitrariness of gender roles is just what we would expect when they emerge via cultural evolution to solve coordination problems (rather than being determined by innate psychological differences).[5] In such an appeal, social structural theorists can present a detailed, dynamical analysis of the emergence of gendered division of labor to counter a speculative, just-so story about sexual selection.

## 4.3  The Evolution of Types

Why do humans have genders at all? Many theorists have argued that gender and gender differences are not innate, but are culturally constructed. But, if so, why should it be the case that every human culture has developed such a construction? Why don't we see some cultures where this particular feature failed to emerge? The universality of gender contributes to the perception described in Chapter 1 of gender as innate

---

[5] One thing to note is that whether or not it is fallacious to employ psychology/biology to justify gender role divisions, people simply do it. And, in particular, in recent studies, it has been observed that men who believe that there are significant biological differences between men and women are more discriminatory and more sexist (Keller, 2005; Morton et al., 2009). This fact means that those working on innate gender differences, or on the evolution of gender roles, face *inductive risk*, as described by philosophers of science, or the risk that they could be wrong and, furthermore, cause social ill by being wrong (Hempel, 1965; Douglas, 2000, 2009; Elliott, 2011). When it comes to work on gender differences, researchers should arguably be taking this inductive risk into account, especially when promoting evolutionary narratives to explain supposed psychological sex differences. This is especially true because work in evolutionary psychology is often built on relatively thin evidence, and is often highly speculative. While there is room for speculative evolutionary narratives in science, in cases where these narratives have the capacity to create social ills, their proponents should arguably be held to higher standards.

and unchanging. It is not impossible that a universal cultural feature could be nonetheless constructed. In order to tell a coherent story along these lines, though, one must provide a good reason for why the cultural feature is so robust. This section presents a toy model that tells such a story about gender.

We have seen how gender can act as a type that human actors take advantage of to solve complementary coordination problems. One further possibility, though, is that gender does not just provide an opportunity for such solutions, but that it arises for the very purpose of doing so. Ridgeway (2011), for example, argues that gender inequality persists in modern, post agricultural, US society *because* of the key role it plays in allowing actors to organize their social relations and thus achieve coordination.

Consider the following model. There is a homogenous group playing a complementary coordination game. Cultural evolution should take this group to a polymorphism, where they manage to coordinate sometimes, but not always.

Suppose that two individuals in this group change strategies. In particular, suppose that these individuals decide to start conditioning their behavior based on some underlying marker that distinguishes them. Now the rest of the group is doing about as well as they were before, but when these two individuals meet each other, they always manage to coordinate, and so do a bit better than average. On cultural evolutionary assumptions, we should expect others to start imitating the behavior of these coordinators, by recognizing the same underlying marker and using it to condition behavior and so coordinate. Once more individuals start to recognize the marker, everyone using it to coordinate will do better than before, because they have more partners who know how to break symmetry. This process will carry the population to a state where now there are types, and everyone uses these to coordinate. In other words, from a completely homogenous group we can see the endogenous emergence of social categories.[6]

Why do we see gender and gender roles in every society? This analysis indicates that the emergence of types is selected for given a need to facilitate coordination and the ability to make use of underlying differences

---

[6] This process is similar to the invasion of actors using correlated strategies discussed by Skyrms (2014, 70).

to do so. Of course, the analysis does not entirely explain why gender in particular has emerged universally, rather than some other sort of type. There are a few observations that can help explain this universality. From a game theoretic standpoint, when it comes to gender, we see almost the best possible conditions for the use of types to solve complementary coordination problems. There are two types that are equally prevalent. (In two-type mixing models, remember, 50–50 between types is the division that allows for the greatest coordination. This is because it maximizes the chances of the different types meeting, and so being able to use their categories to coordinate.) Furthermore, we see actors in many societies grouping into households with one member from each type, or perfectly dividing, leading to the best possible payoffs from a coordination standpoint. Lastly, as Ridgeway (2011) points out, sex differences are already salient for coordinating reproductive roles, leading to a natural salience as an easily observable physical difference upon which to build gender.

Of course, gender categories are probably not the only ones that have emerged to facilitate coordination. There are at least some other cases—class differences and castes, perhaps—where we see types that seem to have emerged for complementary coordination. As mentioned earlier, though, details mean that for every such case careful work will have to be done to fill in and assess the applicability of models such as those presented. In the case of caste, for example, social structures are very different from those associated with gender—the population proportions are not 50–50, there are more than two types, and individuals tend to be raised in environments with only in-group members, rather than the mixed environments we see for gender. (Of course, one might likewise point out that genders vary greatly from culture to culture, and the analysis here surely will be a better or worse fit in different cases. This is absolutely right, but for reasons of space, I will not elaborate further.)

Some sorts of types certainly did not emerge for the purpose of solving complementary coordination games, though some of these may have emerged to solve correlative coordination problems. In particular, consider cultural, racial, or religious groups that constitute types. Richerson et al. (2003) compellingly argue that these sorts of divisions may develop, and persist, in order to facilitate the use of separate correlative coordination conventions in separate groups. In such a case, types allow actors to recognize individuals using similar coordination strategies and interact with them more often. In still other cases, of course, types might play no functional role in coordination, but emerge as a result of innate out-group biases.

### 4.3.1 Learning inequity?

One feature of the toy models just presented is that actors themselves learn to adopt types that, as we have seen, can facilitate the emergence of inequity. Is it realistic to suppose that individuals will themselves be willing to adopt types when this is a consequence?

Remember from Chapter 2 that for many coordination situations, everyone does better to adopt categories, meaning that moving toward an unequal outcome may nonetheless be attractive. In some strategic scenarios, though, one type does less well than they would do in a homogenous group by adopting categories. This happens, remember, whenever actors play hawk–dove, introduced in Figure 1.5. The payoff details mean that doves would rather meet other doves than meet hawks at equilibrium. In a case like this, the evolutionary process just described cannot get off the ground. Note, though, that gender typically solves many coordination problems and not just one. We might imagine a situation where the evolving group encounters a portfolio of coordination problems—some best represented by hawk–dove, others by the leader–follower game, and others by the dancing game or the MFEO game. In such a case the benefits reaped by both sides may be enough for cultural evolutionary processes to promote typing, even if some interactions are straightforwardly worse for one type as a result.

To give a simple example of what I mean, consider a situation where actors interact in two sorts of complementary coordination problems— one that is well represented by hawk–dove and one that is well represented by the dancing game. Furthermore, suppose that the dancing-type interaction is very important to the actors so that they achieve payoffs of 5 when they coordinate and 0 otherwise. Suppose that actors play each of these games 50% of the time when they randomly interact with a group member. Lastly imagine that if actors do choose to condition on types, they do so for both games, not just one. In other words, once they recognize something like gender, they use it for role division in multiple cases.[7]

---

[7] This possibility is somewhat related to explorations of the possibility that humans generalize learning across many games, and that this could influence evolutionary outcomes (Bednar and Page, 2007; Skyrms and Zollman, 2010; Bednar et al., 2012; Mengel, 2012).

In this situation is there cultural evolutionary pressure to adopt types? In a homogenous group, actors will get an average payoff of 2 across the two games. (Half the time they expect to get 1.5 on average from playing hawk–dove, and the other half get 2.5 on average from playing the dancing game.) If two individuals adopt types, and use these for coordination, their payoff improves slightly since on average when they interact in both hawk–dove and the dancing game they will get a payoff of 3 for the type that plays dove and 4 for the type that plays hawk. In other words, when gender is facilitating multiple coordination interactions, the overall benefit from this can swamp any detriment to one type from some of the interactions.

There is an interesting connection, here, to philosophical work on the rationality of women's choices to engage in inequitable social roles. Cudd (1994, 2006) addresses arguments claiming that because women often choose domestic labor over market labor, they cannot be oppressed by the resulting inequitable arrangement. Cudd's response is to highlight the sense in which women's choices along these lines are restricted by social structure, drawing on the work of Okin (1989). So though they may be acting rationally in their own best interest, they may still be oppressed. In the models I have developed in this first half of the book, we see a situation arise where all members of society are restricted in their choices of social roles in the sense that anyone who makes a non-conventional choice will significantly damage their own material well-being. Furthermore, these arrangements are inequitable. And yet, any individual should be rationally willing to enter this social situation (starting from a state of nature), because doing so leads to payoff benefits.[8]

## 4.3.2 Bundling

When it comes to sex and gender, factors that need not necessarily go together *bundle* in individuals. For example, biological sex usually bundles with gender identity (as a man or woman).[9] This bundles with reported sexual preference.[10] These factors, of course, strongly bundle

---

[8] A further requirement Cudd gives for "oppression" is that one group is harmed to another's advantage, and I am unsure whether the social arrangements I have been modeling meet this crtierion.

[9] In a recent survey, only 0.3% of Americans self-identified as transgender. Of course, social stigma against transgender people means that this is probably an underestimate.

[10] About 3.5% of Americans self-identified as lesbian, gay, or bisexual (Gates, 2011).

with how households are formed. Especially in recent Western history, the vast majority of households involved one man and one woman. And all these factors bundle with behavioral regularities regarding division of labor. Women are people with female biological sex, who adopt the gender of woman, signal their membership in this group, sexually prefer men, form households with men, and take the household and workplace roles that are appropriate for women. In learning these behaviors, of course, they use other women as their models for social learning. And men can be defined in a similar way.

It is not just biological sex, or just gender roles, or just learning the appropriate divisions of labor that allow gender to facilitate coordination, but the entire bundle. When these factors are always present in the same types of people, the same social patterns will successfully solve complementary coordination problems. The arguments in the last section suggest that these bundles may even evolve for the purposes of coordination.[11]

Henrich and Boyd (2008) pursue this idea further. They consider cultural group selection in situations where some groups, but not others, have adopted conventions that use types and type-conditioning to divide labor. Cultural group selection, here, refers to situations where the success of competing social groups (as opposed to the success of competing individuals) can act as the mechanism by which cultural variants spread. As they show, in cases where actors play complementary coordination games, this sort of process should select for groups where actors interact more with those of the other type, where they learn only from their own type, where they adopt complementary roles, and where they focus on success-based cultural learning (i.e., adopt learning processes that are well-modeled by the replicator dynamics). In other words, the bundles themselves evolve.

If we consider the resistance of gender-based norms to social change, these bundles for coordination tell part of the story. If they are simply unraveled, a social function is not being performed. While much of the resistance to social change is driven by psychological biases, it is important to also recognize that dynamical factors related to successful

---

[11] Cudd (2006) actually defines social groups via the sorts of constraints these groups face. The fact that this is a plausible move makes salient how tight these bundles tend to be.

social coordination are at play. We must introduce factors to take the place of this complex if we want to change gender roles effectively.

• • •

Why do men make ropes in a certain culture? As we've seen in this chapter, the answer need not appeal to anything special about men, or even about the environment in which this behavior develops. We should expect division of labor by gender to be conventional to at least some degree, and so well explained by appeal to coordination, but not necessarily by other functional features. When it comes to the inequities that emerge because of gendered division of labor, this holds as well. These inequities might well have been otherwise, and appeals to innate differences in preference or abilities won't do the job to justify them.

We also saw in this chapter that from a homogenous group with entirely symmetric roles, categories can emerge spontaneously to solve complementary coordination problems. In the last few chapters, I have described social categorization as a precondition for social inequity. Now we see that this precondition itself can emerge, as well as the bundle of features necessary to get coordination (and resulting inequity) off the ground. This reduces by one the set of preconditions required to generate this sort of inequity via cultural evolution. We see that in a situation where we have 1) a complementary coordination problem, and 2) individuals who learn to do what benefits them, we can end up with social categories that divide people into different groups who get more or less based on their otherwise irrelevant differences.

We'll now move on to Part II of the book.

# PART II

# The Evolution of Inequity Through Division of Resources

Part I of this book focused on the role of types, and especially gender, as solutions for coordination problems. As I argued, typing and type-conditioning allow for a sort of symmetry-breaking when humans face complementary coordination problems. As I further argued, this function of typing means that types such as gender should be expected to emerge spontaneously in human groups for the very purpose of fulfilling that function. And when they do, they have the potential to improve the payoffs of all those involved. In the real world, many aspects of gendered division of labor as a pattern of behavior seem to fit the picture presented where gender emerges on a social evolutionary timescale as a way to break symmetry and improve social coordination.

Part I also discussed the inequitable conventions that emerge once types are established in human groups. In a homogenous group, conventions that evolve are expected to generate the same payoff for all involved—this, remember, is because otherwise the system wouldn't be at equilibrium. Once actors are constrained to different types, we expect equilibria where actors get different payoffs. As I pointed out, we can think of these type-based systems for coordination as having a trade-off in that they improve overall payoff, and often improve the payoff of each actor, but at the cost of equity and equality.

In the second half of the book, we now turn to focus on inequity of the second sort described in the Introduction, where one group simply takes advantage of the other. Chapter 5 starts by introducing a basic framework for thinking about this sort of inequitable norm between types, and focusing, in particular, on the ways in which power differences between groups can impact the course of cultural evolution, potentially leading to serious inequities. Chapter 6 will focus on a different, perhaps unintuitive, way that inequitable conventions can emerge between types. In particular, we will look at how differences in reactivity between groups can be generated either by minority status, or by differential access to institutional memory. These differences in reactivity can lead to disadvantage for one type via cultural Red King and Red Queen effects. Chapter 7 looks at a slightly different set of models, ones that incorporate social network structure, to see how the emergence of this sort of discrimination might impact individuals' choices about interactive partners. Chapter 8 turns to a more specific topic, showing how the evolutionary models from this book can be used to explain patterns of inequitable household bargaining previously treated in economics using rational-choice models. This chapter brings together insights from both halves of the book to show how the two sorts of inequity can interrelate. Chapter 9 concludes by considering, within the cultural evolutionary framework used here, how to change inequitable conventions of division.

Throughout Part II of the book, I will move away from looking at complementary coordination games generally and instead focus almost entirely on various versions of the Nash demand game. The Nash demand game has proven to be an extremely flexible general representation of resource division between actors. While, as I have argued, the coordination games from the first half of the book can also model situations of resource division and of inequity, the Nash demand game is particularly germane because unlike those other models it includes a possibility of equity. We are now focusing less on situations where some inequity arises as a result of coordination (which simultaneously leads to payoff benefits), but instead are looking at situations where because of an existing type division it is possible for non-functional, persistent disadvantages for one group to arise.

# 5

# Power and the Evolution of Inequity

Why do some sorts of people get more and other sorts of people get less? Given the massive inequities in modern human society (of the second, non-functional type), especially those which rest on irrelevant personal characters like race and gender, this question demands attention. Often, the sorts of answers given appeal to the underlying psychology of human beings. Humans have innate in-group preferences. Humans are prone to stereotyping. Humans develop biases against those in certain social categories, including implicit biases, which lead to discrimination. Humans experience stereotype threat, leading to the poor performance of underprivileged groups when it is most crucial. Humans experience confirmation bias, so that events which confirm their stereotypes are salient, while those that oppose them fade away. Recipients of discrimination reasonably disinvest in skill learning on the belief that they will be undervalued in any case, causing further confirmation of stereotypical beliefs that they are unskilled or uneducated (Ogbu, 1978; D'souza, 1995; Loury, 1995; Stewart, 2010).

These sorts of phenomenon are deeply important to understanding inequity, and nothing in this book is intended to suggest otherwise. What I will show now, though, is that another sort of explanation of the second sort of inequity is available. In particular, as I will argue, a modeling perspective can show us that the conditions necessary to generate pernicious inequity in human societies are extremely minimal. Under these minimal conditions, cultural evolutionary pathways will march robustly toward inequitable systems. These models do not prove that real-world systems of inequity have, in fact, evolved via these simple cultural evolutionary pathways, but they tell us that they could. In particular, they show that even if many of the most pernicious psychological facts about humans are removed or mitigated, inequitable conventions of the second sort are still expected to emerge.[1,2]

Part of the message here is that if we hope to reduce inequity in our own societies, working to eliminate the effects of psychological factors such as implicit bias may not be enough. The robustness of the emergence of inequity may mean that it is a fact we have to face again and again. This may require a retooling of our thinking about inequity not as something to conquer and be done with, but as something that will call for a persistent fight.

I'll start by introducing the primary paradigm used in this half of the book—the Nash demand game. I'll then move on to a perhaps unexpected topic—the evolution of fairness. As we'll see, previous evolutionary models of the Nash demand game have been used to argue that fair bargaining is what we should expect in human groups. I'll show why, once types are involved, fairness is often not the expected outcome of evolutionary systems. I'll then turn to the role power plays in the evolution of bargaining conventions. It has been long argued, using rational choice-based models, that power can influence bargaining outcomes between individuals in one-shot interactions. I will show how power, hashed out in a few different ways, can also influence the emergence of bargaining norms between groups. I will conclude with a model where power in one round can translate to advantage in later rounds for members of a type. As I will show, this can generate a process where even small initial differences between types can lead to wildly different outcomes.

---

[1] This sort of explanation bears some similarities to structural explanations of racial inequality. As Stewart (2010) describes such theories, "Race, from the structural perspective, is an integral piece of the social machinery that distributes private rewards and allocates an array of public privileges—it is more than an overt racist attitude/behavior expressed by a faction of dominant group members" (5).

[2] Hoffmann (2006) employs similar models to those presented here in work that he describes as looking at the role of human cognition in economic stratification. However, the only features of his models that represent human cognition are the use of types to condition behavior. Categorization and generalization are entirely general aspects of cognition, and so do not strike me as having much to do with humans' special evolved cognitive mechanisms. This said, the minimal explanations I generate do depend on the psychological tendencies of humans to form and use social categories, but they do not depend on psychological tendencies that we usually think of as the problematic ones.

## 5.1 The Nash Demand Game

The Nash demand game has been widely used as a model of human interaction when actors divide resources (Young, 1993b; Axtell et al., 2000; Stewart, 2010).[3] It involves two actors who each demand some portion of the resource. If these portions are compatible, the actors receive what they demand. If not, the actors receive a payoff called the "disagreement point", often set at 0, the idea being that their inability to settle on a mutually agreeable division leads to poor outcomes for both actors.[4]

Figure 5.1 shows two versions of this game. While in principle actors in the Nash demand game could demand any portion of a resource (53%, say), in practice it is common to look at simplified games where actors instead choose from a limited number of demands, or "mini-games," as Sigmund et al. (2001) have described them.[5] In (a), actors can make either a Low, Med, or High demand, and these correspond to demanding 3, 5, or 7 of a total resource of 10. In (b), the Med demand is dropped, so

(a)

| | | Player 2 | | |
|---|---|---|---|---|
| | | Low | Med | High |
| Player 1 | Low | 3, 3 | 3, 5 | 3, 7 |
| | Med | 5, 3 | 5, 5 | 0, 0 |
| | High | 7, 3 | 0, 0 | 0, 0 |

(b)

| | | Player 2 | |
|---|---|---|---|
| | | Low | High |
| Player 1 | Low | 3, 3 | 3, 7 |
| | High | 7, 3 | 0, 0 |

**Figure 5.1** Payoff tables for two simplified Nash demand games

[3] This game has been given many labels over the years including, at least, the Nash bargaining game, the bargaining game, divide-the-dollar, divide-the-pie, and divide-the-cake.

[4] As in the more purely coordination games, one should not take 0 to have special meaning here. Instead, it is a number that provides a baseline of what actors get for failing to coordinate that can be compared to their coordination payoffs.

[5] For more on evolution and mini versions of the Nash demand game see Young (1993b); Skyrms (1994, 1996); Alexander and Skyrms (1999); Alexander (2000); Binmore (2008); Skyrms and Zollman (2010); Gallo (2014). These authors all employ games with a partition of finite demands.

actors can only choose Low or High. Notice that this second game has the same form as the complementary coordination games from Part I of the book.

For each of these games, the Nash equilibria are the strategy pairings where actors perfectly divide the resource (Low vs. High, High vs. Low, and Med vs. Med). If either actor demands more, they exceed the resource and both get nothing, if either actor demands less she simply gets less.

There is something special to note about the Nash demand game with a fair demand, which is that it has both a complementary and a correlative coordination character. Most equilibria of the game involve complementary demands—80% and 20%, or 63% and 37%. The fair demand is correlative, though, in the sense that actors take the same action to succeed. This makes the fair demand special from a population level and an evolutionary standpoint, which will be discussed in further detail shortly.

It is worth taking a minute to note that many economists think the Nash demand game misses crucial elements of some bargaining processes. For example, actors in bargains often take turns making offers until an agreement is reached, as in the highly influential model from Rubinstein (1982). Because I will focus in this book on an evolutionary scenario, the mini-game presented here can be thought of as having the potential to represent bargaining outcomes that result from all sorts of complicated, interpersonal dynamics. The representation is a rough one. Whatever the process that leads to a bargaining outcome, if the outcome is more preferable to one player than to the other, they have reached the High vs. Low equilibrium, and vice versa. If it is an approximately equal division, they have reached the Med vs. Med outcome. If they have pushed each other so hard that bargaining has failed, they reach the disagreement point.

## 5.2 The Evolution of Fairness and the Evolution of Unfairness

Much philosophical and economic work on the evolution of bargaining starts with the following explanandum: humans treat each other fairly. Suppose that you and Dwayne Johnson are going to share a pie, and you would each like to eat as much pie as possible. How would you split it? Chances are good that your first instinct is to split the pie into two exactly equal portions, and each take one.[6] In general, there seems to be a pull toward equality when it comes to dividing things in human groups. Empirical work backs up this intuitive claim. Humans have stated norms for fair divisions of resources (Yaari and Bar-Hillel, 1984), and in experimental settings involving the Nash demand game players strongly tend toward the 50–50 split (Nydegger and Owen, 1974; Roth and Malouf, 1979; Van Huyck et al., 1997).[7] Economists, for this reason, sometimes build other-regarding preferences for fairness into bargaining models (Fehr and Schmidt, 1999; Camerer, 2003).

To explain this phenomenon, Skyrms (1994) looks at the emergence of bargaining in single groups playing the Nash demand game. As he observes, the most likely outcome in these models (the equilibrium with the largest basin of attraction) is always for every member of the population to play the 50–50 split. One way to understand this result in the language of this book is to observe that the 50–50 split is special because it is the only equilibrium that involves a correlative, and not a complementary, solution to the underlying coordination problem. An entire population demanding 50% of a resource will always manage to coordinate their demands when they meet. On the other hand, a population with any other set of demands will sometimes mis-coordinate, for the same reasons as in any other complementary coordination problem. In a population where some actors make low demands, when they meet other low demanders they will waste the resource. In a population where some actors make high demands, when they meet other high demanders they will get the disagreement point.

Sometimes other outcomes arise. In particular, a "fractious" outcome, where some actors make high demands, and some low, sometimes emerges. In the service of explaining fairness, philosophers have looked for conditions under which these fractious outcomes disappear. Skyrms (1994) points out that correlation between strategies, so that Highs tend to meet Highs, Meds meet Meds, and Lows meet Lows, will push the population to the fair outcome. (This correlation prevents the complementary outcomes where Highs and Lows meet from occurring,

[6] Just kidding, obviously you would give all the pie to Dwayne Johnson.
[7] Except you, Mina Pedersen.

making it worse to demand High or Low.)[8] Alexander and Skyrms (1999) point out that this correlation can be generated by network interactions, where people tend to meet their neighbors again and again for interaction. And Alexander (2007) argues extensively that such repeated neighbor interactions can lead to the emergence of equitable bargaining. Lastly, as Skyrms (2014) points out, communication between neighbors—the simple ability to transfer information—tends to generate fair demands. Furthermore, the fair demand in the Nash demand game will always be the only evolutionarily stable strategy, or ESS of the game (Sugden, 1986), and the only stochastically stable equilibrium as well (Young, 1993b).[9,10]

If there is so much evolutionary pressure for fairness, though, the obvious question is: why inequity? To give one example, women regularly receive less in negotiations, and are punished for high demands (Bowles et al., 2007; Babcock and Laschever, 2009).[11] Why do we see these sorts of patterns, rather than the expected equitable ones? This is where types and type-conditioning come into the story. As I made clear in the first half of the book, populations with types are importantly different from populations without types because there is an extra piece of information available when an actor meets someone of another type. There we focused on the functional role this extra piece of information can play in facilitating coordination. When it comes to bargaining, though, this extra information can play a more sinister role. As we will see, it makes

[8] But see D'Arms et al. (1998) who counter that anti-correlation of strategies can lead to the evolution of unfair norms. Anti-correlation can, in effect, create a population that mimics a perfectly divided one. If two bargaining strategies evolve in the population, and only meet the opposite strategies, they end up in the same situation as actors who only meet different types and who evolve to play different strategies.

[9] Maynard-Smith and Price (1973) introduced this concept of evolutionarily stable strategies to identify strategies that are stable against invasion of mutants. ESSes in games can be identified through payoff tables alone. In this way, although a dynamic concept, ESSes do not depend on the choice of dynamic, and are stable for any dynamics that increase the proportion of strategies with higher payoffs. A strategy $x_i$ is an ESS if $u(x_i, x_j)$ is the payoff of strategy $x_i$ played against $x_j$ and : 1) $u(x_i, x_i) > u(x_i, x_j)$ or 2) $u(x_i, x_i) = u(x_i, x_j)$ and $u(x_i, x_j) > u(x_j, x_j)$ for all $x_j \neq x_i$.

[10] A stochastically stable equilibrium is obtained by finding the limiting behavior of the system as the probability of experimentation goes to zero (Foster and Young, 1990; Young, 1993a,b).

[11] In a key study, Bowles et al. (2005) find that when women negotiate for others, they are more aggressive and demanding. In other words, they conform to non-aggressive normative behavior when bargaining, but in different circumstances are perfectly capable of behaving aggressively—indicating that the difference between men and women is not in ability, but in choice.

unfair solutions to the Nash demand game go from an impossibility to a commonplace. Typing creates new equilibria, not possible in single populations, where one group gets less and the other more. Axtell et al. (2000) label these outcomes as "discriminatory" in two-type models because they involve populations who treat out-group members differently from the in-group, to the detriment of one out-group. It is hard to understate the importance of this simple observation—add types to an evolutionary model of bargaining and now fairness is not the expected outcome. Instead, inequity and discrimination emerge.[12]

A number of previous authors have used this fact to model inequity, class stratification, or racism in two-population models. In economics, Axtell et al. (2000) look at the emergence of inequity in two populations playing the Nash demand game (as do Poza et al. (2011) in a follow-up paper). Bowles and Naidu (2006) and Hwang et al. (2014) look at the conditions under which inequitable conventions are stable in two-population models where actors from both groups try to move toward conventions that benefit themselves. Hoffmann (2006) considers the impacts of tags on populations evolving to play hawk–dove, and uses these models to explain social stratification. Smith and Choi (2007) present a rather complicated agent-based model where actors without types divide into upper and lower classes based on initial resource disparities. In sociology, Stewart (2010) shows how small numbers of discriminators can generate a system of persistent racial inequality in a bargaining model where actors sometimes engage in typing and type-conditioning. All of these models employ the base assumptions that allow inequity to emerge in the models

---

[12] Regarding gender and bargaining, there does not seem to be much experimental work looking at the effects of gender on play in the Nash bargaining game, though D'Exelle et al. (2017) find that women in rural Uganda make lower demands when playing with men than with women. It is worth noting that experimental evidence on asymmetric bargaining games, though, shows that inequity is common between social groups in such games. In the ultimatum game, one player offers another some portion of a resource. The second player has the opportunity to accept the offer or to reject it, leaving both players with nothing. In the dictator game, the second player must simply accept their offer. Solnick (2001) finds that women receive smaller offers from women and men in the simultaneous move ultimatum game (where actors choose strategies at the same time), and offer more to men. In the sequential ultimatum game, women receive lower offers, and are more likely to accept low offers, than men (Eckel and Grossman, 2001). Eckel and Grossman (1998) also find that women make larger offers in the dictator game than men do. (But see Frey and Bohnet (1995) and Bolton et al. (1998) who find no gender differences in the dictator game.)

here—actors are divided into types, they bargain, and via some dynamical process they adopt actions which benefit themselves.

To see how common unfair outcomes are in the simplest model that adds types to an evolving population, let us look at some evolutionary results. Figure 5.2 shows results from a simulation where actors in a group with two categories learn to bargain.[13] I assume, for now, that there are three strategies—Low, Med, and High—and I vary the values of the Low and High demands. In the figure, shaded patches in each bar represent the sizes of the basins of attraction for the three possible equilibria (which correspond to how often a simulation reaches them)—discrimination by one type, the fair outcome, and discrimination by the other type. When the Low and High demands are more inequitable (for example when Low = 1 and High = 9) the fair outcome has a relatively large basin of attraction, though the two inequitable outcomes are still possible. When Low and High are closer together the probability that the populations end up at a discriminatory bargaining convention becomes quite high.[14]

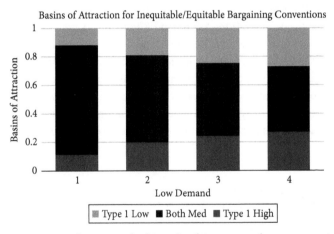

**Figure 5.2** Basins of attraction for fair and unfair outcomes between types in the Nash demand game with three strategies

[13] These results use the discrete time-replicator dynamics and a perfectly divided population, but the results will be similar in a two-type mixing population. As elsewhere in the book, reported results are from 10k runs of simulation.

[14] This is somewhat similar to a result from Henrich and Boyd (2008) who find that the more inequitable the equilibrium for a two-strategy complementary coordination game, the less likely it is that an inequitable type-based convention emerges, and the more likely that

When Low $= 4$, the probability that the population ends up at one of the unfair conventions is 55%, meaning that more than half the time these simulations head to an unfair convention, despite the fact that there is perfect symmetry between the types. There is no reason, other than chance initial conditions, that one type or the other should get more, but the simple fact of types and typing means that they do. Notice that in these simulations there is perfect symmetry between the two types, so it is equally likely that each type ends up discriminating against the other.

Let us look at one more set of results. Consider again a population with two types playing a Nash demand game, but suppose we now have a strategic situation that allows for a more fine-grained division of resources. In particular, we will consider three models with increasingly fine partitions of demands. In the first actors have five available demands corresponding to 1, 3, 5, 7, or 9 of a resource of value 10. The second has 9 available demands (1, 2, 3, 4...), and the third 19 demands (0.5, 1, 1.5, ...). The equilibria for each of these models will correspond to the fair outcome and the unfair outcomes where one type takes a low demand and the other type a complementary high demand, such as 0.5 and 9.5, or 3 and 7. This means there is a range of levels of inequity that might evolve, from the most serious to more minor. Figure 5.3 shows the size of the basin of attraction for each of these equilibria in each of the three models. In all three cases, the black patch represents the basin of attraction for the fair norm. Each slightly lighter patch represents the basin of attraction for an unfair norm, with lighter colors corresponding to greater inequity. (There is no legend for this figure since there are 10 possible equilibria for the model with 19 possible strategies.) One thing to note is that the fair equilibrium is always the one with the largest basin of attraction, and the less inequitable equilibria will have larger basins of attraction than the more inequitable ones. In all three models, though, inequitable conventions emerge more than half of the time. Furthermore, as the partitions grow finer, the chance that the population ends up at the fair equilibrium gets smaller and smaller. In the model with 19 possible demands, the population goes to the fair convention only 19% of the

---

a fractious but equitable outcome emerges. Bowles and Naidu (2006); Hwang et al. (2014) similarly find that inequitable conventions are more likely to be the stochastically stable equilibria of evolutionary models when the conventions themselves are less inequitable.

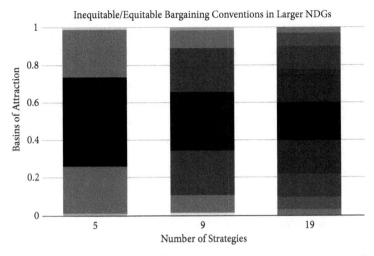

**Figure 5.3** Basins of attraction for fair and unfair outcomes between types in the Nash demand game with various numbers of strategies

time. In many real-world cases, of course, fine partitions of resources are possible.[15]

Hopefully now the claim made at the very beginning of this chapter—that the preconditions to generate inequity of the second sort are very minimal—is starting to become clear. In the bargaining models we have just considered, inequitable conventions are expected to emerge between groups despite the possibility of an equally good fair convention, and despite the lack of any sort of asymmetry between groups that might explain why one and not the other should be disadvantaged. The preconditions for this emergence are 1) a strategic scenario well modeled by a bargaining game, 2) actors who learn to repeat strategies that work well for themselves and others, and 3) typing and type-conditioning. Notice that these conditions hold broadly in human groups.

---

[15] Of course, one might point out that as we increase the number of strategies, many of the possible outcomes are quite close to fair (i.e., one side receives a resource of 4.5 and the other 5.5). We might instead consider the expected payoff difference between the two groups to see whether inequity increases as partitions grow finer. On this measure, inequity is actually less serious for finer partitions in the models in Figure 5.3. (For Figure 5.2 there is no straightforward trend, though the worst inequity emerges when the low demand is 2.) This is to point out that there are different ways to measure inequity in this model, but the main point stands that once we add categories, inequity of some sort or another becomes commonplace.

## 5.2.1 *Is fair, fair?*

In the next section, we will start to look at models where there is some sort of asymmetry between groups to clarify the conditions under which a social group will be more likely to be disadvantaged by bargaining norms. First, though, a brief discussion about what fairness even means in bargaining models is in order.

What, exactly, does a medium demand consist in? Surely we are not trying to represent just those real-world cases where actors divide a cake (or some other resource) into exactly equal parts. Instead, we are trying to capture an approximately fair division of resources. Of course, what a fair division is might be quite different depending on the background context in which a game is played. As Bicchieri (2005) puts it, "Fairness, reciprocity, trust, and so on, are *local* concepts, in the sense that their interpretation and the expectations and prescriptions that surround them vary with the objects, people, and situations to which they apply" (76). If I buy ingredients and do the extensive work of baking a cake while you laze around, no one would expect me to split it 50–50 with you. It would be fair for me to keep the entire thing, and generous to give you a piece. A 50–50 split in this case would be a division falling heavily in your favor. What I am trying to highlight here is that what a Med vs. Med split corresponds to in a society will itself often be a culturally evolved notion. In our society, we think that people should possess those things that they buy or build (or bake). But we might have had other norms for what is fair, and many societies do (Henrich et al., 2001).[16] Experimental work on ultimatum games—a type of asymmetric bargaining game—show a surprising amount of variation cross-culturally in what is taken to be a fair split. In addition, framing effects will create within-culture differences in beliefs about fairness (Bicchieri, 2005). (For example, the addition of factors that imply one player is deserving will tend to skew percepts of fairness in their favor (Hoffman and Spitzer, 1985; Frey and Bohnet, 1995; Falk et al., 2008).) Note that these evolved standards play an important role. Without them, the sort of special coordination that the fair outcome provides is not possible. In order for fairness to be special, everyone has to agree on what fairness means.

---

[16] Fiske (1992) describes cases where authority rankings create perceptions of fairness for behaviors (like simply taking goods from group members) that seem objectively one-sided.

Now, though, suppose that a society can have norms of fairness where social categories come into play. Perhaps in a society what everyone (implicitly or explicitly) agrees to be "fair," for example, is that immigrants get less and natives get more in situations of bargaining. In such a society, a Med demand in a representative model could correspond to one group literally demanding 60% and the other 40% of a resource. On this interpretation, the extensive results supporting fair divisions in the Nash demand game described above do not necessarily tell us that fairness should be expected in human cultures at all. If asymmetries are exploited to redefine "fair," the payoff benefits of fairness are recovered to some degree in the new scenario. Actors still manage to coordinate in a correlative way when they meet, but the extra information provided by social categories allows for this coordination to involve asymmetric outcomes.

Sen (1987) pursues a similar argument in claiming that household bargaining models from economics ignore what he calls "perceptions" of dessert. He points out that divisions may be judged fair between parties as a result of social conventions that, objectively, are not.[17] Of course, one might rightly ask what objective measure of fairness is possible if "fair" itself is an emergent, conventional social norm. Sen (1987) identifies unfairness between genders with variable outcomes on measures like mortality, morbidity, health, income, etc., as well as "well-being," which he describes as, ". . . a person's functionings and capabilities: what he or she is able to do or be" (8). Where these diverge as a result of household divisions of goods and labor, he labels the division as inequitable. This, of course, requires assuming that our stated (if not always practiced) social norm that factors like gender and race should not determine dessert is a good one.

This is all to say that there are two different ways of thinking about the role types and typing play in inequitable norms. Either we can think of them as creating an asymmetry that allows inequitable divisions to arise (as in the models discussed here), or as creating an asymmetry that allows for a culturally evolved notion of fairness to emerge that treats types differently. I will not model this second possibility explicitly.

---

[17] Relatedly, he points out that in many studies women do a disproportionate amount of work contributing to a household, but are perceived as contributing relatively little.

## 5.3 Power

Nash (1950) was the one who first introduced a bargaining problem similar to the Nash demand game, along with his famous solution to it (which I will say more about in a minute). Just a few years later he produced another paper thinking about his bargaining model in a slightly different way (Nash, 1953). Suppose that before engaging in a bargaining scenario, two actors each have an opportunity to make threats about what will happen to the other should bargaining break down. If you and Dwayne Johnson are dividing your pie, say, you might threaten him with your annoyed glare should bargaining go south and he might threaten you with a crushed spine. These threats can then be taken as the disagreement points of the model, which, under this interpretation, are relabelled as *threatpoints*.

In this version of the game, power differentials between bargaining agents become salient. Suppose one player is able to issue a more credible threat than the other, for whatever reason. Because the less powerful player now stands to lose more should bargaining fail, the more powerful player derives an advantage.

The Nash bargaining solution starts with four axioms that he argues any solution to the bargaining problem should hold to.[18] From there Nash derives a unique division, which is that players should maximize $(v_1 - t_1)(v_2 - t_2)$, or the product of each player's expected payoff $(v_i)$ minus their disagreement (threat) point $(t_i)$. On this formulation, the player with the higher disagreement point, or ability to make a more credible threat, will get a higher value, holding other things fixed. One question that arises given the framework we are working with is the following: how does power influence not individual bargaining outcomes in one-shot games, but the emergence of bargaining conventions between social groups? This is the question that I will focus on for the rest of the chapter.

In order to address this question another question must first be answered and that is: what is power? There are many ways in which

---

[18] The details of these axioms are beyond the scope of this discussion. They are *Pareto efficiency*, essentially that there should be no resource gone to waste, *symmetry*, that if players have completely symmetric positions they should get equal amounts of the resource, *invariance to affine transformations*, that an affine transformation of a player's payoffs should not influence the outcome, and *independence of irrelevant alternatives*, basically that the removal of options that are not chosen should not change the expected outcome.

one person can have power over another person, and many ways in which members of one social group can have more power than members of another social group. For our purposes here, I will not give a conceptual analysis of power, or try to otherwise pin down this notion, but will instead look at a number of different ways of operationalizing power within a cultural evolutionary framework. As I will argue, these operationalizations fit well with at least some properties of social groups that we associate with power. And, as I will show, there are a number of different ways in which these operationalizations can impact the chances that certain social groups are disadvantaged with respect to bargaining norms. This part of the book draws heavily on joint work with Justin Bruner (Bruner and O'Connor, 2015).

The models we are about to consider are particularly important for the following reason: in almost every case, the social situation for members of two social categories will be asymmetric. When it comes to gender, we have already seen one important reason why—division of labor by gender means that men and women are always in asymmetric positions with respect to social roles. These small differences of inequity between genders, as we will now see, can feed into evolutionary processes that generate more serious inequity. In general asymmetry rather than symmetry is the rule in the social realm. If we have one group, there is only one way for a second group to be identical to it, and uncountable ways for it to be different. As we will see, these differences increase the chances that inequitable conventions will emerge.

### 5.3.1 *Evolution with threats*

Suppose that members of one social group tend to be able to issue credible threats to members of another social group to be carried out should bargaining between them fail. Scenarios that fit this assumption might include household bargaining between genders where there is a more serious threat of domestic violence for women owing to size dimorphism, or bargaining between classes when one class holds greater economic or political power than another, or bargaining between members of different races when there is a similar economic or political divide. (For an example where both race and class play such roles, consider the negotiations taking place between landowners and sharecroppers in the American South post-Civil War.) In Bruner and O'Connor (2015), where Justin

Bruner and I first explored evolutionary bargaining models with power differences between groups, we use the models to represent bargaining across the academic hierarchy, where members of one group (professors) can make choices that more seriously impact the careers of the other group (grad students). Notice that although the source of "power" in these examples is different—physical strength versus economic advantage versus asymmetric working conditions—in each case the difference creates potential for one side to lower the payoffs of the other.

Figure 5.4 shows an underlying game that might capture such a situation. We see a Nash demand game with Low, Med, and High demands, but now instead of both actors receiving the same disagreement point of o, we have actors receiving threatpoints of $t$ and $T$ where we assume (without loss of generality) that $t \leq T$. In other words, if bargaining should go south, one player can lower the payoff of the other more effectively than the converse.

In an evolutionary model where $t = T = o$, as we know, inequity can emerge, but it is equally likely that each type ends up at an advantaged equilibrium. As we vary the values of $t$ and $T$, though, we no longer see this sort of symmetry. Let $t = o$ and let $T$ vary between o and 3.5. Figure 5.5 shows results for evolution in such a model. As before, there are three possible outcomes to this model—two discriminatory outcomes where one side demands High and the other Low, and one fair outcome. What we see now, though, is that as $T$ increases, or as the difference between the threatpoints for the two groups becomes wider, three things happen. First, the likelihood that the fair outcomes is reached decreases. Second, the likelihood that the powerful group demands High goes up. And last, the likelihood that the less powerful group demands High goes down. When $T = 3.5$, 61% of simulations go to the outcome where the powerful type discriminates, and only 4% of simulations go to the outcome where the less powerful type discriminates.

|  |  | Player 2 | | |
|---|---|---|---|---|
|  |  | Low | Med | High |
|  | Low | 4, 4 | 4, 5 | 4, 6 |
| Player 1 | Med | 5, 4 | 5, 5 | t, T |
|  | High | 6, 4 | t, T | t, T |

Figure 5.4 Payoff table for a three-strategy Nash demand game with threatpoints

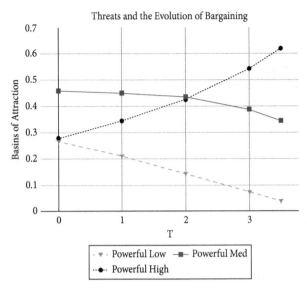

**Figure 5.5** Basins of attraction for a model where one type has a higher disagreement point in the Nash demand game

From the Nash perspective, a higher threatpoint can translate into a bargaining advantage between individuals. Why, though, do high threatpoints translate to advantage in the emergence of bargaining conventions between social groups? The explanation for this phenomenon has to do with the incentives actors have for learning various strategies. For actors with a high threatpoint, the difference between receiving Low and getting the threatpoint is relatively small, meaning that there is relatively little incentive to learn to demand Low. On the other hand, demanding High is not as risky for them, and still generates the same rewards, so there is a greater incentive to learn to play High. This asymmetry creates a selective environment where the powerful group then tends to move toward demanding High. In this case, the details of the game matter little. A similar effect will be observed for Nash demand games with different demands, or finer partitions, for the very same reasons.[19]

---

[19] For example, see Bruner and O'Connor (2015). In LaCroix and O'Connor (2017) we show the robustness of this effect in models with different dynamics, finite populations, and cases where disagreement points are heterogeneous across the groups.

Note that there is another sort of threat that members of one social group might be able to wield that shifts payoffs in a different way, but still advantages the powerful group. Suppose that instead of issuing a threat contingent on bargaining breakdown, actors of one type threaten to punish their opponents for making high demands simpliciter. (Bowles et al. (2007), for instance, find that women are directly punished for making high bargaining demands.) Suppose that a powerful actor can decrease the payoff of their opponent by 2 should the opponent choose High. This induces a payoff table like the one in Figure 5.6. Notice that unlike changes to the threatpoint of the model, this sort of threat disrupts one of the Nash equilibria of the game. Now the strategy pairing where player 1 chooses High and player 2 Low is no longer an equilibrium. In an evolutionary model, this strategy pairing will no longer emerge as a stable population convention either. In this sort of threat scenario, then, one side can entirely eliminate the possibility of ending up at the disadvantaged outcome via a threat.

Notice that these models are applicable only to cases where, for some reason, the members of one social group are actually more able to change the payoffs of the other group. This is importantly different from the role that threats play in standard game theoretic models, as I will now elaborate.

In many game theoretic analyses, the way threatpoints impact outcomes is by changing the beliefs and expected payoff calculations of the players. Importantly, threats impact bargaining outcomes without ever having to be carried out! Of course, it is important that they be credible. Threats are not expected to have an impact on outcomes if the other player does not believe them. (If you tell Dwayne Johnson you'll crush his spine, for example, you will not end up with more pie.) In fact many economists have pointed out that carrying out threats is often costly (in terms of time,

|          |      | Player 2 | | |
|----------|------|-----|-----|------|
|          |      | Low | Med | High |
|          | Low  | 4, 4 | 4, 5 | 4, 6 |
| Player 1 | Med  | 5, 4 | 5, 5 | 0, 0 |
|          | High | 4, 4 | −2, 0 | −2, 0 |

Figure 5.6 Payoff table for a Nash demand game where one player carriers out a threat in response to a High demand

energy, social standing, etc.), and so once bargaining is over one is not incentivized to make good on a threat. This means that threats should only work if one is precommitted to them. Nash (1953) says that "... it is essential for the success of the threat that A be *compelled* to carry out his threat T if B fails to comply. Otherwise it will have little meaning. For, in general, to execute the threat will not be something A would want to do, just of itself" (130).[20]

This seems to lead to a problem for the inclusion of threats in evolutionary models. Unlike models of rational choice, threatpoints do nothing in an evolutionary scenario unless they are actually carried out. They must, in fact, lower the payoffs of some actors to impact how learning happens in cultural groups. The thing to consider, though, in assessing whether evolutionary threatpoint models are good ones is not whether it is rational to punish, but whether actors who are physically stronger, more economically powerful, or more politically powerful *do* in fact carry out threats in the real world.

The evidence suggests that, yes, humans carry out threats and punish one another. This is despite sometimes clear irrationality from a short-term payoff point of view. Evidence for this claim can be derived from empirical work. Domestic violence, for example, is almost always directed toward women and it has not been lost on researchers in sociology and economics that this sort of violence is often used to improve men's bargaining power.[21] Goode (1971) argues that men use physical threats to gain resources for themselves in the household. Eswaran and Malhotra (2011) use empirical data to argue that men in India use domestic

---

[20] Similarly Schelling (1960) says that "[t]he distinctive character of a threat is that one asserts that he will do, in a contingency, what he would manifestly prefer not to do if the contingency occurred" (123).

[21] Blood and Wolfe (1960), in their influential study of the family, argue that "[t]he dominance of men in marriage is often attributed to physical strength. While men do have more muscle power, any factor which operates purely in a biological fashion would be expected to have a universal effect. If superior musculature were the only reason for male dominance, we would expect men to dominate everywhere and in all times. The fact that they do not suggests that other factors must, as least, contribute to the picture" (Blood and Wolfe, 1960, 15). These authors reason from the incomplete dominance of men in the household to an argument that biology cannot be causally responsible for this dominance. Like the social-structural theorists discussed in the last chapter, they fail to recognize that cultural evolutionary processes need not be deterministic. The models here show how physical dominance can lead to preferential bargaining outcomes, even though this outcome is not determined.

violence to prevent women's autonomy for the purposes of household bargaining. (Rao (1998) uses modeling work to show how domestic violence might increase bargaining power.)

Experimental work also provides strong evidence that humans do, in fact, carry out threats and punishments in bargaining-type scenarios, even when doing so is costly to themselves. Güth et al. (1982), in a seminal study, had experimental subjects play the ultimatum game. This game is sometimes interpreted as a type of asymmetric bargaining situation because actors divide a resource. One actor offers some portion of a resource to the second, and the second has the option to either accept the offer or reject it. Rejection means neither player gets anything. Unlike the Nash demand game, the sequential nature of the ultimatum game means that there is a single *subgame perfect equilibrium*. (This concept is slightly different from the Nash equilibrium concept, and applies to sequential games. It assumes that actors play Nash equilibria of every *subgame*, or part of the sequential game.) Upon receiving an offer, the second player will do their best to accept it, no matter what it is. Knowing this means that the first player will make the smallest possible offer. The unique equilibrium of the game is then that the first player takes almost the entire resource.

What Güth et al. (1982) found was that experimental subjects behaved nothing like what this concept would predict. Instead, most offers were significant. Importantly, second actors regularly rejected offers that were too low. As the authors point out, "Subjects do not hesitate to punish if their opponent asks for 'too much'" (384). Here actors forgo taking payment in order to decrease the payoff of the other actor, or accept personal costs to punish. Subsequent experiments find cross-cultural variation in the ultimatum bargaining game, but confirm that actors punish norm violators, even when it is costly for them to do so (Güth and Tietz, 1990; Henrich et al., 2006). Henrich et al. (2006) find that, cross-culturally, humans are willing to pay to punish those who offer too little in the ultimatum game even if they are third-party bystanders.[22]

---

[22] Costly punishment has been observed under many other experimental paradigms as well, such as public goods games (Fehr and Gächter, 1999). Costly punishment can evolve for the ultimatum game under the replicator dynamics (Gale et al., 1995; Harms, 1997; Skyrms, 2014). Page et al. (2000) derive similar results for actors learning on a network.

If humans are willing to punish, even at cost to themselves, threatpoint models can tell us something about the emergence of bargaining behavior across types. In particular, they suggest that when members of one social group can wield a credible threat, and at least sometimes actually carry it out, they gain an advantage with respect to emerging bargaining conventions.

### 5.3.2 Threatpoints without threat

While I have just defended the real possibility that powerful social groups can gain bargaining advantages via threats and punishment, importantly in many real-world scenarios power differentials can translate directly to advantage, no threat needed. This is because differences in the economic, political, or social spheres of those in different social categories can often impact disagreement points directly.

A classic example comes from the economics of the family, and will be discussed in further detail in Chapter 8. Suppose that men are more economically advantaged than women within a society. When household bargaining breaks down, men need not make threats against women for the two groups to have very different disagreement points. The facts of the economic situation mean that women will tend to be at risk of poverty, and its attendant discomforts, should the household dissolve, while men will not.[23] This creates a scenario well represented by the threatpoint models just described. As discussed, in a situation like this, men should be expected to end up at a better outcome by dint of their higher disagreement points.

This sort of asymmetry between types is extremely prevalent in the real world. These scenarios arise whenever two groups engage in bargaining and one side generally has a better fall-back position. Especially relevant is the impact that different economic situations of social groups can have on bargaining norms. Whenever members of one social group tend to have more, this means that they are also likely to get more as a result of cultural evolution. This observation helps us start to understand one of the claims I made in the introduction to this chapter—that initial differences in power between types can compound into greater differences. An

---

[23] Sen (1987) also focuses on pregnancy as a biological factor that creates different disagreement points for women and men upon breakdown of a household, with the woman's disagreement point lowered by the physical facts of pregnancy.

economic advantage today can yield an economic advantage tomorrow via the emergence of bargaining conventions. As I will argue later in the chapter, this can create a sort of runaway process that leads to serious, persistent inequity between groups.

One further thing to note about this sort of structural power asymmetry, briefly mentioned earlier, is that it can arise via gendered (or class or race) division of labor. Suppose that actors in a society divide labor by type, and this creates benefits for both types, but in an inegalitarian way. Perhaps women in a society control crop production, and so have more direct access to the food supply. If women derive greater economic benefits as a result of this conventional division, they are expected to end up at preferred bargaining conventions in other arenas as well. These sorts of asymmetries may even emerge in a previously egalitarian regime and provide new power imbalances as technology changes. Imagine, for example, that ploughs are made much more efficient. This might mean that men in a plough-based agricultural society gain a sudden boost in disagreement points.

Before continuing, as a sort of robustness check, let us discuss models from Young (1993b). Young's framework, remember, involves actors from two different classes who randomly interact in a bargaining engagement. Actors always choose the strategy that yields the best expected payoff in response to a sampling of past play. This, remember, leads to the emergence of bargaining conventions just like those from replicator dynamics models, but the process of change appeals only to the bounded rationality of agents, and not to cultural imitation or individual learning. In this quite different evolutionary model, high disagreement points also advantage social groups, but in a way that is closer to Nash's original findings. Young finds that the stochastically stable equilibrium of these models is for actors to play the Nash bargaining solution, so that an advantage in disagreement point for one type will translate into an advantage in the unique, expected convention that populations evolve to play. Binmore et al. (2003) expand these results for different versions of best-response dynamics, and for some related coordination games. These results can increase the weight we give to claims about the cultural evolutionary impact of disagreement (threat) points on the emergence of bargaining conventions. Even under quite different assumptions, the benefits of high disagreement points for a bargaining social group are robust.

In LaCroix and O'Connor (2017) we use simulations of this sort to show how even one or two individuals with high disagreement points can improve the chances that one group ends up with a bargaining advantage. We also look at populations with distributions of disagreement points, and show that ones with higher means tend to be advantaged. These results, which introduce heterogeny into the two populations, demonstrate an extra point—when it comes to the emergence of bargaining norms, individual power matters less than average power across a group. An economically advantaged woman may still engage in extra household labor, because she is part of the social category "women" and this generally low-powered category has ended up conventionally disadvantaged.

### 5.3.3 Outside options

As I said at the beginning of this section, I will operationalize power in a few different ways to investigate the impact of power on bargaining conventions. To this point, power has been operationalized as a threat that impacts either the threatpoints, or the payoffs for high demands of actors. It has also been interpreted as a disagreement point that emerges from the asymmetric situations of social groups. Now I will consider another mechanism whereby power differences, especially those created by economic or social asymmetries, can impact bargaining conventions.

An *outside option* in a game allows actors to essentially opt out of a strategic scenario. In a bargaining game, an outside option means that rather than bargaining, an actor can instead engage in some sort of solo work that generates a predetermined payoff. In Bruner and O'Connor (2015) we show that when members of groups have different outside options, this impacts the basins of attraction for bargaining outcomes between them. Consider again household bargaining in a society where men make more money than women. In this case, men may be able to survive perfectly well without ever forming a household. Instead, they can use their solo income to support themselves. Women, on the other hand, might not have that option. In the case of landowners and sharecroppers, those who own the land may be able to use it in many different ways that do not involve a bargain, while sharecroppers depend on a bargain being struck for any sort of livelihood.

Figure 5.7 shows a Nash demand game with three demands—Low, Med, and High—and an outside option. In this case, player 1 gets $X$ and

Player 2

|  | Low | Med | High | Outside |
|---|---|---|---|---|
| Low | 4, 4 | 4, 5 | 4, 6 | 0, Y |
| Med | 5, 4 | 5, 5 | 0, 0 | 0, Y |
| High | 6, 4 | 0, 0 | 0, 0 | 0, Y |
| Outside | X, 0 | X, 0 | X, 0 | X, Y |

Player 1

Figure 5.7 Nash demand game with different outside options for each player

player 2 $Y$ for solo work. For simplicity's sake assume that $Y \leq X$.[24] This figure should help make clear the difference between asymmetries in outside options and disagreement points. Disagreement points are reached only when players bargain and fail, outside options are reached only when players choose not to bargain. Of course, in many scenarios actors with high disagreement points will also have high outside options and vice versa. This will occur if, for instance, one class of actor has better access to jobs, and so has both a better non-bargaining outside option, and a better fall-back position if bargaining fails.

Changing the values of the outside options in this game will alter the Nash equilibria. Why? If an actor expects to receive a low bargaining demand, and her outside option provides a better payoff, she can unilaterally switch strategies and do better. If an outside option is higher than the Low bargaining demand, the equilibrium where the actor with that option receives Low disappears. If an outside option is higher than the Med demand, the fair equilibrium disappears.

For simplicity's sake, assume $Y = 0$. Let $X$ vary between 0 and 6. When $X \leq 4$, all three bargaining outcomes are still Nash equilibria. When $4 < X \leq 5$, only the bargaining outcomes where player 1 receives Med or High remain Nash equilibria. When $5 < X \leq 6$, only the bargaining outcome where player 1 demands High is a Nash equilibrium. The elimination of these equilibria means that the corresponding outcomes no longer emerge in evolutionary processes. Importantly, this means that the type with the higher outside option is expected to end up at an advantaged

---

[24] Wagner (2012) uses this game to model actors who first play a stag hunt and then a Nash demand game to divide the fruits of their labor. On this interpretation, the outside option is hare-hunting—individual work that yields some decent payoff. The other options represent attempts to work together to yield a higher joint payoff, but where this adds the requirement that actors then must bargain either explicitly or implicitly to divide their group yield. More on this interpretation in Chapter 7.

bargaining convention by dint of having that outside option. If we return to the sharecropper example, we should never expect landowners to accept a portion of crop yield that pays them less than, say, letting goats graze on the land. In the case of household bargaining, if men can have perfectly successful solo households and women cannot, we should expect conventions to emerge where men do no more household labor than they would on their own.

## 5.4 Compounding Power

In the last section we saw that power differences between types can translate to bargaining advantage over cultural evolutionary time. This observation begins a narrative that will be expanded in this section. One way to gain economic power in the first place is through successful bargaining. This means we can observe circular patterns where economic advantage lead to better bargaining outcomes, leads to further economic advantage. Sen (1987) focuses on a similar phenomenon, which he calls "feedback transmission" in the context of rational choice models. As he says, "The asymmetries of immediate benefits sustain future asymmetries of future bases of sexual divisions" (27). His compounding of power and bargaining advantage happens when social conventions lead to improved bargaining outcomes for individuals in the household, though he does not analyze the emergence of these social conventions in the first place.

We'll explore the possibility of this sort of feedback loop using a toy model—one that tells a how-possibly story about the accumulation of power for one social group. Suppose that two types play a Nash demand game where they have different levels of power operationalized as varying disagreement points. Assume that there are multiple arenas of bargaining where types develop conventions of interaction. And, in particular, assume that in each of these arenas, the disagreement points for each type are determined by their success in previous bargaining interactions.

For our model, let's use the game displayed in Figure 5.4. Demands are 4, 5, and 6, and the disagreement points for the two sides are $T$ and $t$. To instantiate the assumptions just described, about past bargaining success influencing current power, we'll start simulations with $T = t = 2$. Then after conventions develop, if one type is demanding High, we'll increase their disagreement point, and decrease the disagreement point for the other type.[25] If they make equal demands, the disagreement points will remain the same. The question is: does this carry-over of bargaining outcomes to future disagreement points mean that one side tends to keep power for themselves?

Suppose we run this model without the disagreement-point adjustments just described. In this case, over the course of many arenas of bargaining the two sides will each be equally likely to end up demanding High (in about 25% of simulations each), though the fair outcome will be the most likely one (about 50% of simulations). If we add the adjustment, things change. One side tends to gain an advantage fairly early on in the simulation and maintain this advantage. Each side is equally likely to gain the advantage, but once they do, they'll end up demanding High for a large percentage of simulations (around 70%), making fair demands less often (around 30%), and essentially never demanding Low (less than 1% of simulation outcomes). In other words, we see that a process by which current power feeds into the emergence of bargaining conventions can preserve power for one group over a long period of time and across bargaining arenas.

There is one more observation I'd like to make here, addressing cases where there are some innate asymmetries between groups. This is particularly germane to understanding gender and power, where differences in strength between men and women could have acted as an initial asymmetry that allowed men to generally end up with greater power across societies and over time. Suppose that in many different cultures genders developed bargaining conventions across arenas and over time, and suppose that previous success in bargaining impacted later interactions as above. But suppose that one side tended to have a slight power advantage to start with. To capture this possibility, I'll run the models described above, but many times, seeing each time which side tends to

[25] I do this by taking the difference between 4 (the Low demand) and the current higher disagreement point. I then increment/decrement the disagreement points by 10% of this difference. So say men currently have $T = 2.2$ and women have $t = 1.8$. If men end up demanding High, I calculate $4 - 2.2 = 1.8$, and change the disagreement points by .18 so that they are now $T = 2.38$ and $t = 1.62$. This method is somewhat arbitrary. I use it because it keeps the disagreement points from ever exceeding the Low demand or going below 0. Note that this keeps the powerful side from accumulating too much power since the outcome where they demand Low always remains an equilibrium of the model. On the other hand, as the disagreement points become more disparate, they change more slowly, meaning that the less powerful side will have a harder time recovering lost ground.

end up empowered. And I'll also vary the initial disagreement points in the model from equal (2 and 2) to quite unequal (3 and 1).

As we see in Figure 5.8, introducing an initial asymmetry to the model makes it more likely that one side gains and keeps power over time. The greater the initial asymmetry in disagreement points, the more likely it is that the more powerful side remains that way.

This set of models shows how random initial events that advantage one group over another can ultimately lead to a sustained power difference between groups, and to enduring economic advantage for the powerful group. One thing this result tells us is that when we see persistent inequity between groups, the explanation need not always appeal to anything in particular about those groups. Random chance can advantage one group over another, and the dynamics of bargaining conventions can sustain that advantage indefinitely.

This model relates to sociological work on the concept of "cumulative advantage," or the idea that "current levels of accumulation have a direct causal relationship on future levels of accumulation" (DiPrete and Eirich, 2006, 272). For example, Gould (2002) and Lynn et al. (2009) provide models where displays of deference to other individuals create status hierarchies which are not based on merit, because current status deter-

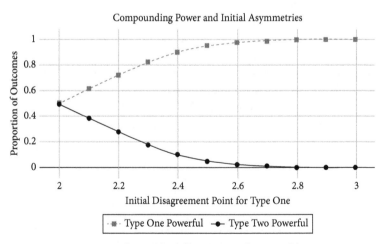

**Figure 5.8** Proportions of outcomes where an initially powerful group maintains power for a Nash demand game where disagreement points are determined by past success

mines level of deference from others. Merton et al. (1968); Merton (1988) outlines how academic communities that use past success as a predictor of future productivity will develop hierarchies only loosely based on merit, and significantly impacted by chance initial conditions. Some of this work addresses status and wealth differences between those in different social groups (DiPrete and Eirich, 2006). Tilly (1998) focuses on social categories, and illustrates detailed causal processes by which members of one group can use power to compound advantages in terms of resources, much like processes in the models just described. Okin (1989) makes clear how gender inequities in the context of marriage can lead to cyclical processes which prevent women from gaining power. (See also Cudd (1994).) Note that these approaches focus on how different conditions caused by social group membership lead to inequitable outcomes for individuals, but, unlike the model here, have not typically focused on how the existence of types simpliciter is a causal factor in the emergence of inequity.

Notice that these observations about the compounding of power have meta-implications regarding inequality and innate ability. Sometimes gender and racial inequality are taken as evidence that women or members of some race must be less innately talented than men or members of another race. But if we expect categorization to lead to inequity, and we expect inequity to generate further inequity, we need not appeal to innate ability in explaining these inequities in the first place. They are easy to get.[26]

* * *

In this chapter we began to explore the dynamics of inequity of the second, more pernicious sort. There are a handful of takeaways that the models discussed underscore. First, although previous evolutionary models of bargaining have focused on explaining fairness, once types

---

[26] For example, in *The Origin of Species* Darwin argues that "[t]he chief distinction in the intellectual powers of the two sexes is shewn by man's attaining to a higher eminence, in whatever he takes up, than can woman—whether requiring deep thought, reason, or imagination, or merely the use of the senses and hands. If two lists were made of the most eminent men and women in poetry, painting, sculpture, music (inclusive both of composition and performance), history, science, and philosophy, with half-a-dozen names under each subject, the two lists would not bear comparison" (361). In other words, Darwin takes the "eminence" of men to be evidence that women are inferior to men. These models indicate that social position provides little evidence with regard to the qualities or abilities of those in power.

are introduced to an evolutionary model, unfairness is just as likely an outcome. This sort of inequity requires very little to emerge beyond the simple fact of typing in a group. Furthermore, we have seen how power for a social group can lead to advantage when it comes to bargaining conventions. Groups with power are more likely to end up with resources, groups with less get less. And lastly, these sorts of processes can lead power and resources to concentrate for the same groups meaning that the same sorts of inequity persist over time.

In the next chapter we'll look at a different sort of causal variable which can impact inequity—asymmetries in the learning environments of different types. Before moving on though, a word about the epistemic role of the models presented here and in the next chapter. All of these models instantiate causal variables that mimic those seen in the real world. For this reason, it is plausible that the processes observed in these models can tell us something about what really happens when groups learn to divide resources. They are how-potentially models. At the same time, they are how-minimally models. Even if their processes don't fully match the real processes that generate divisional inequity, they give us counterfactual information about how easy it is to generate this sort of inequity that, as I will elaborate in Chapter 9, may be helpful in thinking about intervention.

# 6

# The Cultural Red Queen and the Cultural Red King

According to the Red Queen hypothesis in biology, it is better to evolve quickly. Van Valen (1973), who first described the effect, named it after a quote from Lewis Carroll's *Through the Looking Glass* where the Red Queen says to Alice, "Now, *here*, you see, it takes all the running you can do, to keep in the same place" (Carroll, 1917, 46). In a predator-prey interaction, for example, one species might gain an advantage by quickly evolving to run faster than the other. In parasite-host interactions, likewise, there is a benefit in evolving quickly to either take advantage of a host, or avoid parasitism.

Counterintuitively, Bergstrom and Lachmann (2003) use evolutionary game theory to show that in mutualistic interactions a species can, in some situations, actually obtain a benefit by evolving more slowly. They call this the "Red King Effect." To explain this effect, it's useful to appeal to a rational-choice scenario introduced by Schelling (1960). Suppose two people (you and Dwayne Johnson) are playing the chicken version of hawk–dove. One way to win this contest is to throw your steering wheel out the window, or to visibly make yourself unable to change strategies. We can predict that any sensible opponent will choose to swerve should you do so. Under the Red King effect, we can think of a fast-evolving species as swerving in evolutionary time. They evolve toward a strategy that yields higher payoffs in the short term, but ultimately allows the other species to take advantage.[1] Alternatively, as Bergstrom and Lachmann (2003) show, and Gokhale and Traulsen (2012) and Gao et al. (2015)

---

[1] Thanks to Jean-Paul Carvalho for this connection to Schelling.

outline in detail, sometimes in mutualistic interactions a fast-evolving species gains an advantage because they quickly evolve toward strategies that garner higher payoffs in the end. They term this alternative scenario a Red Queen effect.

The goal of this chapter will be to outline, in detail, how these effects can occur in a cultural context rather than a biological one. When cultural groups evolve, or adapt, at different rates, or more generally show asymmetric levels of reactivity toward one an other, we can observe a *cultural* Red King or Red Queen as a result of this asymmetry (Bruner, 2017). On the face of it, this might not seem like a situation that will emerge commonly in the real world. Why would members of one social category evolve faster than another?

There are actually several important situations where such an asymmetry is expected. The first was identified by Bruner (2017), who makes the important observation that when a minority group interacts with a majority group, minority types tend to meet out-group members much more often than majority types do. As a result, he argues, the minority group will learn to interact with the majority more quickly. Another such asymmetry (as Justin Bruner notes in his dissertation work) has to do with differences in what we might broadly label as institutional memory for different types. Young (1993b) shows that types with more information about previous bargaining interactions can gain an advantage in the emergence of bargaining norms. And similarly Gallo (2014) finds that groups of actors who are more tightly networked, and so see more information about past interactions of their neighbors, can gain a bargaining advantage. These results are deeply related to the cultural Red King effect because they are created by differences in the reactivity of the two groups. Finally, I'll show how one last operationalization of power—higher background payoffs for one group—can potentially yield advantages for the powerful group via a cultural Red King effect.

The set of results discussed in this chapter complement those in the last by filling out the scenarios under which one social group is expected to end up at an advantaged bargaining convention. In a way, we can see these two sets of results as exploring asymmetries between groups in the two main elements of our evolutionary game theoretic models. The last chapter looked at asymmetries in the games played by two types. This chapter looks at asymmetries in the dynamics, or the learning situation of the types.[2] Although, there are, as discussed, many more complicated aspects of discrimination and inequity, these two realms will treat the most important causal factors of inequity in our simplified modeling framework.

At the end of this chapter, I will present models that make use of the results from both the previous chapter and the current one to show further how the dynamics of inequity can impact real-world populations. In particular, I will show how in groups with intersectional identities the cultural Red King effect and various power effects can combine to create serious disadvantage for intersectional types. As we argue in O'Connor et al. (2017), these models can provide specific hypotheses as to the emergence of intersectional disadvantage.

## 6.1 The Red King and the Red Queen

It will be useful to start by gaining a better sense of the Red King and Red Queen effects and how they work. This section will be on the technical side, so some readers may wish to skip it.

The first thing we'll want to understand is the conditions under which a Red King/Red Queen can even occur. Under these effects one species, or in our cultural interpretation one type, will gain an advantage in that its members will be more likely to end up at a preferred convention than members of the other. This will only be possible in a strategic situation where there are different preferred conventions for the two types, or a game with multiple equilibria and at least some conflict of interest between players. Bergstrom and Lachmann (2003) explore a general version of a two-player, two-strategy game with this character. Figure 6.1 shows the payoff table of the game they consider.[3] Notice that it corresponds to the exact class of game we have been considering in this book. When $x < 1$, we have a leader–follower game, when $x = 1$, we have a version of the two-player Nash demand game, and when $1 < x < 2$, we have hawk–dove. In addition to these two-strategy games, versions of the

---

[2] Things are not actually this simple and, in the last section of this chapter, we'll look at a case where payoffs impact dynamical speed.

[3] They actually look at a correlative version of the game. Because they consider two species who interact only with the other, the difference does not matter. Since we will look at a cultural population where members of different types can interact with both in- and out-group members, I use the complementary version.

|            |   | Player 2 | |
|------------|---|------|------|
|            |   | A    | B    |
| Player 1   | A | X, X | 1, 2 |
|            | B | 2, 1 | 0, 0 |

**Figure 6.1** A general game where we can potentially observe a Red King/Queen effect

|            |      | Player 2 | |
|------------|------|------|------|
|            |      | Low  | High |
| Player 1   | Low  | 4, 4 | 4, 6 |
|            | High | 6, 4 | 0, 0 |

**Figure 6.2** A Nash demand game with demands 4 and 6

Nash demand game with any number of demands will also have the right character for the Red King/Red Queen to potentially occur—there will be multiple equilibria and conflicts of interest between players over them.

So, now we know that the sorts of strategic situations we are considering in this book are exactly those where the Red King/Red Queen effects have the potential to impact evolutionary processes. Since this part of the book is primarily about understanding inequitable resource divisions between types, we'll focus, though, on how this effect can impact emerging bargaining conventions in particular. To do so, let's start by looking at the two-strategy Nash demand game shown in Figure 6.2.

As we know, when two types evolve to play this game there are two possible outcomes—type one demands High and type two Low or vice versa. Under the standard model, these two outcomes are equally likely, or have equal basins of attraction under the replicator dynamics. Figure 6.3 shows the phase diagram for this model with complete symmetry for the two types. The equilibria, remember, are represented by the dark circles at the top right and bottom left corners of the diagram. This diagram adds a darker region corresponding to the basin of attraction for the top right rest point, and a light region for the bottom left rest point. The top right region is the one where population one ultimately gains an advantage by demanding High. In the bottom left region, on the other hand, the dynamics move to the outcome where population two demands High instead. The black line between the two basins of attraction represents the *separatrix,* or the divide between them, which will be important to subsequent discussion.

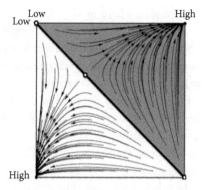

**Figure 6.3** Phase diagram for two populations playing the two-strategy Nash demand game

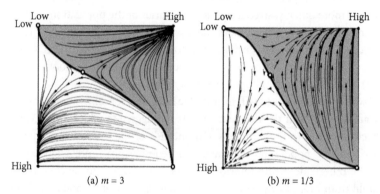

(a) $m = 3$          (b) $m = 1/3$

**Figure 6.4** Phase diagrams for two populations playing a Nash demand game where one population evolves $m$ times as quickly as the other. We see a Red King effect

The Red King and Red Queen effects in this game occur when evolutionary speed advantages one of two evolving populations in terms of their likelihood of ultimately demanding High. To see how this works in general, we can simply speed up evolution for one side versus the other by adding a multiplier $m$ to the replicator equation for population one. When $m = 1$, then, both sides evolve at the same rate. When $m > 1$, population one evolves faster than population two, and when $0 \leq m < 1$, population two evolves faster. Figure 6.4 shows what happens when $m = 3$ and when $m = 1/3$.

Let's consider Figure 6.4(a), where $m = 3$, first. As we can see, the separatrix between the two basins of attraction is no longer a straight line. Instead it snakes to the left and to the right. The reason for this is that the increased evolutionary speed of population one stretches the trajectories of population change in the x-direction. As a result, some areas of the state space that would have gone to the top right corner now go to the bottom left, and vice versa. Importantly though, there is an asymmetry in how the speed change affects the two basins of attraction. The one for the bottom left is now larger than the one for the top right. This means that now more population starting points move to the outcome where population two demands High. In other words, the slow evolving population has gained an advantage in terms of likelihood of ending up at the preferred equilibrium. This is the Red King effect.

If we look at Figure 6.4 (b), the situation reverses. Now population two evolves more quickly, stretching the trajectories of the population in the y-direction. This, again, changes the separatrix, but now so that the top right equilibrium has a larger basin of attraction. Again, we see a Red King effect where the more slowly evolving population (this time population one) is more likely to end up demanding High.

Notice that the location of the unstable interior rest point—represented by an empty dot in the diagram—limits the degree to which speed can affect outcomes in these models. On one side of the interior rest point, speed in one population will make one equilibrium more likely, and on the other side of the interior rest point, speed will make the other equilibrium more likely. For the entire state space, this balancing effect means that the basins of attraction for one equilibrium can only get so large. (This is unlike some other models we've looked at, where changing payoffs could increase the basins of attraction for one outcome indefinitely.) Figure 6.5 shows phase diagrams for this model as $m$ increases from 2 to 100. As is clear, even as $m$ grows very large, the strength of the Red King effect is bounded. (Though, as we'll see, this bound is not robust across modeling choices.)[4]

What about the Red Queen effect? The location of the interior rest point also determines whether speed provides an advantage or a disadvantage to a population. In the case just described, learning more quickly

---

[4] In particular, suppose that at the interior rest point population two is at 2/3. Then the biggest the basin of attraction for one equilibrium can get is 2/3 of the state space.

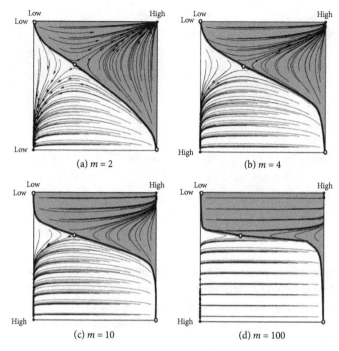

**Figure 6.5** Phase diagrams for two populations playing a Nash demand game where one population evolves *m* times as quickly as the other. As *m* increases, the Red King grows stronger, but is bounded

takes the fast population to the worse equilibrium. But suppose instead that we have a Nash demand game where the two demands are 2 and 8. Figure 6.6 shows the phase diagram for this model when $m = 1$ and when $m = 3$. If we look at (a) we see that when $m = 1$, as with the last game, the basins of attraction are exactly equal. But notice that the interior rest point is shifted toward the bottom right of the phase diagram. Now, when $m = 3$, the separatrix curves just like before, stretched along the x-axis, but this curvature means that the top right basin of attraction gets larger than the one for the bottom left. Now population one, the faster population, is more likely to end up demanding High as a result of their speed, and the slower population two is more likely to end up demanding Low.

So what does all this tell us about the real-world populations? Not much yet, but in the rest of the chapter I will use the theoretical framework just laid out to explain how the cultural Red King/Red Queen effect

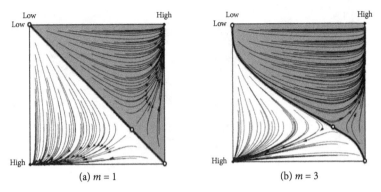

**Figure 6.6** Phase diagrams for two populations playing a Nash demand game where one population evolves $m$ times as quickly as the other. We see a Red Queen effect

can impact the emergence of actual bargaining conventions. As we will see, when it comes to bargaining there is particular reason to think the cultural Red King effect is especially important, and this has impacts for groups with minority status, and groups without access to institutional memory.

## 6.2 Minorities and the Red King/Red Queen

To this point in the book, in looking at our highly simplified models with two types, I have always assumed that the types are equally prevalent. As I briefly mentioned at the beginning of this chapter, though, Bruner (2017) shows that relaxing this assumption can have surprising effects on the outcomes of evolutionary models. Of course models where one type is in the majority and one in the minority correspond to many real-world situations. In businesses and in academic communities, for example, it is often the case that one gender is in the minority. In the same situations, and also more broadly within any culture, there are almost always some racial/cultural/religious minority groups.

The important observation for our exploration here, is that minority/majority status creates asymmetric learning environments for those of different types. Suppose, for example, that you are part of a company that is 90% white and 10% Latinx. Suppose further that, as in our models, you condition your learning and behavior based on the type of your interactive partner. If you interact with others in your company approximately randomly, and you are Latinx, this means that you will meet out-group members about 90% of the time, and in-group members only 10% of the time. Now suppose you are white. Under the same conditions, you will meet in-group members about 90% of the time, and the out-group about 10% of the time. In other words, Latinx agents will meet their out-group 9 times as often as white agents will, and vice versa with respect to the in-group. This, of course, impacts how quickly the two groups learn to interact with each other. For Latinx agents, the out-group is extremely important to them from a strategic standpoint, as out-group interactions make up 90% of their payoffs. For white agents, the Latinx group is relatively unimportant. This means that we can see a cultural Red King/Red Queen effect emerge solely as a result of the minority status of a group. Group size alone can act as the asymmetry that leads to disadvantage as a result of the social dynamics of bargaining.

Let's explore this in more detail. In minority/majority models of the Red King/Red Queen, we now no longer need a speed multiplier, $m$, for one side. Instead, we have a variable, $p_i$, that represents the prevalence of each type. Let's assume that $p_1 \geq p_2$, and that $p_1 + p_2 = 1$, or that there are only two types in our population and $p_1$ is in the majority. We can generate a version of the replicator equations for such a population that looks just like the two-type mixing equation, except that the payoffs for each type are weighted by how often they meet members of the two types. (See the Appendix for more.) As in the example above, this means that the behaviors of the out-group will more significantly impact the payoffs of minority types, and they will more quickly learn to deal with out-group members.[5]

Consider a population playing a three-strategy Nash demand game with a fair outcome and two unfair equilibria. Suppose that we have a minority and majority group learning bargaining conventions. It won't be possible to show the phase diagrams for this model, because there are too many strategies, but Figure 6.7 shows proportions of outcomes when the Low demand is 4 and High is 6.[6]

---

[5] For more on this equation and for the minority/majority effect generally see Bruner (2017); O'Connor and Bruner (2017).

[6] These results, like the rest in this section, are from 10k runs of simulations at each parameter value using the discrete time replicator dynamics.

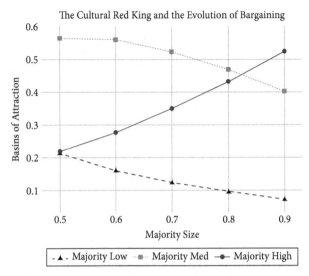

Figure 6.7 Basins of attraction for two types playing the Nash demand game with a minority group

As we can see from this figure, increasing $p_1$, the size of the majority population, impacts the sizes of the basins of attraction for the three outcomes. This is for just the reason outlined in the last section—the minority type evolves more quickly and this shifts the separatrices between the basins of attraction. Now that we're considering a Nash demand game with three strategies, there are three basins of attraction whose sizes change. First, the proportion of simulations that go to the fair outcome decreases. Second, the proportion of outcomes where the majority type discriminates by demanding High increases considerably. And last, the proportion of outcomes where the minority type demands High drops to nearly 0. When the majority type makes up 90% of the population, the most probable outcome is that they end up discriminating.

In the last chapter, I pointed out that the explanation of inequity offered there rests on minimal assumptions about human psychology. The results just presented provide a similar explanation for minority disadvantage in particular. Again, we can ignore the possibility of out-group bias, implicit bias, etc. Again, we can assume that members of two types are completely identical with respect to abilities, preferences, etc. Inequity emerges endogenously in the model, and furthermore the simple fact of minority status alone leads to a disadvantage as a result of the dynamics of interaction.

In order to see whether group size alone might really cause such an effect among real people, in Mohseni et al. (2018) we did a human subjects experiment. We separated lab participants into two groups and had them play a version of the Nash demand game over the course of many rounds with randomly chosen out-group partners. We found that those in the minority group were significantly more likely to demand Low, and those in the majority significantly more likely to demand High. We also found that this discrepancy arose over the course of the experiment. In other words, subjects learned this behavior. Importantly, we did not give the subjects any information about the groups they were in. We did not even tell them they were in groups at all! This might sound like an odd choice, but we wanted to let the minority/majority learning dynamic, and not any expectations on the part of our subjects, do all the work. This result is underpowered, but combined with the modeling results described in this chapter it helps provide evidence that the cultural Red King might truly influence bargaining behavior.

## 6.2.1 The cultural Red Queen

In Nash demand games, we can also see a cultural Red Queen effect. For the game with three demands, this happens for value of the Low demand, $L < 3$ (approximately). Again, this switch between the two effects occurs because of the locations of interior rest points in the model, but we can also give a more intuitive explanation. When $L$ is relatively high, it tends to be better for a population to choose Low at the beginning of simulation because Low generates a decent payoff and is less risky than more aggressive choices. The fast evolving population then tends to move toward Low and ends up eventually at a disadvantage. When $L$ is small enough, although it is less risky, it still tends to yield higher payoffs to make high demands at the beginning of simulation, meaning that fast evolving populations learn to do so and eventually gain an advantage.

Figure 6.8 shows outcomes for the model where $L = 2$ and $H = 8$. Here we see a cultural Red Queen effect. As the size of $p_1$ grows, the fair outcome becomes less prevalent, and the outcome where the small population demands High becomes more prevalent. Notice, though, that the strength of the cultural Red Queen is relatively small compared to the cultural Red King in the last model. This is because when the Low

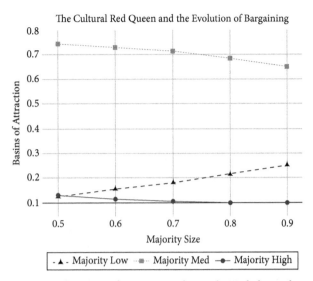

**Figure 6.8** Basins of attraction for two types playing the Nash demand game with a minority group

and High demands are more disparate, remember, bargaining models are more likely to evolve toward the fair demand. For this model, even when the minority group is very small, the fair demand remains quite likely to emerge, and so the Red Queen has relatively little impact. When the majority type makes up 90% of the population here, the fair demand is still the most likely one to emerge by far.

What about Nash demand games with a finer partition of demands? Let's consider one more model, this time of a population with two types evolving to play a game with demands 1, 3, 5, 7, and 9. With finer demands we again see a cultural Red Queen so that minority groups get an advantage. Figure 6.9 shows outcomes for simulations of this model. I use a bar graph here rather than a line graph to make the prevalences of the five possible equilibria more clear. Lighter areas represent outcomes where the majority is advantaged. As we can see, when the majority gets larger, the outcomes where its members are advantaged become less likely. In Nash demand games with even finer partitions—nine possible demands, or nineteen—the same slight Red Queen is observed. For these games, there is on average an advantage at the beginning of simulation to making higher demands, and so the small, fast evolving group tends to end up better off.

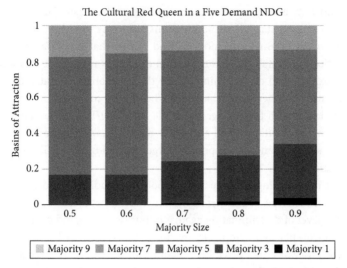

**Figure 6.9** Basins of attraction for two types playing the Nash demand game with a minority group

This last observation—that the Red Queen effect occurs in models with a finer partition of demands—might lead one to believe that this is the more significant effect in a cultural bargaining scenario. Or one might conclude that because different bargaining games yield different effects, generally these models will not have much explanatory/predictive power when it comes to the emergence of bargaining norms. In the next two subsections I will explain why these conclusions are overly hasty, and why the cultural Red King effect in particular has the potential to significantly impact bargaining conventions in the real world.

### 6.2.2  Starting places

One important target arena for cultural Red King/Red Queen effect models is the workplace. There are two reasons for this. First, these effects are expected when there are minority/majority populations, and in many workplaces this is indeed the case when it comes to gender/race. Second, when gender and racial minority groups enter traditionally male- or white-dominated workforces, or when men enter traditionally female-dominated workforces, initially the two populations are very skewed with respect to size. Almost the entire population consists of one gender or race, and only a very small fraction consists of the other. This means that these groups start off in the situations best represented by the most extreme minority/majority models. And notice that once bargaining conventions are established, the addition of further minority types will not be expected to change things, since the populations are already at equilibrium. In other words, bargaining norms are solidified in a situation, typically, with the strongest possible Red King/Red Queen effects. (These sort of conditions will also apply when a new immigrant group enters a society—another important target for cultural Red King/Red Queen models.)

There is something more we can say about the conditions under which these norms emerge. While there are strong differences across workplaces as to the level of discrimination against minority groups, indicating that different workplaces develop different conventions for this behavior, none of these processes take place in a vacuum. In our replicator dynamics models, it has been the case to this point that population starting points are selected randomly, and then outcomes over these are measured. In other words, it is equally likely that simulations start with lots of minority types demanding High, or lots of majority types doing so. In the real world, workplace dynamics emerge within a cultural context where, often, minority groups are already being discriminated against.

Suppose that we consider models where we do not select population starting points equiprobably over the entire state space, but instead where it is more likely that we select starting points from the portion of the state space where the majority group discriminates. This reflects an assumption that actors are drawn from a larger population where many already follow discriminatory conventions, and that they transfer their learned behaviors to the new context.[7] Under this assumption the relatively quick adaptation of a minority group will always be detrimental to them. We see a cultural Red King in these cases, even if the strategic structure of the interaction would lend itself to a Red Queen (O'Connor and Bruner, 2017; O'Connor, 2017a)

To make this claim more clear, consider Figure 6.10, which shows the phase diagrams from Figure 6.6. This is the two-strategy Nash demand

---

[7] Relatedly, Bicchieri (2005) elaborates how, when presented with a new interactive scenario, humans attempt to draw analogies, and use existing cultural scripts to coordinate behavior. These scripts include conditioned behavior based on gender and race.

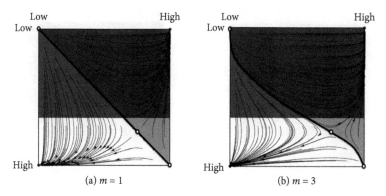

(a) $m = 1$    (b) $m = 3$

**Figure 6.10** Phase diagrams for two populations playing a Nash demand game. With restricted starting points, a general Red Queen can translate to a Red King

game with $L = 2$ where we see a Red Queen effect. Imagine, though, that populations only start in the area of the phase diagram that is not shaded out. (This is the area where the larger population tends to be demanding High.) While there is a Red Queen effect over the entire space, for this limited section there is a Red King effect. The smaller the minority, the more likely they are to end up demanding Low.

This claim makes intuitive sense when it comes to minority/majority scenarios. If a minority population is reacting to a majority that is likely to make strong demands of its members, and they react quickly, then they tend to move towards accommodation. If they were less reactive, the other side might update to accommodate their demands instead. Whenever conventions of bargaining emerge within a larger context of discrimination, then minority status should always lead to disadvantage. The Red King is expected to prevail.[8]

As I argue in O'Connor (2017a), when actors display even minimal in-group preferences, we should expect the cultural Red King to occur quite generally. Suppose that a minority and majority group develop bargaining norms in a society, and suppose further that each side shows some tendency to discriminate against their out-group. (Notice that now we appeal to the possibility of psychological in-group favoritism, which

---

[8] Of course, if our sub-population is drawn from a larger group where the minority type tends to demand High, and the majority Low, we should again expect a Red Queen. Swift minority responses will tend to recreate existing social patterns.

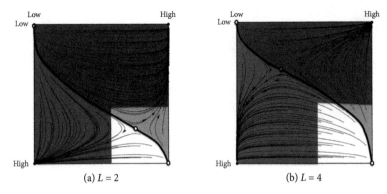

**Figure 6.11** Phase diagrams for two populations playing a Nash demand game. If actors tend to display in-group preference, the cultural Red King is strengthened

has heretofore been ignored.) In other words, population starting points tend to be in the area of the phase diagram where both sides often demand High. Again, in this scenario minority groups will tend to be disadvantaged by dint of the cultural Red King. Figure 6.11 drives this home. The first figure (a) shows a phase diagram for a Nash demand game where $L = 2$ and there is a Red Queen, the second (b) for a game where $L = 4$ and there is a Red King. If populations start in the portion of the state space where they both discriminate against the out-group (the area that is not shaded out), there is a Red King for both models. Again, this makes intuitive sense. The fact that one side is more reactive means that they will be more likely to cave if both sides are making high demands.

These observations about the context in which the cultural Red King/Red Queen occur are the first part of the story behind why the Red King, rather than the Red Queen, is expected to shape the emergence of bargaining conventions. In the next section, I will fill in this claim, while also giving a robustness check for the cultural Red King/Red Queen effects.

### 6.2.3 Robustness and risk aversion

Throughout the book, I've appealed to models developed by Peyton Young, especially those from Axtell et al. (2000), to provide a robustness check on the results I've presented. In their model, remember, instead of infinite populations, deterministic dynamics, and cultural imitation/learning, we assume finite populations, stochastic dynamics, and boundedly rational best response. And yet, for a number of important results, the outcomes of these two sets of models are very qualitatively similar. As I will now show, the cultural Red King/Red Queen can be reproduced in this set of models (O'Connor, 2017a). Changing the numbers of agents interacting on either side shifts outcomes, and in just the ways we'd expect given the replicator dynamic results. As I will also show, and perhaps more importantly, this modeling framework allows us to investigate the influence of a well-established economic phenomenon—risk aversion—on our results. As we will see, when agents display risk aversion, the Red King becomes significantly more important.

Consider a model with $N$ agents of two types. Let's call the proportion of type one $p_1$. Each round, two agents are randomly chosen to interact. Each agent has a finite memory of past interaction with each of the two types. They choose a strategy that would have generated the highest payoff if played in each previous interaction that they remember.

Over time, agents in these models head toward absorbing states, or conventions, that correspond to the equilibria of the model—types make fair demands, or else compatible but unfair demands of each other.[9] When types are of equal sizes, each is equally likely to gain an advantage. When one type is larger, however, we observe cultural Red King/Red Queen effects just as before. Again, in these scenarios, the minority type meets majority members more often than the reverse. In this model, the minority types are then updating their majority memories much more quickly than vice versa. As a result their strategies change more quickly. (See O'Connor (2017a) for a more in-depth presentation of these results.)

So the cultural Red King/Red Queen is robust to significantly different modeling choices. This can increase our confidence that these effects may truly impact the real world. And, as I will now show, this set of models also allows us to incorporate new assumptions, and, as a result, to deepen our understanding of these effects.

### 6.2.3.1 RISK AVERSION

Young (1993b), in a similar model of the emergence of bargaining norms, assumes that his agents display *risk aversion*. This means that the value they place on a good decreases over each unit of it they receive. If given

---

[9] Moving away from the Young framework, I assume that the probability of erring for agents is 0, so that models reach and stay at absorbing states.

a choice to simply receive $x$ units of some good, then, or to engage in a lottery with an expected outcome of $x + \epsilon$, there will be positive values of $\epsilon$ for which an agent will pick the sure thing even though it has a smaller expected payoff.[10] Risk aversion is a common assumption from economics since it reflects the actual preferences of humans under many circumstances (Kahneman and Tversky, 1984).

Let us add to the models just described an assumption that agents have risk-averse preferences. In choosing their best responses to their finite memories, they show preference for smaller, sure outcomes over larger riskier ones.[11] This change significantly impacts the Red King/Red Queen effects in these models.

Consider a model with nine demands ranging from one to nine. Just as under the replicator dynamics, this model displays a cultural Red Queen effect. As $p_1$ gets larger and larger, it becomes increasingly likely that members of the type in the majority end up making lower demands. Figure 6.12 shows these results. Notice that as $p_1$ gets larger, we see the lighter patches expand slightly, reflecting a greater likelihood of disadvantage for the majority group.[12]

Once we add risk aversion, however, the results flip. Now, as type one becomes more prevalent, they are also more likely to end up making high demands. Figure 6.13 shows results from the model with risk-averse preferences. As we can see, it is now increasingly likely that the majority gains an advantage as their numbers expand. When $p_1 = .9$ the majority group discriminates more than 60% of the time, and the minority group discriminates in only about 15% of simulations.

---

[10] An example can perhaps make clear why this is an intuitive preference. Suppose you were offered either $1000 or a 50% chance to win $2001. While the expected payoff of the second offer is slightly higher, you would still be quite reasonable to take the guaranteed $1000. Kahneman and Tversky (1984) detail at length the conditions under which people tend to display risk-averse or risk-seeking choices.

[11] This is done by adding a concave utility function. I choose $u(x) = 3ln(x + 1)$ for the simulations shown because it respects the 0 payoff point, is concave, and is monotonically increasing, but not too steep. To give a sense of how this influences preferences, individuals with such a utility function would be indifferent between receiving a payoff of five for sure, and a 75% chance of getting a payoff of ten. An individual with no such function would, obviously, be indifferent between receiving five and a 50% chance of ten. Other functions with these properties might just as well have been chosen.

[12] Results are from 10k runs of simulation of these models, measuring outcomes once they have settled into a stable absorbing state.

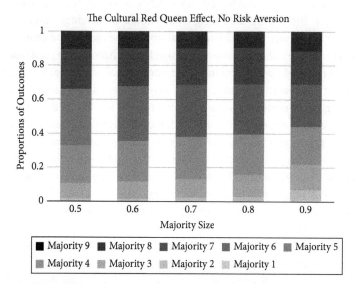

**Figure 6.12** Basins of attraction for two types playing the Nash demand game with a minority group

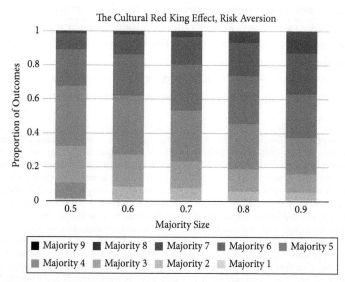

**Figure 6.13** Basins of attraction for two types playing the Nash demand game with a minority group

So what do these results tell us? Inasmuch as actors display risk-averse preferences, the cultural Red King effect should disadvantage minority groups with respect to emerging bargaining conventions. The intuitive explanation here is that risk aversion makes low demands more preferable to all agents because low demands guarantee a small, dependable payoff while high demands present a risk of getting the disagreement point. Although every actor is now more drawn toward low demands, minority groups react more swiftly and in doing so create a scenario where majority types can then take advantage by making high demands. This same reasoning applies to other versions of the model—those with fewer demands, or more, or other levels of risk aversion—in general risk-averse tendencies strengthen the cultural Red King and weaken the cultural Red Queen, meaning that minority groups are the ones who tend to end up disadvantaged.[13]

There are a few reasons to care about this finding, in particular, in the case of minority/majority interactions. Guiso and Paiella (2008) show that individuals with more assets are less risk averse than those with fewer, and that respondents who expect to be under future risk are more risk averse. In other words, the cultural Red King effect might be particularly strong at the intersection of poverty and minority status. When disadvantaged minority groups interact with less disadvantaged majority groups, the cultural Red King should be stronger. When a financially secure minority group interacts with a disadvantaged majority, we would expect the effect to be lessened.

To sum up, the cultural Red King effect has real potential to disadvantage minority groups with respect to the emergence of bargaining conven-

---

[13]  There is a set of results from Bowles and Naidu (2006) and Hwang et al. (2014) yielding an opposite finding—that when it comes to preferred conventions of division, actors in a larger social class are disadvantaged. In their models, the disadvantage is generated by the fact that actors tend to err in their own favor, and small classes of actors are more likely to do so in a way that shifts a convention to one they prefer—essentially the small numbers make a coordinated shift of a significant proportion of them more probable. (Note that this is not a cultural Red Queen, because reactiveness has nothing to do with the asymmetry.) They employ myopic best-response dynamics with inertia, representing a case where each round every agent revises their strategies with some probability to play a best response to the other population. Bruner (2017), however, finds that in models with this dynamic the cultural Red King does not arise. Because the same portion of each population best responds at every time step, they are equally reactive to each other. In reality, a small group may find it hard to shift the behaviors of a large one under these conditions because the large group is relatively un-reactive.

tions solely by dint of their minority status. Several realistic conditions—the existence of discriminatory norms, risk aversion, especially in disadvantaged groups, and in-group preference—exacerbate this effect.

There are actually a few more results contributing to robustness of this claim. As I will outline in the next chapter, in Rubin and O'Connor (2018) we find something similar to the cultural Red King in agent-based network bargaining models. Bruner (2017) in his original work shows that the effect is robust across several further dynamics, and that positive assortment with in-group members does not disrupt the effects. In O'Connor and Bruner (2017) we show how the effect occurs even when actors have outside options. This perhaps surprising set of findings means that besides the usual problems with bias that minority groups face, they are at further risk of disadvantage from solely dynamical effects.

### 6.2.4   Doubling down

There is one more observation to make about minority/majority models before continuing. Computer scientist Karen Petrie has pointed out that if men and women each make equal numbers of sexist remarks to the other gender, the number of remarks one man or woman receives scales exponentially with the gender ratio. So, for example, if the gender ratio is 1 : 2 women to men, women will receive 4 times as many sexist remarks as men. If this gender ratio goes up to 1 : 5, women receive 25 times as many sexist remarks.

This so-called "Petrie multiplier" is somewhat analogous to a further disadvantage that minority groups undergo in the types of models we have just been exploring. A minority/majority asymmetry creates not just different learning environments for those in different types, but also different interactive environments once bargaining norms have developed (O'Connor and Bruner, 2017). Return to the example of a company that is 90% white and 10% Latinx. If a norm develops between types that disadvantages Latinx people, then in 90% of interactions they will end up demanding Low. If a norm develops that disadvantages whites, then they will only receive the Low demand in 10% of their interactions. In other words, a disadvantaged bargaining convention is especially damaging to those in minority groups because they meet the out-group so regularly. Of course, this asymmetry also means that minority types who end up at an advantaged convention reap more significant rewards as a result.

## 6.3 Institutional Memory

Imagine a situation where two types of agents learn to bargain, but where one side has better access to what we might call institutional memory. In particular, they are able to find out more about the past bargaining experiences of their in-group. This sort of situation might hold in the real world if one group is better networked—they have access, for instance, to social clubs where they share information about their past bargaining experiences, or have old-boy mentoring networks to transfer information about past interaction. As Hwang et al. (2014) point out for the case of household bargaining, "men who can publicly fraternize with other men have an informational advantage vis-a-vis women confined to domestic roles and family networks" (34).

Young (1993b) argues that in a situation like this, the type with more information should have an advantage with respect to bargaining conventions. His model differs slightly from the ones I just explored. Each agent does not have a private memory, but rather obtains a random sample of the last $m$ bargaining interactions that have occurred. This means that in each round agents best respond to what they have seen happen to others as well as to themselves. When Young analyzes this model for the stochastically stable equilibrium, he predicts that actors will arrive at the fair demand between groups. But, if members of one group have a longer institutional memory, this prediction shifts. The longer the memory of one side (compared to the other), the more resource they get at the equilibrium. Gallo (2014) provides a very similar proof, but where the difference in memory results from network structure specifically. He looks at situations where members of one group are more tightly networked, and, as a result, get larger samples of past interactions from their neighbors to react to. In this context, network density provides an advantage to a group with respect to the predicted bargaining convention. Bowles and Naidu (2006) and Hwang et al. (2014) look at models of actors who engage in a different best-response dynamic and who play what they call a "contract game"—basically a coordination game where one outcome is equitable, and the other inequitable. Again, they find that information provides an advantage. In their case, when one side can observe a greater portion of the other type, they are more likely to end up favored by convention.

Why do we see these results? Why should memory length or network density matter with regard to which side gets more? These results, in fact, are a sort of cultural Red King effect. In all three cases, the fact that one side sees more makes them less reactive, and less likely to change strategies quickly. As Hwang et al. (2014) put it, "a larger scope of vision among the well off reduces their responsiveness to the idiosyncratic play of the poor" (6). To make this clearer, imagine two agents in the Young and Gallo type models, one with a memory of a single interaction and one with memories of ten interactions. The agent with the single memory will always best respond to whatever she last experienced, and so could flip strategies every round if she meets different interactive partners. The agent with ten memories maintains some consistency over rounds. A single interaction will probably not impact their best response. Because both Young and Gallo assume that their actors have risk-averse preferences, the side that is less reactive—the one with longer institutional memory—then gains an advantage. The reactive side becomes more likely to flip toward low demands than the better networked agents and then to eventually end up making low demands at the emergent convention.[14] (In the Bowles and Naidu (2006); Hwang et al. (2014) case because actors err in their own favor there is always an advantage to being unresponsive to the other side.)

## 6.4  Power and Learning

In the last chapter, I discussed at length how power can advantage members of a social group with respect to bargaining conventions. In Bruner and O'Connor (2015) we instantiate power in one more way that I have not yet discussed. This is because this last instantiation of power in fact works via a Red Queen/Red King effect.

Suppose that two groups bargain, but that for one group this bargaining scenario is just one of many that they engage in. Or suppose that they tend to have payoffs coming in from another source—land holdings, or a trust fund, or a cushy job. The idea is that for one group the bargain is their

---

[14] See O'Connor (2017a) for a more in-depth discussion of the connection between these results and the cultural Red King effect.

Player 2

|  | Low | Med | High |
|---|---|---|---|
| Low | 4+b, 4 | 4+b, 5 | 4+b, 6 |
| Med | 5+b, 4 | 5+b, 5 | 0+b, 0 |
| High | 6+b, 4 | 0+b, 0 | 0+b, 0 |

(Player 1 labels the rows Low, Med, High)

**Figure 6.14** Payoff table for a Nash demand game with background payoffs for one actor

only source of payoff, while for the other it is a relatively unimportant interaction. A natural target for a model like this is bargaining between landholders and sharecroppers, or between genders when one gender tends to make more money. Figure 6.14 shows a payoff table representing this scenario. Here $b$ is the extra background payoff to the more powerful side.

This addition impacts how quickly one side learns to interact with the other. The intuition is that because the interaction is less important or less salient to members of the more powerful class, they are less quick to update their strategies. And, in particular, this change to the payoff table can induce a cultural Red King/Red Queen effect in just the way that minority status, or asymmetries in institutional memory, can. The takeaway is that inasmuch as reactivity of a type is impacted by their economic empowerment, they may gain a bargaining advantage via this difference.

## 6.5 Intersectional Oppression

This chapter and the last one have dealt with the evolution of the second sort of inequity, where one group exploits another. In particular, they have tackled the various ways in which differences between groups can lead to an advantage for one side as far as bargaining conventions go. As we have seen, power, operationalized in multiple ways (note that we can include networking and institutional memory under this broad heading as well) and also majority status can lead to advantage for a particular group. Now I will use these effects to explore what sorts of inequity can happen at the intersection of social groups when individuals have multiple aspects to their social identity.

The inspiration for this exploration comes from intersectionality theorists who argue that understanding inequity via binary social categories is short-sighted. As they point out, we sometimes have to look at the intersections of demographic categories to understand oppression. For instance, the effect that being a black woman has on one's expected salary might not be a simple combination of the effects that being a woman and being black have on one's salary. As Collins and Chepp (2013) put it, "the first core idea of intersectional knowledge projects stresses that systems of power . . . cannot be understood in isolation from one another; instead systems of power intersect and coproduce one another to result in unequal material realities and the distinctive social experiences that characterize them" (60). One strong theme of intersectional research is the observation that sometimes disadvantage for those who share two intersecting disadvantaged identities is non-additive. In other words, this disadvantage is more than the sum of its parts.

This raises a series of questions. Can we model special intersectional inequity using the framework developed in this book? What patterns do these effects follow? Do those in multiple disadvantaged social categories experience particular inequity as a result of intersectional effects? In O'Connor et al. (2017), Liam Kofi Bright, Justin Bruner, and I set out to answer these questions, and, in doing so, to provide a general methodological contribution to the more empirically minded areas of intersectionality theory. (For more on these methodological contributions, see the original paper). Our paper looks at a number of scenarios in which intersectional disadvantage can arise in evolutionary bargaining models. Here, I will discuss just one model that illustrates why those with intersecting disadvantaged social identities may be especially disadvantaged. To be clear, we by no means think our simplified models will capture all the social features relevant to intersectional oppression, and the question, again, is how far we can get with relatively minimal conditions.[15]

Imagine a population with two dimensions of personal identity that are relevant to bargaining interactions—gender and race. Suppose in

---

[15] Hoffmann (2006) considers a model where actors with multiple social identity markers evolve to play hawk–dove. He considers situations where actors have up to seven dimensions of identity that are relevant to interaction. In his models, actors generalize their learned responses over all the categories that an opponent belongs to, so that an interaction with a black man will be used to learn about all black people and all men. This is slightly different from the models we employ, but also involves potential for intersectional disadvantage (though he does not identify his models as applying to this area of theory).

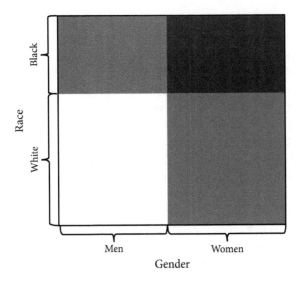

**Figure 6.15** A population with two dimensions of demographic category, gender and race

particular that this population has equal proportions of men and women, and a white majority and black minority. Figure 6.15 shows a representation of this population. As we can see, these two intersecting aspects of identity generate four types in the population: white men, black men, white women, and black women.

Now imagine the following scenario. (This will be slightly jerry-rigged, but I will explain why momentarily.) Actors bargain in two arenas—in the workplace, they bargain for their level of compensation and at home they bargain over what proportion of this compensation they keep control of. Further suppose that in the workplace race is a more salient social category. Actors tend to pay attention to race and condition behavior on it when choosing how to bargain. In the home, on the other hand, gender is the more salient social category. This scenario generates two interrelated processes where bargaining conventions emerge. Conventions emerge for cross-racial bargaining in the workplace, and simultaneously emerge between genders in the home.

One might point out that this set-up seems to deny the fundamental thesis of intersectionality theory—that various aspects of identity cannot simply be detangled for the purposes of understanding inequity. We could instead look at a model where there are simply four intersectional types and bargaining conventions emerge between all of them. Indeed in O'Connor et al. (2017) we do so, and find that the smallest intersectional types can be especially disadvantaged by the cultural Red King. Here I focus on this two-arena model because it will allow us to easily compare two scenarios, one which assumes a less robust level of intersectional identity, and one which assumes a more robust level. As we show, as the intersectional assumptions grow more robust, the inequity between advantaged and disadvantaged intersectional types increases.

Assume actors play a Nash demand game with two strategies. In these two-arena models, this generates four possible joint evolutionary outcomes. In the workplace either white people or black people demand High and at home either men or women demand High, so a joint outcome would be, for example, that black people and women demand High. When the types are symmetric, each of these joint outcomes arises equally often. But let's add the possibility of a majority/minority split in the workplace, and a power imbalance in the home. In particular, let's consider a model with demands of 4 and 6, where $p_1$, the proportion of white people, varies from .5 to .99, and where the disagreement point for men varies from 0 to 3.9 (but is always 0 for women). These changes mean that there are two possible sources of disadvantage for social groups. Black people are disadvantaged in the workforce as a result of the cultural Red King, and women are disadvantaged in the home as the result of a power imbalance.

As we've said, for the purposes of type-conditioning race matters in the workforce and gender at home. For the model with weaker intersectional assumptions let's also assume that for the purposes of social imitation the same is true. People imitate those of their own race in the workplace and their own gender in the home, but do not pay attention to their intersectional categories. This means that the outcomes of this model are simply a combination of the outcomes of two separate models of bargaining. (That is, the two processes take place entirely independently.) Figure 6.16 shows results from this model. I only focus on a small subset of the parameter space to give an idea of what happens when both the minority disadvantage and the power disadvantage increase. On the x-axis, both $p_1$, proportion of whites, and the disagreement point for men increase. Each data point shows basins of attraction for the four outcomes. As we can see, there is particular disadvantage for black women. They

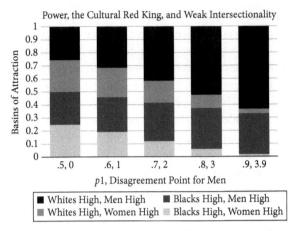

Figure 6.16 Basins of attraction for actors with four intersectional types playing a Nash demand game

are most likely to end up demanding Low in the workplace and in the home, so jointly they are most likely to end up demanding Low in both places. White men, in contrast, are particularly advantaged by their intersectional identity.

In this case, although the evolutionary processes occur separately, we still see a special intersectional disadvantage that is more than the sum of the two processes because the payoffs from the actors are determined by what happens at work and at home. For instance, at the most extreme parameter values for disadvantage (where $p_1 = .99$ and the disagreement point for men is 3.9) on average over all runs of simulation white men receive payoffs of 3.22, white women 2.24, black men 2.68, and black women 1.86. If we considered just the disadvantage that black people face in the workplace, or just the disadvantage women face in the home, we would miss this particular disadvantage for black women. If we studied overall disadvantage we would find that black people make less than whites on average (2.27 versus 2.73), and that women make less than men (2.05 versus 2.95), but we would have to study black women in particular to capture their level of disadvantage.

Now let's look at a second model. Suppose that instead of choosing role models from their binary types in each arena of interaction, actors now imitate only those of their intersectional types in both arenas. That is, black men imitate only black men at work, even though their status

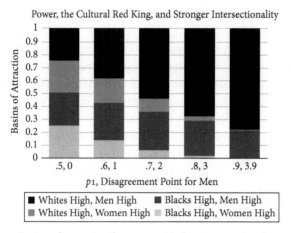

Figure 6.17 Basins of attraction for actors with four intersectional types playing a Nash demand game

as men is irrelevant for bargaining interactions in this case. Figure 6.17 shows results for this model. We see a similar pattern to the last model, but with a more dramatic difference between the outcomes for advantaged and disadvantaged types. In this case, whites and men demand High in nearly 80% of simulations, compared to 63% of the time in the previous simulations. This is a direct result of the stronger intersectional assumptions. Because actors only imitate their own intersectional type, the size differential between the types is more significant, leading to a stronger cultural Red King effect.

As with all the models investigated in the last two chapters, intersectional disadvantage arises here as a result of agents who type-condition and learn to behave in their own best interest. Again, we can explain intersectional oppression via solely dynamical effects (even though there is little reason to think that these explanations capture the full picture in real-world populations). Again, it takes very little to generate special disadvantage for intersectional groups compared to their binary social groups.

•   •   •

This chapter wraps up the main body of our discussion of the dynamics of pernicious inequity. In particular, we explored the effects that reactivity differences can have on the emergence of bargaining norms. As we saw, one of the most important implications of this set of results is with regard to minority populations. In bargaining scenarios, the cultural Red King can lead to bargaining disadvantage by virtue simply of minority status and absent any other asymmetries between groups. Besides minority status, this same sort of disadvantage can arise for groups that lack institutional memory, or who are more economically insecure with respect to background payoffs. We also explored some more specific applications of these models. As we showed in O'Connor et al. (2017), special intersectional disadvantage can arise in these models as a result of dynamics. In the next chapter, we will turn to a slightly different question—once the sort of inequitable conventions we have been addressing arise, how does this impact interactive choices?

# 7

# Discrimination and Homophily

Feldon et al. (2017) asked 336 first-year PhD students in the biological sciences to record their research hours biweekly over the course of a year. At the end of the year, they administered surveys asking, among other things, how many publications these students had been included on as authors. What they found was that, controlling for relevant variables, women students spent significantly more time on research than men students. They also found that for each 100 hours worked, men were 15% more likely to earn an authorship position than women. In other words, the women suffered an inequity in terms of academic credit assigned per hour worked.

This is not the only study to identify gender-based credit inequities in academia. West et al. (2013) and Sugimoto (2013) find that across various disciplines women are less likely to hold first and last author positions. Sarsons (2017) looks at the impact of research publications on the likelihood that economists receive tenure. She finds that men receive an equal boost for co-authored and single-authored publications. Women's chances of tenure, on the other hand, increase by about 8% for a single-authored publication (similar to a man's) or for a paper co-authored with another woman, but by only 2% for a publication with a male co-author (and only 4.5% for a publication with mixed gender co-authors). In other words, even in cases where the collaborators themselves might attempt to give fair authorship credit, the ultimate credit payoffs for collaborative work significantly disadvantage women (at least in economics).

Another set of results indicate that in many academic disciplines women are less likely to choose to co-author, and that when they do co-author, they tend to choose other women as partners. Ferber and Teiman

(1980); McDowell and Smith (1992); Boschini and Sjögren (2007); West et al. (2013) find these results for women in disciplines where they are underrepresented, including economics. In addition, Del Carmen and Bing (2000) find that black criminologists are less likely to co-author than their colleagues. And Botts et al. (2014) find that black philosophers tend to cluster into sub-disciplines, where those sub-disciplines such as philosophy of race, have lower proportions of white academics.

The goal of this chapter is to use the framework developed thus far in the book to address the question: how do discriminatory conventions and norms influence patterns of interaction? In particular, the models presented will highlight causal processes that can lead to homophily, or disproportionate in-group interaction, as a result of discrimination.

While these models apply generally to the dynamics of strategic interaction, I'll use academic communities as a case study throughout the chapter. This case is a useful one since discrimination with respect to credit sharing in academia has been extensively studied, as have collaboration networks. The models will draw a causal link between the two sets of empirical results from this literature described above. The suggestion is that when women get less credit, they learn to avoid collaborating with men as a result.

I will start by looking at models where those who face discrimination can opt out of scenarios of joint action/division of resources. As we'll see, in these models, those who face discrimination are less likely to collaborate and more likely to work alone as a result of receiving relatively low shares of jointly produced resources. Next, I will turn to models that more explicitly represent interactive structure—network models. Using this framework, I'll explore how interactive network structure and discriminatory behavior are mutually influential, noting especially the emergence of homophily. I'll also look at what happens in these models when social groups have differential access to resources that create asymmetries in their productive abilities. As we'll see, this kind of asymmetry can dramatically change outcomes. I'll conclude by discussing the special relevance of these models to academic communities. It has often been argued that diversity is a boon to scientific research. But discriminatory practices may decrease the effective diversity of scientific teams. In this vein, I will address the possibility of intervening on homophillic collaboration networks, and the potential consequences of such intervention.

## 7.1  Taking the Outside Option

In O'Connor and Bruner (2017), we consider a case where a community composed of two types (men and women, white and black, etc.) adheres to discriminatory bargaining conventions. This means that when members of the two types divide a resource, it is always the case that the advantaged type receives more than the disadvantaged type. The question we ask is: how does this assumption impact agents' choices about strategic interaction?

In particular, we look at the Nash demand game with an outside option. (See Figure 5.7.) But we twist the interpretation slightly, and take it to represent cases where the resource that is divided is one that actors jointly produce. In general, joint action often improves human productivity, but raises the issue of 1) who will do what work and 2) who will get how much of the resource produced. In other words, situations of joint action are also almost always situations of resource division (Wagner, 2012).

Under this interpretation, we have to change our understanding of the Nash demand game's strategies slightly. In particular, we take them to represent demands for some level of payoff given an amount of work invested.[1] A medium demand, in this version of the game, might correspond to a demand for most of the resource by an individual who also did most of the work to produce it. Or it might correspond to a demand for about half the resource if both actors shared labor fairly. A high demand might be for 70% of a resource that an individual did not contribute much to producing. As mentioned, later I will further discuss an academic interpretation of these models. Under that interpretation, a high demand might represent a researcher who wants to be first author on a research paper where they only did 30% of the work. Notice that this interpretation transforms the question above to: how do discriminatory conventions impact *joint action* between those in different social groups? (And: does discrimination increase homophily in these cases?)

---

[1] In Cochran and O'Connor (2018) we describe a model that more explicitly represents joint production followed by bargaining. I do not present results from this paper here, since they are more complicated than those from the basic Nash demand game. We find that in this two-stage game the presence of social categories like gender and race also tend to lead to inequitable conventions, even when actors can condition their demands for compensation on the contribution level of their partners.

Remember that in the Nash demand game with an outside option, actors have the option of choosing a low, dependable payoff, rather than risking a bargaining interaction. This model creates a framework where we can investigate whether actors tend to learn to opt out of joint action under discriminatory conditions. That is, if they face discrimination, do they respond by learning to simply work alone?

Consider such a model where the outside option is always 2, and where actors follow a discriminatory norm such that one type always gets L and the other H. Figure 7.1 shows the proportion of outcomes of these models that end up at collaboration rather than solo work.[2] As the inequity between the two groups increases (L gets lower), the likelihood of collaboration also decreases. Notice that this happens despite the fact that collaboration is *always* better from a payoff standpoint, that is, $L > 2$. The relatively low payoff of the disadvantaged type, plus risks associated with collaboration, make them more likely to opt out of collaboration and simply work alone. This effect is stronger for small minority groups. Notice that when the minority makes up only 1% of the population, and when the Low demand is very small ($L = 2.2$), collaboration only emerges between types about 10% of the time. Again, this is despite the fact that

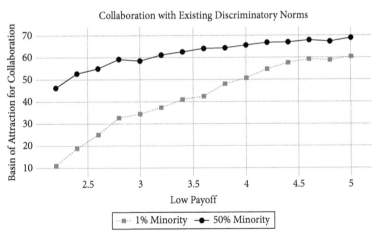

**Figure 7.1** Basins of attraction for collaboration for two types playing a Nash demand game with an outside option

[2] As with previous models in the book, we use the discrete time replicator dynamics to generate these results.

the payoffs for the discriminatory collaboration outcomes are better for both parties.

This result suggests that when those in disadvantaged groups are discriminated against, they should be more likely to learn to abstain from joint projects that require bargaining. In other words, based on these results, we might think there is a causal link between the empirical results described in the beginning of the chapter. In particular, when women are subject to credit discrimination, they should also be more likely to single-author. This said, the model just described cannot represent more specific interactive choices (such as to replace an unsatisfactory interactive partner with another who demands less compensation). For that reason, I now move on to discuss network models of similar phenomena.

## 7.2 Networks and Homophily

In Rubin and O'Connor (2018), philosopher of science Hannah Rubin and I further explore the possibility that discriminatory norms disincentivize joint action between diverse groups. The rest of this section will describe our work together. In particular, we look at *networks* of agents who play Nash demand games with their neighbors on this network. Each *node* of the network represents an individual, and each *edge* an interactive connection. Figure 7.2 gives an example of what such a network might look like. In this figure, we see eight individuals of two different types, with eight links between them.

We use simulations to explore the interactions between discriminatory conventions and network structure. To fully describe these

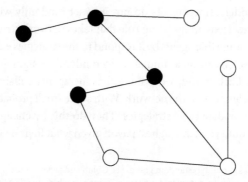

**Figure 7.2** A network with two types represented by black and white nodes. Edges represent interactive links between agents

interactions, we break our investigation into three parts. First, we hold one aspect of our model—the network structure—fixed while allowing actors to develop conventions of bargaining. Second, we hold the other aspect of our model—bargaining behavior—fixed and allow actors to choose their network partners. Then we allow both of these elements to vary. As will become clear, in these models (as in the infinite population models from O'Connor and Bruner (2017)) discrimination disincentivizes collaboration between different social groups. The network structure here, though, lets us explore, in particular, the possibility of homophily—preferential in-group interaction—that can arise as the result of discrimination.

### 7.2.1 Fixed network, evolving bargaining

In this section, I describe models where we assume a fixed network and see how it influences the emergence of bargaining behavior. The question is: on network models, do we see discrimination emerge just as in the infinite population models from the last chapters? And: how does network structure influence this emergence? We begin by specifying networks with two types of actors. In particular, we create random networks using an algorithm where for each possible combination of two agents an edge is formed with some probability, $p$. We allow the possibility that agents might have different probabilities of linking with those in their in- and out-groups.[3] If the probability of forming each in-group edge $p_{in}$, is greater than for each out-group edge, $p_{out}$, the network exhibits homophily.

In the models throughout the rest of the book, I have mostly assumed that actors change strategies according to the replicator dynamics. But in network models, since agents do not interact randomly within their population, one needs an updating rule that takes network structure into account. We assume that agents best respond to the strategies exhibited by their neighbors.[4] We begin a simulation by randomly assigning strategies to each agent. Each round, we assume that the agents collaborate with each of their neighbors on the network. With some small probability, each agent will then update their strategies. They do this by changing to the strategy that would yield the highest payoff given what their neighbors are

---

[3] This generates a multitype random graph. See Golub and Jackson (2012).

[4] To this point, we have considered a number of models where agents best respond to some set of memories, as in Axtell et al. (2000). Here, we assume agents myopically respond to whatever is happening with their partners at a particular moment.

doing. For example, suppose Suzy has three neighbors who are women, all of whom demand Medium, and four neighbors who are men, all of whom demand Low. Her best response is to switch to demanding Medium of the women, and High of the men. Notice that this is a boundedly rational updating rule—Suzy does not try to predict what her neighbors will do in the next round, or how they might respond to her. She simply myopically responds to her environment. Over time, the agents in these simulations reach stable patterns of behavior, which, again, we take to represent something like a convention for bargaining over joint action.

Reflecting previous work by Poza et al. (2011), we find that these models always evolve to conventions like those described in the previous chapters. In particular, we looked at a Nash demand game with Low, Med, and High demands, so the evolutionary outcomes are that one group demands High, or the other does, or they make fair demands of each other. Payoff details determine how likely these outcomes are, but, as in previous chapters, we find that fair conventions are most likely between groups, but inequitable ones also commonly emerge.

Perhaps surprisingly, the level of homophily in these networks seems to have no effect on the emergence of between-group conventions of bargaining. In other words, discrimination emerges in the same way whether or not agents prefer to interact with those of their own type. Why might this be? In these models, there really are three separate cultural evolutionary processes occurring—one within each in-group and one between groups. A convention develops for each of these—for what actors do in the first in-group, in the second in-group, and between groups. The between-group process is thus insensitive to the level of connectivity within each group.

In Chapter 6 I briefly mentioned that the cultural Red King effect shows robustness across a number of different models, including network models. Hannah and I find that for smaller majority groups, the likelihood that they end up demanding Low at emerged conventions is higher. Figure 7.3 demonstrates this result.[5] As is evident, as one group grows in size, the likelihood that they demand High increases.

---

[5] This figure averages over a wide set of parameter values. We always considered models with probability .1 that agents updated their strategies in each round, and high demand $H = 6$. We kept $p_{in} = .4$ and varied $p_{out}$ from .2 to .8, meaning that agents went from half as likely to link with out-group members to twice as likely. Network size ranged from 20 to 100 agents. Minority group size ranged from 10% to 50%. Each set of parameter values was run 100 times, in a simulation with 1000 rounds.

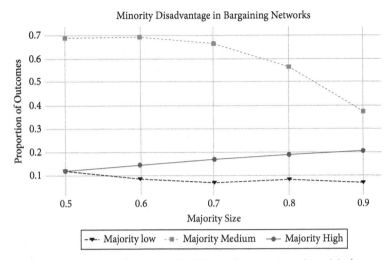

Figure 7.3 An analog of the cultural Red King effect in a network model of agents playing the Nash demand game. Results are averaged over parameter values with H = 6

Perhaps surprisingly, the reason for this trend is actually different from that described in the last chapter. There, minority size caused a difference in learning speed which could lead to disadvantage (or advantage). Here the asymmetry has to do with the average number of between-group network connections for each type. Consider, for example, a community with eight white people and four black people. And suppose that there are eight between-group connections. On average, each white person will interact with one out-group member, and each black person with two out-group members. This sort of asymmetry in out-group connections will exist whenever one group is in the minority.

What this means, for the Nash demand game, is that minority group members will have a greater probability of updating toward lower demands, on average. For example, consider a game with demands 4, 5, and 6. For each white person who has one out-group partner, and for random starting strategies, there is a 1/3 chance that their best response is High (ditto for Medium and Low), because there is a 1/3 chance their single partner starts by playing Low. For each black person with two out-group partners, there is only a 1/9 chance that their best response is High, because this only occurs when both partners demand Low. On the other hand, there is a 5/9 chance that their best response is Low, and 1/3 for Medium. We do not find an analog to the cultural Red Queen in these models, for combinatorial reasons described in Rubin and O'Connor (2018). (The Red King occurs as long as $H < 7$.)

### 7.2.2 Fixed bargaining, evolving network

Now let us assume a community where discriminatory norms for dividing work and rewards in joint action are already established. In other words, hold bargaining strategies fixed. What happens if we allow the network structure of this model to evolve?

To investigate this question, we consider models where agents use expected payoffs from strategic interactions to update network structure (see Watts (2001)). We assume that agents are making fair demands with their in-group (and so receive a payoff of 5 for each in-group connection) and unfair demands with their out-group. This means that one type gets 6, and the other 4, for each out-group connection. We begin with an empty network. In each round we choose an updater and a potential collaborator. Whenever both of these players are willing to form a link, they do so. Any agent who has not reached their maximum number of links will be willing to form a new one because some payoff from joint action is better than none. For agents who have reached their maximum number of links—essentially the number of interactive partners they can sustain—they consider whether the new potential link will provide more payoff than any of their current ones. If so, agents drop their lowest payoff link and form a new one.[6] Over subsequent rounds of simulation, agents change collaborative partners until the entire network reaches a stable state where no pair of agents is willing to form a new, different link.

We find that these networks always evolve to a state where they are fully homophilous. In other words, each type only interacts with their in-group, and there are no links between the groups. Why? The type that is discriminated against always prefers to interact with their in-group, where they receive a fair payoff. At the beginning of a simulation, links of all kinds form. But once agents reach their maximum number of links, the oppressed type breaks off contact with their oppressors. Once

---

[6] If the two agents chosen are already collaborators, the updater has the option to break the link and form a new one with another randomly chosen agent. See Watts (2001); Rubin and O'Connor (2018) for more details.

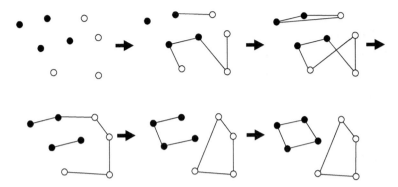

**Figure 7.4** An evolving network where eventually agents break all out-group links, leading to total homophily

this happens, the discriminating type forms links with their in-group members, even though they would prefer out-group links that would allow them to get a bigger portion of the pie. Figure 7.4 shows an example of what this might look like in an eight-agent network where the maximum number of links is two. First, agents form links indiscriminately. Once they reach their maximum number of links the oppressed agents (white) break out-group links to form in-group links. The oppressing agents (black) then form in-group links as well.

Returning to academic communities, we see here a potential explanation of why women might tend to collaborate with other women in, say, economics. On the expectation that they will have to do extra work, and receive less credit, should they collaborate with men, they choose a woman partner instead. Notice that one result of homophily in these models is a complete eradication of discriminatory behavior. One group has discriminatory *tendencies*, but since they never get a chance to deploy them, equitable divisions happen across the community. (That sounds unrealistic, and it should. As we will see in the next section, many realistic conditions should shift this picture to one where inequitable behavior is maintained in the group.)

### 7.2.3 *The coevolution of bargaining and network structure*

Of course, in real interactive networks, we rarely see complete homophily. The last set of models Hannah and I investigate show what happens when both bargaining and interactive choices update simultaneously. To test this we considered simulation models that began with empty networks, and random strategies. In each round with probability .1 every agent takes one action. The agents either update their bargaining strategy via best response as described above, or else update their network partners as described.[7]

In this model, we observed an emergence of heterogenous strategies throughout the network. Some agents developed discriminatory strategies, and others fair strategies. In response to this, partial homophily emerged at the same time. In particular, agents learned to avoid discriminatory out-groupers, but to maintain links to out-group members who treated them fairly. This meant that there was variety from simulation to simulation as to the level of homophily that emerged in these models. If many agents happened to evolve discriminatory practices, more homophily emerged.

Figure 7.5 shows this trend.[8] As is evident, the greater the level of discrimination, on average, the greater the homophily. To quantify

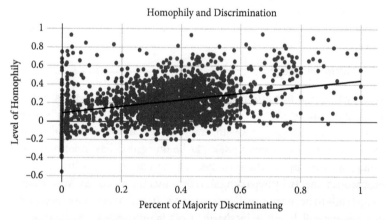

Figure 7.5 Increasing discrimination corresponds to increasing homophily in network bargaining models

---

[7] Whether an agent updated their bargaining or their network was chosen probabilistically. We considered a .8 probability of updating bargaining strategy and a .2 probability of updating a network link. Similar results emerge for different values.

[8] These results were from simulations with 100 agents and $H = 6$. We varied minority proportion from 10% to 50%. The maximum number of links varied from 3 to 9. We ran 100 simulations for each set of parameter values, running each for 20,000 rounds.

homophily here we use a measure from Currarini et al. (2009) called *inbreeding homophily*. Basically, this measures the proportion of within-group links in the network, controlling for the size of each group.[9]

## 7.3 Bigger and Smaller Pies

The analysis presented thus far predicts that when two groups engage in joint action, discrimination toward one group should lead to homophily. This does seem to be what we observe in the case of collaboration in academic communities—when women receive less credit for joint work, they are more likely to collaborate with women (as well as to opt out of collaborating). This pattern is not perfect, and the last model we saw predicts that actors will maintain out-group links with those who treat them fairly, while avoiding those who treat them unfairly.

The models discussed thus far, though, also make a key assumption, which is that joint action yields equal amounts of resource, or credit, regardless of who is engaged in it. There are a few cases in which such an assumption will not hold. In Rubin and O'Connor (2018) and Schneider et al. (2019) we consider these cases, and how they impact the results above.

### 7.3.1 *Group privilege*

Suppose first that one group generally has special access to resources—social, political, or physical—that increase its productivity. Maybe one group tends to hold greater wealth, and so can get access to the bank loans necessary to start new businesses. Maybe one group has more political capital, and so can use these connections to remove impediments to a joint project, that is, by bypassing slow bureaucratic processes. Maybe one group tends to be more prestigious, and so will tend to get more credit for an academic collaboration by sharing work at prestigious conferences.

We can represent this kind of case by supposing that the size of the "pie" that must be divided between two individuals is biggest if it is produced

---

[9] Inbreeding homophily ($I_i$) is defined by:

$$I_i = \frac{H_i - w_i}{1 - w_i}$$

where $H_i$ is the proportion of links for group $i$ that are within-group, and $w_i$ is the proportion of the population that $i$ makes up.

by two members of type A, smallest if produced by two members of type B, and intermediate for one member of each. For instance, maybe two women can generate a resource of value 10, two men one of value 16, and a mixed-gender pairing one of value 12.

What happens in this sort of case? The relative sizes of the pies will define a few different regimes with different interactive outcomes. Consider a model, like those discussed in section 7.2.2, where we assume discrimination happens between groups. Let the Low, Med, and High demands now correspond to demands for .4, .5, or .6 of the resource. And further suppose that those who do the discriminating (type A) are also those with more access to resources.

As we have seen, when the two groups produce similar amounts of resource, homophily occurs because the B types choose to disengage with discriminatory partners. But there are also stable regimes where both types will prefer to interact with their out-group. This occurs, for instance, when the three pie sizes are 15, 14, and 10. Within groups, the expected payoffs are 7.5 and 5, because actors divide their resources fairly. Between groups, the expected payoffs are 8.4 for the A types and 5.6 for the B types. Notice that these payoffs are better than what they would get by collaborating with in-group members, so under an evolving network, we would instead expect actors to maximize their number of out-group connections (Rubin and O'Connor, 2018). Notice also that unlike the models described in the last section, these outcomes are persistently inequitable. The advantages of the A group mean that members of the B group are willing to engage in unfair partnerships to gain access to their partner's extra resources.

If the advantages of the A group are too great, we again expect homophily, but now because A types are unwilling to interact with B types, even though they discriminate against them. Instead, it is better to interact with an in-group member who brings their own special advantages to the table, even if they in turn demand a fair portion of the good that gets produced. In an outcome like this, the groups are homophilic, and B types also receive lower payoffs. Consider, for example, a situation where two As make a pie of value 18, two Bs one of value 10, and a mixed group one of value 13. At stable network outcomes, the A types all receive 9 for each in-group interaction, and the Bs get 5.

To summarize, when one group produces resources of more value, for whatever reason, the picture described in the last section where we expect completely fair treatment, and homophily, breaks down. We sometimes expect homophily, though we do not necessarily expect fair outcomes, and in some cases we expect inequitable between-group interactions to dominate. As an example of this last, think of collaborations between professors and graduate students—in such interactions, the expectation is often that graduate students will perform the lion's share of the work and receive less credit from the community. The opportunity to tap into the personal and monetary resources of an established academic, however, makes the trade-off worth their while. The professor, in the meantime, is willing to collaborate with someone who does not bring as much to the table, but who will do most of the work.

### 7.3.2 Diversity and synergy

There is one other possibility to consider, which is that in some situations diverse teams may be able to generate resources that homogenous teams cannot. This is often the case when groups interact whose members, by dint of different background training, have complementary skill sets. (See Part I of the book.) In Schneider et al. (2019) we outline several case studies from academia where, by dint of different social training, experience, and access, cross-gender collaboration was especially successful. For example, the early field of sexology, for obvious reasons, benefited from input by both men and women researchers.

There are also empirical results suggesting that in some situations simply combining individuals with different life experiences and social identities can create synergistic effects vis a vis joint production or collaboration. To give a few examples, Sommers (2006) finds that racially diverse juries deliberate more effectively by sharing more information. Phillips et al. (2006) looks at small groups solving problems, and finds that racial diversity improves their decision-making for similar reasons. And, in experimental "markets," Levine et al. (2014) find that prices are more accurate when traders are ethnically diverse because they are more likely to scrutinize the decisions of others. In academia, some authors have found that culturally diverse groups are more productive (Barjak and Robinson, 2008). And Campbell et al. (2013) find that gender-diverse collaborative research is cited more (which they argue is a result of its higher quality).[10]

---

[10] Freeman and Huang (2015) also find that papers produced by ethnically diverse groups are cited more, but this may result from the relative diversity of their social networks.

Suppose we consider a model where the size of the resource produced between groups is larger than that produced by in-group collaboration. In this case, there is an incentive to drop in-group links, and to form out-group links instead, so as to reap the benefit of this synergy. In other words, we expect negative homophily to emerge. In such models, though, we also expect discrimination between groups to be stable in many cases. For example, suppose one group demands 60% of the resource and the other 40%. If production was the same regardless of group membership, we would expect homophily. If between-group pies are of size 14, while in-group pies are size 10, we expect heterophily (because 5.6 is better than 5). So, again, although one group is disadvantaged with respect to the other group, they still choose out-group partners.

## 7.4 Discrimination and Academic Progress

Before concluding this chapter, I would like to discuss, in further detail, the interpretation of the models from this chapter as representing bargaining and collaboration in epistemic communities—groups of knowledge-makers such as academics and industry researchers. Philosophers of science are interested in understanding how interactions among members of such communities influence the process of science. This is part of *social epistemology*—the study of knowledge creation emphasizing the role of knowledge-making communities.

In the last few decades, and especially recently, philosophers have used formal models to attempt to understand epistemic communities. Landmark papers by Kitcher (1990), Strevens (2003), Weisberg and Muldoon (2009), and Zollman (2007), for example, have used models to explore questions related to the division of cognitive labor, the role of diversity in science, and how communication networks influence scientific consensus.[11] More recently, in O'Connor and Bruner (2017), Bruner and O'Connor (2015), and Rubin and O'Connor (2018) we've used models to explore not the progress of science directly, but rather the emergence of norms between social categories in scientific communities and the potential impacts of these norms on knowledge.

How do these models translate into an epistemic context? As I have hinted at throughout this chapter, explicit or implicit negotiations are key

---

[11] Though see Alexander (2013), Thoma (2014), and Rosenstock et al. (2017).

to joint action in academia, and, importantly, to collaborative research projects. This is because in such collaborations academics must decide who will do what work, and also must decide author order on papers produced, which is a proxy for academic credit.[12]

What implications do our results on inequity hold for epistemic communities? Philosophers of science such as Longino (1990), Solomon (2001), and Okruhlik (1994) have convincingly argued that not all knowledge-makers are the same. The experiences and personalities of scientists will matter in how they go about doing science. And in particular diverse communities may be more successful than uniform ones. There are many arguments given in philosophy of science in support of diverse scientific communities. I will not outline them at length here, but will just give an example.[13] Haraway (1989) details how the entrance of women into the field of primatology revolutionized the field, which had previously focused largely on the behaviors of male primates. In this case there is a clear connection between the personal identities of the researchers as women and their research, and a clear benefit to inquiry from this connection.

The implication is that factors that decrease the diversity, or the effective diversity, of scientific fields, may negatively impact science. This seems especially likely in fields where individual experiences impact research choices, like biology and the social sciences. Thus, if discriminatory conventions lead to homophily in academic groups, we might create situations where the benefits to science of diverse collaboration are lost.

### 7.4.1 Incentivizing collaboration

Given the work just described from philosophy of science, and on the benefits of diverse collaboration more generally, one natural question is: can we incentivize diverse collaborations in science? The framework described in this chapter suggests possible ways to do this. In particular, as we have seen, when individuals expect special benefits from between-group collaboration, we expect them to choose these sorts of interactions.

---

[12] These models are part of the literature in philosophy of science using a "credit economy" to understand science. The assumption (obviously not always realized in the real world) is that what academics want is credit—recognition from their community, and all that attends it.

[13] Interested readers can find an overview of arguments in support of scientific diversity in O'Connor and Bruner (2017).

In response to this possibility, funding bodies might create special grants for those who wish to form international, or otherwise diverse collaborative groups. Such grants could increase the productivity of these collaborations by, for example, facilitating hiring of research assistants. There is a worry, though, which we raise in Schneider et al. (2019). If discriminatory norms are entrenched between two groups, any initiative to increase interaction between them will also increase the number of discriminatory interactions occurring. Even if we create a situation where the overall payoff outcome is better for both groups (by increasing the between-group pie), we entrench inequities between the groups by incentivizing interaction. As we point out, in the case of academic collaboration, measures intended to improve epistemic outcomes might have unintended social consequences.

. . .

Schelling (1971), in a famous paper, provides an explanation of group-level segregation via appeal to individual discrimination. In particular, his agents prefer to live in neighborhoods where they are not in a small racial minority (less than 30% or so). The result of these preferences is a series of moves that almost inevitably result in spatial segregation by race. While very elegant, this model has been criticized for failing to capture the key causal factors involved in real-world segregation. Among these are a number of structural policies, such as exclusionary mortgage practices and steering by real estate agencies (Galster and Godfrey, 2005; Denton, 2006; de Leeuw et al., 2007). In addition, empirical work indicates that where preferences for racial make up play a role in housing choices, they do not match the minimal discrimination described by Schelling. Instead, Farley et al. (1997) find that black people report hesitation to live in largely white neighborhoods for fear of bias and discrimination. (And, additionally, while black people report preferring mixed neighborhoods, white people's willingness to live in a neighborhood decreases steadily as the proportion of black neighbors increases.)

The framework described in this chapter is not about housing segregation, but rather about interactive segregation—why do people often choose those in their own social identity groups for interaction, and strategic interaction in particular? The answer provided, though, is in line with that developed by Farley et al. (1997). If people are sensitive to the negative effects of discrimination, they should learn to avoid discriminators. This leads to homophily, but also to largely fair patterns of behavior. Where the benefits of out-group collaboration outweigh the detriment of discrimination, we should expect this pattern to reverse, potentially at the cost of equity.

I would like to add one caveat before moving on. All the dynamic network models presented in this chapter assume that actors may freely choose to form and leave collaborative endeavors. In reality, there may be serious constraints to doing so. Actors may be coerced into arrangements that they would not freely choose. Even when actors have freely chosen arrangements, there may be costs to leaving them. A further extension of this work might involve adding such features to these models.

# 8

# The Evolution of Household Bargaining

Recent media attention has focused on a perhaps surprising observation from the perspective of rational choice. Even when women in modern families earn as much as their male partners, they tend to do a larger portion of the housework (Bianchi et al., 2006; Coltrane, 2000; Treas and Drobnic, 2010).[1] The reason this poses a rational-choice conundrum is that when it comes to household bargaining over labor, one would expect that symmetric positions with respect to income and external labor would lead to symmetric outcomes. If both actors work extensively outside the home, this framework would predict that they should divide home labor fairly.

This topic has generated quite a lot of work both in sociology and in household economics. The latter discipline has developed models based in assumptions of rational choice to explain these inequitable household divisions of labor. While these models shed light on the phenomenon, they tend to de-emphasize the role of norms and conventions in patterns of household behavior. As I will argue, there are many reasons to think that norms and conventions influence such patterns, and so models that incorporate their emergence are important here. The idea is not that rational choice-based models are uninformative, but that they fail to capture the relevance of social transmission and cultural evolution to these phenomena. At the end of the chapter I'll discuss how these two approaches can provide complementary accounts of different aspects of household divisions.

---

[1] I will focus on modern, heterosexual households, not because they are the only ones that matter, but simply because treating all households is beyond the scope of this chapter.

In this chapter, I do two things. First, drawing on the work from the rest of the book, I present an explicitly evolutionary model of the emergence of coordination in modern households. In particular, I show why certain conditions might favor market labor for one gender and home labor for the other. The goal is to provide a proof of concept for the usefulness of evolutionary models in this domain. I also argue that once these patterns have emerged, they should be relatively stable in the face of changing social conditions. (This is a theme that will become particularly relevant in Chapter 9.) Using these patterns of coordination as a starting point, I then show why emerging patterns of household bargaining, that is, over who does more total work, and has more total leisure time, should favor whichever gender tends to be employed in market work. The idea is that this gender is more powerful in the senses outlined in Chapter 5, and so will tend to end up at preferred outcomes.

This how-possibly story brings together the two halves of this book. The first set of models looks at the first sort of inequity—actors involved in joint action take complementary roles to benefit themselves, and end up with unequal rewards. This feeds into the second part of the story, where this small initial difference contributes to the second sort of inequity, where one type exploits the other. In other words, we see how the two kinds of inequity are interrelated in a special case of gendered division of labor.

## 8.1 The Evolution of Household Coordination

The model I am about to describe is intended to give a "how-possibly" story for the emergence of norms that favor housework for one gender, favor labor market work for the other, and are sticky in the face of changing external environments. The idea is to show the potential usefulness of evolutionary, rather than choice-based, models in this area, rather than to carefully capture the details of how household division of labor actually emerges.

Start by assuming that two actors in a household must coordinate who does how much market labor and who does how much unpaid household labor. An insufficient level of either of these leads to an unsuccessful household. If household labor is not performed, the household is in poor shape, and the actors are unhappy. If market labor is not performed,

Player 2

|  | Low–High | Med–Med | High–Low |
|---|---|---|---|
| Low–High | 0, 0 | 0, 0 | 1, 1 |
| Med–Med | 0, 0 | 1, 1 | 0, 0 |
| High–Low | 1, 1 | 0, 0 | 0, 0 |

Player 1 labels the rows (Low–High, Med–Med, High–Low).

**Figure 8.1** A three-strategy complementary coordination game

the household does not generate income to meet basic needs. Figure 8.1 shows a payoff table of a game where actors do best when they perform complementary levels of household and market labor. Each actor chooses Low–High (low household labor, high market labor), Med–Med (moderate levels of both), or High–Low (high household labor, low market labor). Complementary splits receive the best payoffs. I assume there is a viable even split so that actors can mutually do well by evenly dividing market work and household labor (though this may not always be a good assumption).[2]

This game assumes that the actors are completely symmetric in that each arrangement will generate the same amount of goods. In modern societies, however, it is usually the case that the average earning power of men exceeds that of women, and in recent history this disparity has been even greater. For this reason, let's add to the model a factor $\alpha$ that determines how much one actor versus the other earns. When the higher-earning actor chooses High–Low, this increases the total payoff at that equilibrium, compared to their Medium amount of work, by $\alpha$ percent. When the higher-earning actor chooses Low–High, this decreases the payoff at that equilibrium by $\alpha$ percent. To give an example, assume that $\alpha = .5$. The resulting payoff table (modified from the one in Figure 8.1) is shown in Figure 8.2. Of course (not to bury the lede) this aspect of the model assumes payoff asymmetries for roles to get an asymmetry in the evolution of these roles. But the idea is that an asymmetry in workplace wages leads to an asymmetry in household division of labor.

---

[2] One might complain that the payoffs for miscoordination here are unrealistic. Actors who are both engaged in market labor can use the money earned to pay for household labor. In such a case Low–High vs. Low–High might be better than High–Low vs. High–Low. Likewise, one might point out that equal sharing might lead to production of a greater total resource since partners are more satisfied. The goal with this model is to give a sort of easy to understand proof of possibility, so I ask the reader to tolerate a few inaccurate assumptions.

Player 2

| | Low–High | Med–Med | High–Low |
|---|---|---|---|
| **Low–High** | 0, 0 | 0, 0 | 1.5, 1.5 |
| **Med–Med** | 0, 0 | 1, 1 | 0, 0 |
| **High–Low** | .5, .5 | 0, 0 | 0, 0 |

(Player 1 labels the rows)

**Figure 8.2** A three-strategy complementary coordination game with better equilibria for both players

Player 2

| | Low–High | Med–Med | High–Low |
|---|---|---|---|
| **Low–High** | 0, 0 | 0, 0 | .75, 2.25 |
| **Med–Med** | 0, 0 | 1, 1 | 0, 0 |
| **High–Low** | .75, .25 | 0, 0 | 0, 0 |

(Player 1 labels the rows)

**Figure 8.3** A three-strategy complementary coordination game where players have some conflict of interest

This is similar to the influential analysis by Okin (1989) of how wage asymmetries can lead to cycles of inequity based on the rational choices of men and women who divide household labor.

This game, like the last one, assumes full common interest between the actors in the household. But, as I will elaborate shortly, this is not a particularly good assumption. Studies have shown that control over goods or money provides direct, personal benefits to members of a household that do not accrue to those who do not control these resources (Beblo, 2001; Eswaran, 2014). For this reason, let's add the assumption that the player who controls the money also derives some benefit from doing so. Let $\beta$ be a factor that determines the total proportion of household resources that the actor doing more market labor receives. If $\beta = .5$, each actor receives half the total generated household resources. If $\beta > .5$, the player with greater outside earnings gets a greater percentage of the earnings. Figure 8.3 shows the game above with $\beta = .75$, so that the actor doing household labor receives only 25% of generated payoff at each outcome.

The payoffs in this game combine two factors—benefits from efficient coordination of labor at home, and benefits from monetary gains associated with certain coordination arrangements. The payoffs, of course, cannot be taken as tracking monetary compensation directly. Rather the idea is that under the feasible household divisions of labor from a work perspective, some of these will be more or less preferable to the actors as a result of the money that they gain and their control of it.

In this final version of the game, things look different from the first version I presented. In the first version of this problem, every equilibrium generates the same amount of total good. Once we add the assumption that one actor earns more than the other, we see a spectrum of total good generated. This change moves the game further from the conventional end of the spectrum, and more toward the functional end of things on the measure outlined in Part I. Once we add the assumption that players prefer to control money, the equilibria can be ordered for efficiency in the sense that one yields the greatest total payoff, but now players can have conflict of interest in the sense that they nonetheless prefer different equilibria. In this particular example, player 1 prefers the Med–Med vs. Med–Med equilibrium, while player 2 prefers the Low–High vs. High–Low equilibrium. Notice that in this game the equilibrium that generates the most total good will also be the most inequitable one. This is because the total amount of available payoff at that outcome is highest, so an unequal division of this larger amount will more strongly favor the working partner in terms of total payoff.

What happens when populations of potential partners evolve to divide labor in the household in a situation well-modeled by this game? In the first version presented, where coordination is the only thing actors care about, the populations evolve to any of the three equilibria with equal probability. As $\alpha$—the factor determining how much one actor makes compared to the other—increases, evolution will tend to drive populations to the Low–High vs. High–Low equilibrium where that actor works outside the home. Thus, intuitively, we expect that if one type of member of the household can earn significantly more than the other, conventions will emerge where that type works outside the house. In situations like this there is a functional explanation for the emergence of such a convention—it benefits both actors in that it brings more resources home. Figure 8.4 shows how the basins of attraction for the three equilibria change as $\alpha$, the relative earnings of one spouse, shifts. $\beta$ in this figure is held fixed at .6, or a moderate inequity in who controls household resources.

As $\beta$—the factor determining which actor gets more benefits from earned income—shifts, it makes the equal work split more attractive. Inequitable outcomes have smaller basins of attraction because they yield relatively low payoffs for one type of actor, who will then be disincentivized from learning the relevant behavior. This can mean that, in

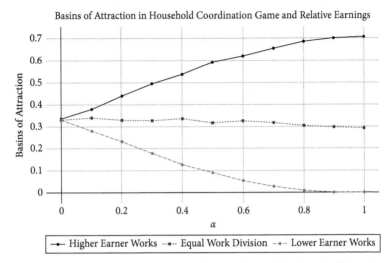

**Figure 8.4** Basins of attraction for the three equilibria in the household coordination game as a function of $\alpha$, $\beta = .6$

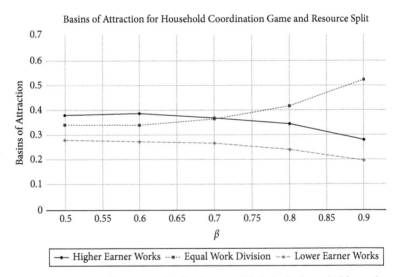

**Figure 8.5** Basins of attraction for the three equilibria in the household coordination game as a function of $\beta$, $\alpha = .1$

this model, the equilibrium with the largest basin of attraction may not be the one that generates the most total payoff. Figure 8.5 shows an example. Here $\alpha = .1$, so one type can earn only slightly more outside the household. When the split between actors is only somewhat inequitable, the highest payoff outcome is the most likely to emerge, when the split is very unfair, though, the most likely outcome is Med–Med vs. Med–Med. In cases where $\alpha$ is higher, though—where one actor can earn much more—the Low–High vs. High–Low equilibrium will remain the most likely one to emerge for a wider range of $\beta$.

This example shows how external conditions, such as those related to the working world, can influence the development of conventions surrounding household division of labor. When one partner can earn more, outcomes where they work will be more attractive, even though they are the least equitable available equilibria.

### 8.1.1 Changing the environment

Suppose that a convention of household coordination is reached in an environment where members of one gender can generate greater payoffs outside the home. It might seem that the way to change this convention is to simply legislate equal pay for equal work across genders. This takes away the initial pressures that made it more likely for one gender to end up at a convention where they work outside the home.

Once the population has reached a convention, however, changes to $\alpha$ and $\beta$ will not actually shift it away from the current convention. Under such changes, the convention still remains an equilibrium, meaning that no one is incentivized to switch. (Note that this is true even if we reverse $\alpha$ so that it becomes jointly much more efficient for the gender spending time at home to work.) What this tells us is that rules for equal pay, even when they work, may not be enough to change gendered patterns of household coordination when conventions and norms are at play. Conventions have staying power.

Changing levels of pay for the two genders does matter in a (perhaps more realistic) model where there is some stochasticity to the behavior of actors. Under such a model, it is possible for random changes in the population (or directed changes, as will be discussed in Chapter 9), to shift an equilibrium once it has been reached. In such a situation the size of the basin of attraction surrounding an equilibrium for household coordination will determine how easy it is to unseat. In the case where pay is more equal, this will decrease the size of the basin of attraction around the Low–High vs. High–Low equilibrium, meaning that other kinds of shifts in the population can move it away. In the next chapter, I will address this sort of convention change at length.

## 8.2 Household Bargaining

Now let us move on to the puzzle introduced at the beginning of this chapter—why do women who work outside the home continue to perform a greater amount of household labor than men with similar earnings and working hours? More generally we can also ask—why do women tend to do more labor overall, and to have less leisure time, than men?

First, let me add some detail to the phenomenon. Findings from sociology and economics are that 1) as women's share of household earnings increases, they perform a smaller portion of household labor and 2) nonetheless, regardless of circumstances in the household, women average significantly more household labor than men (Brines, 1994; Bittman et al., 2003; Gupta, 1999; Greenstein, 2000).[3] In addition, the United Nation's *Human Development Report* in 1995 found that in thirty-one countries women consistently enjoyed less leisure time and worked longer hours when household labor and labor force work were combined.

Sociologists have considered various explanations for this data. The perspective of "exchange theory" suggests that when women earn more relative to their husbands, this translates into a more powerful bargaining position which they can use to lessen their portion of household labor. Sanjiv Gupta's "autonomy" model holds that women's house-

---

[3] This difference in division of labor seems to lead to advantages for married men. Married men have been found to earn more than single men, and this seems to be a direct effect of having a spouse who provides domestic support (Ginther and Zavodny, 2001; Bardasi and Taylor, 2008; Eswaran, 2014). There is also some data indicating that for households where women earn more than men, this trend switches in that women start doing *more* household labor on average than women whose salaries approach, but do not exceed, their husband's (Bittman et al., 2003; Berk, 2012). Authors have explained this by claiming that in these cases women and men 'do gender', in the sense famously outlined by West and Zimmerman (1987). In other words, this trend is an attempt by these households to maintain the appearance of gender conformance in the face of the woman's superior salary. This finding has been convincingly challenged by Gupta (2006, 2007); Gupta and Ash (2008) and by Sullivan (2011), though, who explain it as a statistical mistake, so I do not elaborate these findings here.

hold labor decreases as a function of their absolute earnings, with little dependence on their relative income, or their husband's absolute income (Gupta, 2006, 2007). In other words, household labor is the domain of women, and wealthier women get out of it by paying others to do the work. Both frameworks explain the variation in bargaining across households, but not the general social trend where women work more. Sociologists acknowledge that the large gap between men and women generally in doing household labor is a result of gender norms. These theories do not, though, say much about how these norms emerge in the first place.

Economists have also generated a substantive body of work intended to explain this phenomenon. The household is a paradigmatic case of Schelling's "mixed motive" game. Interests among members of the household are strongly aligned. Beblo (2001), for instance, in her work on bargaining over time allocation in the household, points out that forming a household saves members from transaction costs that arise in the usual processes of trading goods, advantages members in terms of information-sharing, improves efficiency in the consumption of public goods, and provides an insurance policy should one member of the household become sick or unemployed. For these sorts of reasons, traditional economic approaches to the household treated it as a single unit of interest (Gronau, 1973, 1976; Becker, 1981). But a wide swath of studies has since provided strong evidence that, in fact, different members of the household often have separate interests (Thomas, 1990, 1993, 1994; Hoddinott and Haddad, 1995; Udry, 1996; Doss, 1996). Lundberg et al. (1997), for example, in a landmark study observe that in a natural experiment where the British government changed a tax break in men's paychecks to a direct payment to women, there were observable changes in spending—for example, purchases of women's and children's clothing increased whereas purchases of men's clothing and tobacco decreased.[4] (Okin (1989) makes a similar critique in philosophy, in response to theories of justice that treat the family as a univocal unit.)

Recognizing both the common and conflicting interests present in a household, economists have used bargaining games to model division of material resources and time in this domain. Some of this work has

---

[4] See Beblo (2001) and Eswaran (2014) for an excellent overviews of this, and other literature, indicating that treating households as units is problematically simple.

applied Nash's axiomatic approach to household bargaining. Here the disagreement point can be interpreted as the payoff to individuals should they divorce (Manser and Brown, 1980; McElroy and Horney, 1981).[5] Systematic differences in these payoffs can result from "extrahousehold environmental parameters" (McElroy, 1990)—factors like differences in social network support, legal structures, access to communal goods, social norms, education, work experience, ownership of assets, chances on the marriage market, and laws such as divorce and inheritance laws (Eswaran, 2014). Lundberg (2008) points out that extremely different expected disagreement points from divorce can result from traditional division of labor with women doing home and men market labor. This is because the latter leads to private goods (money) and is more relevant to single life.[6] (Philosophers have attended to this sort of asymmetry in thinking about justice and morality. Goodin (1986) identifies symmetric ability to leave a relationship as a key factor in preventing exploitation, and Okin (1989) makes explicit how this requirement often fails in marriages.)

These models can explain systematic patterns in household bargaining in the following way. Earned income and the other social factors described above will determine the disagreement point for each couple. If women's wages are lower, on average, than men's wages, their disagreement point will tend to be lower and, as a result, they will be expected to receive less preferable outcomes in household bargaining scenarios. This can occur even in couples where partners work the same hours because these other social factors matter to the disagreement point.[7]

---

[5] The disagreement point can also be interpreted as payoffs from remaining in a non-cooperative marriage where actors revert to traditional marriage roles (Lundberg and Pollak, 1993), or where actors treat each other poorly (Bergstrom, 1996). As Bergstrom (1996) argues, "If one spouse proposes a resolution to a household dispute and the other does not agree, the expected outcome is not a divorce. A more likely outcome is harsh words and burnt toast until the next offer is made" (1926).

[6] Other work using bargaining games to model the division of labor and goods in the household employs models with deeper levels of conflict between actors, where, for example, one actor is dominant and may make unilateral choices on how to allocate their time, while the other must react to this sort of decision (Beblo, 2001). Still others have used dynamical models to understand household bargaining where actors' possible outcomes at each stage are determined by previous choices (Konrad and Lommerud, 2000; Ott, 2012). A decision to invest capital in education, for example, might translate into a better outside option later on.

[7] Stevenson and Wolfers (2006) provide empirical evidence for this theoretical prediction. When the United States changed to unilateral divorce laws, thus raising the divorce

What these models do not explain are cross-national differences in household division of labor even when factors such as women's wages are held constant (Treas and Drobnic, 2010). These features are arguably accounted for by norms that govern household division of labor. Fuwa (2004), for example, finds that gender norms impact household bargaining beyond what any individual monetary/power differences might explain. In countries with norms for high gender equality, women are better able to make use of their bargaining chips. Evolutionary models where behavior emerges at the group or society level provide simple, compelling explanations of the norm-like aspects of household bargaining inequities.

## 8.2.1  Evolving household bargaining

How do we go about providing a conventional or normative explanation for inequity in the household division of labor? We can apply the evolutionary bargaining models discussed previously in the book directly to the case of household bargaining over time spent working.

If we assume that household partners value time away from housework, and that types have different disagreement points, the prediction is that conventions of division are more likely to emerge that favor the type with the higher disagreement point. If one interprets this disagreement point as divorce (as we have discussed), it is clear that in Western (and many other) societies men have had a higher one. This is a direct result of men typically working outside the home, and so having the capacity to singly support a household in the case of divorce, and earning higher wages on average. Other factors contribute to this sort of difference, as outlined in the previous section—differences in the social networks, assets, and access to communal goods, etc. Men have also tended to have greater potential to issue and carry out threats when household bargaining breaks down both because of physical differences, and differences in economic status. If men are better able to threaten their spouses in the case of divorce—say by hiring an expensive lawyer—this can lead to different disagreement points between genders in the case of divorce.

If one type has better outside options than the other when it comes to household formation, that type, likewise, may have an advantage in that

threatpoint for women, their outcomes in marriage, including suicide rates, domestic violence, and homicide, improved.

conventions of division that do not favor them will not be equilibria. In societies where women are incapable of earning their own living, their only option is typically to form a household or else suffer greatly. People in this sort of situation will be willing to form a household even if they expect to receive the short end of the stick when it comes to labor. On the other hand, someone who can capably support themselves may not be willing to enter a household, or remain in one, if they do not receive the benefit of preferable bargaining outcomes. As we discussed in Chapter 5, this means that social conventions that emerge will favor the group with higher outside options.

The insight from section 8.1.1, that even when social conditions change, conventions surrounding household division of labor are not necessarily going to shift in response, is relevant here. Presumably, the disagreement points and outside options of men and women have become more equal but on the evolutionary picture we should still expect household division of labor to continue to favor men as a result of established population level equilibria.

Overall, these models predict that in industrial and post industrial societies, emerging household bargaining norms should favor men, who tend to have higher wages and greater economic security, meaning higher disagreement points *and* better outside options. This direct application of the models helps explain the emergence of social conventions, and attendant norms, that favor men when it comes to overall time spent working.

•  •  •

As hinted at in the introduction to this chapter, rational-choice models and evolutionary models of household bargaining provide not alternative explanations, but complementary accounts that clarify different features of the same phenomenon. When it comes to household bargaining and division of labor, we see both between-household variation, and across-society regularity.[8] Evolutionary processes of social imitation and repeated interaction may lead to general divisional norms between men and women in the household. Differences in wages, social networks, utility functions, etc. between any two partners may influence how, given these divisional norms, each actual pair determines their levels of labor.

---

[8] Young (2015) calls this sort of social regularity of norm-governed behavior *compression*.

On this picture, social norms provide the regularity, and rational choice the variation, between households.[9]

Sen (1987) provides an extended analysis suggesting something similar. As he points out, "perceptions" of desert and legitimacy may mean that women and men do not perceive household divisions as unequal, even when they are, from a more objective standpoint. He points out that "[o]ur agency role is often overshadowed by social rules and by conventional perceptions of legitimacy. In the case of gender divisions, these conventions often act as barriers to seeking a more equitable deal, and sometimes militate even against recognizing the spectacular lack of equity in the ruling arrangements" (45). The idea here is that social conventions influence what actors believe they deserve in the household, or what would be fair, thus shifting bargaining outcomes for individual households. The account here complements this work by explaining how these social conventions might arise.

Altogether, this chapter should be taken as showing how, in principle, the evolutionary framework developed throughout the entire book—for the emergence of both the first, and the second, sorts of inequity—can be applied to illuminate a real-world case. These two aspects of inequity can intertwine to create persistent disadvantage to those in one social category, even in the face of changes intended to improve things.

---

[9] Lundberg and Pollak (1993) suggest a different way of combining approaches. Their model of household bargaining includes a threatpoint that returns behaviors to socially sanctioned gender roles (and Lundberg (2008) re-emphasizes the importance of norms and conventions to our understanding of household divisions).

# 9

# Evolution and Revolution

Power concedes nothing without a demand.

Frederick Douglass

At this point in the book, I have argued for a number of things that might make the possibility of gender, race, and class egalitarianism seem unlikely. First, I have argued that the adoption of types and typing can lead to efficiency when groups are faced with coordination problems. Second, I have argued that, in some cases, the adoption of types benefits all the individuals involved, not just those who end up at preferable outcomes. I've shown that under a number of modeling assumptions, these facts mean that types emerge spontaneously to solve coordination problems.

But, as mentioned, these sorts of solutions to coordination problems are often inequitable. Furthermore, as the second half of the book shows, types set the stage for inequity of a more serious sort to emerge. In particular, perniciously inequitable conventions emerge even without factors that we usually blame for them—such as bias or stereotype threat. They are simply the common end products of cultural evolutionary processes where everyone learns to do what is best for themselves.

In this chapter, I will look at a cluster of topics centered on the following question: what can be done about inequitable conventions of division between types? This is not a new question by any means, but the evolutionary framework used in this book does provide some new insights into it.

This discussion will be broken into two subparts. First, I will outline the social preconditions that must be in place in order for inequitable type-based conventions to arise at all. I'll briefly discuss the possibility of eliminating these preconditions. As we will see, while there might be some ways to minimize the features of groups that allow for type-based conventions, the likelihood of really eliminating these features seems low, especially given the observations from Part I of the book—that these features often have the potential to improve social coordination.

We will then move on to consider how one might go about moving groups from inequitable to equitable norms for division of resources. As mentioned in the last chapter, there is a sort of stickiness of convention, a persistence that resists environmental changes. This is because all the sorts of conventions and norms we are concerned with here are equilibria. No one is personally incentivized to change given the state of the group. This does not mean that change is impossible, though. When individual behavior deviates, as a result of random exploration, or purposeful attempts to buck social norms, there is a chance that a group will be pushed out of the basin of attraction for the current convention, and into a new one. We would then expect the processes of cultural evolution to push the group towards a new pattern of behavior.

As I will point out, there are ways to make undesirable conventions less stable to these sorts of shocks by decreasing the sizes of their basins of attraction. This leads to a perhaps surprising observation: that the behaviors of a group can look just as inequitable as ever, while the stability of an inequitable norm is nonetheless eroded. Ultimately this erosion is useless, though, if no one actually does something different. We will look at how behaviors such as protest can act as the fulcrum that levers a population toward a new equilibrium.

This is not the end of the story, though. Social dynamical forces can just as easily carry groups back toward inequitable norms. Ultimately, I will present a picture in which social justice is an endless battle. The forces of cultural evolution can pull populations toward inequity, and combating these forces requires constant vigilance.[1] Those concerned with equity, then, need to reconceptualize inequity not as a static state, but as part of a continual dynamical process. Not something to be solved, but something to keep solving.

---

[1] Liam K. Bright, philosopher and Marxist, insists that this picture is similar to the idea of the 'permanent revolution' first introduced by Marx (see Marx and Engels (1975)). The similarity is that Marxists advocated a permanent state of revolutionary behavior and attitude for the proletariat.

## 9.1   Preconditions for Type-Based Conventions

Butler, in her work on gender as performance, wrote that "[i]f the ground of gender identity is the stylized repetition of acts through time, and not a seemingly seamless identity, then the possibilities of gender transformation are to be found in the arbitrary relation between such acts, in the possibility of a different sort of repeating, in the breaking or subversive repetition of that style" (Butler, 1988, 520). The idea that gender is nothing more than a series of social acts contains a powerful possibility—that gender, and of course, gender inequity, could be dissolved if this performance just stopped. There are three sorts of behaviors in our models that allow for the emergence of inequity based on types—typing, social learning, and type-conditioning. In what follows, I will discuss the possibility of intervening on these factors to prevent the emergence of inequity.

In the models I have focused on, social learning and other forms of cultural change play a key role in the emergence of type-based conventions. In replicator dynamics models, because actors learn from their own types, they can evolve to employ different strategies from those of other types. But if actors learned from all types, this categorization by different strategies would not be possible. This suggests that if type-based social learning could be broken down, this should improve outcomes. Henrich and Boyd (2008) consider this possibility explicitly, and show that when actors do not learn from their own types, equitable, if inefficient, outcomes are more likely for actors playing complementary coordination games. But, as mentioned earlier, in models where actors do not engage in social learning, and instead learn individually, inequitable type-based conventions can also emerge (Young, 1993b). In societies where actors recognize types and engage in type-conditioning, members of different types exist in different environments and so individual learning, or rational reactions to their environment, or social learning can carry them to type-based conventions. Is it truly possible to expect that actors should not engage in behaviors that simply are their best strategic choices under the conditions they have observed? This seems like an unpromising place to intervene on the processes that lead to inequity.

In our models, removing typing—the ability of actors to differentiate each other into clear categories—also removes the possibility of type-based conventions. Without recognizable types, type-conditioning is not possible even if someone wants to do it. There are two sorts of ways this can happen. One is to actually remove, or allow actors to vary, the physical markers that allow type recognition. Of course, when it comes to markers such as race and gender, this possibility is not particularly relevant.

The other way to stop typing is to somehow stop the process on the recognition side—so that actors no longer perceive different people as belonging to relevantly different types. It has been widely argued that gender and race are constructed.[2] This means that gender and racial categories, or types, are socially created, although they clearly piggyback on biological markers. While the biological markers used for this construction are very difficult to change or remove, the social aspect of the construction presumably can be. Is it possible to actually stop people from noticing or caring about gender and racial categories? Of course, many have criticized those who attempt to "not see" or dissolve race and gender (Butler, 1988). Doing so means also ignoring the fact that these social categories are currently associated with massive social inequities. It seems a tricky (and unpromising) line to walk to both try to stop the recognition of types for current interaction, while recognizing their importance to historical disadvantage and somehow also trying to rectify or account for this disadvantage in current decision-making. In addition, as I argue in Part I of the book, categories like gender seem to emerge for functional reasons. Even if we were somehow able to eliminate gender recognition, this does not remove the need to use social categories for coordination purposes. As a result, we might expect the re-emergence of social categories for coordination.

Another precondition for the emergence of type-based conventions (and one that seems more promising to push on) is type-conditioning. As addressed in Chapter 2, type-conditioning comes naturally to humans. This does not mean, however, that it is inevitable. There are two sorts of ways to stop type-conditioning, one internal and one external. The internal way involves incentivizing, or convincing, actors to decide to stop treating members of different types differently in cases where this involves discrimination. This is more plausible when it comes to explicit forms of type-conditioning. We know, though, that people also have implicit biases which result in type-conditioning that they are not consciously aware

---

[2] For work on social construction of gender see, for example, Butler (2004, 2011b); Fenstermaker and West (2002). For work on social construction of race see Du Bois (1906); Jeffers (2013); Omi and Winant (2014). Haslanger (2000) discusses both sorts of identities.

of (Greenwald and Banaji, 1995). Empirical work, however, indicates that it is possible to reduce the effects of implicit bias in a number of ways. Establishing communal norms against behavior that results from such biases, and making community members aware of these norms, can reduce the behavior. Making people aware that implicit bias occurs reduces it. And giving people time to make choices more deliberately in situations where they may be biased is effective in reducing its impact. (Lee, 2016; Hofmann et al., 2005; Hopkins, 2006).

The second sort of way to stop type-conditioning is externally—through explicit rules, norms, or laws preventing type-conditioning from influencing those it is directed against. These sorts of rules are common in our society—title IX in secondary education and blind review in academia, for example. In the US there are a host of laws to prevent discrimination against women, people of color, the elderly, pregnant people, and those with disabilities. While these rules and laws may miss inequities occurring in small, day-to-day interactions, they are an important tool to employ against type-conditioning.[3]

One lesson from the models in this book, however, is that simple processes of cultural evolution should lead to the emergence and re-emergence of inequitable conventions. Types and type-conditioning arise spontaneously under the right strategic conditions. Once this happens, inequity can emerge as well. While we can study and regulate particular instances of discrimination and inequity, if such instances arise spontaneously under ubiquitous social conditions, such explicit regulations may be temporary fixes on an ever-evolving problem.

On the other hand, it is clear that even in the last hundred years there have been massive changes in the kind and level of type-based conventions in, for example, the United States. There is also cross-cultural evidence of conventionality as far as the strength of typing and type-conditioning. For example, the Mbuti of Africa have traditionally not had words for man, woman, boy, or girl, have de-emphasized gender differences in their rituals, and have had little division of labor by gender. In contrast, the Mundurucu Indians of central Brazil strongly divide

---

[3] To give a little example of an accidentally successful rule—in academic disciplines like math, author order is determined alphabetically. This disciplinary rule means that in math, unlike many other fields, women are as likely to hold prestigious first author positions as men (West et al., 2013).

economic roles, have an antagonistic relationship between genders, and have highly different lives including separate residences (Oakley, 2015). This indicates that functioning societies can do perfectly well with lower levels of typing and type-conditioning, and that this lower level is psychologically achievable for humans. Additionally, resource distribution varies cross-culturally from highly inegalitarian to more egalitarian. Highly inequitable divisions are not inevitable. We need not despair. In the next part of the chapter we will address, in particular, how a group can move from one sort of convention to another.

## 9.2 Convention and Norm Change

When it comes to resource division, there is often an equitable option—a fair division, or something close to it. We know, however, that inequitable conventions of division are likely to arise. This raises the question: how do we move from less to more equitable conventions?

Social movement theory is a cross-disciplinary area of study that looks at social mobilization. Of course, not all social mobilization involves attempts to change inequitable norms of division between types, but this is, of course, a recurring theme in social movements—consider the women's suffrage movements, labor/workers' movements, the civil rights movement, feminist movements, and, more recently, the Black Lives Matter movement.[4]

There are (at least) two levels of focus that one might employ in thinking about such social movements. The first treats individuals as the units of rationality and behavioral choice. The second treats groups involved in social movements as the units of rationality and choice. Early work on social movements maintained focus on this second level. How do groups act to achieve their collective interests? In 1965 Mancur Olson published *The Logic of Collective Action*. This work criticized the group-level focus of previous social movement theories, such as Marxism, by pointing out that groups involved in joint action often suffer from public goods problems (Olson, 2009). A public goods problem occurs when a group of people generate a good that all members can benefit from. The

---

[4] The gay rights and trans rights movements are less clearly about division of resources, though they are about inequity.

problem is that for any individual, it is preferable to avoid doing the work or paying costs to create the good if they can benefit from it nonetheless. When it comes to a social movement, say a protest for equal legal rights, each member of the oppressed class would like to benefit from those rights, but under some conditions will be disincentivized from protesting by the costs in time, risk of punishment, etc., especially if others will do this unpleasant work.[5]

More recent collective action theorists analyzing social movements have been highly critical of those who ignore the individual level for this reason (Lichbach, 1998; Opp, 2009).[6] They are right to think that this level of analysis is key to a full picture of social movement. In what follows, I will nonetheless focus on the group level in thinking about convention change when it comes to inegalitarian divisions between groups. The idea is not that understanding how groups manage to engage in social movements, given public goods problems and other such conundrums, is unimportant. Rather this discussion will table these issues and ask, what are the strategic situations under which collective action will be more or less easy, and more or less effective? And, in what ways does collective action shift the broader strategic structure of a population?

To tackle this problem, it will be necessary to pull apart the concepts of norm and convention. In Chapter 1 I made clear that, for the purposes of this book, they should not be understood as coextensive, in contrast to some previous authors. Conventions, for our purposes, are patterns of behavior that mimic equilibria in coordination games. (Remember, I claimed that these are conventions, not that all conventions are well modeled by such equilibria.) Some conventions, but not necessarily all, acquire varying degrees of normative force.

### 9.2.1 Conventions

Even when social conventions are well represented by equilibria in a game, and so exhibit the sort of stability that equilibria entail, some are relatively easy to change. For example, September 3, 1967 was Sweden's

---

[5] Subsequent social movement theorists focusing on rational choice have discussed solutions to this, and related problems, at length (Roemer, 1985; Lichbach, 1998; Opp, 2009; Chong, 2014). Philosopher Margaret Gilbert attempts to resolve such problems by appeal to joint commitment in groups of actors (Gilbert, 2006).

[6] Opp (2009) argues that a "macro–micro" approach, which looks at both levels of organization, and causal links between them, is necessary for a thorough theory of social movement.

famous "H-day" when the country switched from left- to right-hand-side driving. This equilibrium was preferred because it allowed for better coordination with nearby countries.

Things are not always so simple, though. The correlative coordination game that represents the Swedish scenario is one where actors have generally similar preferences over the possible equilibria. This facilitated a situation in which a large majority of citizens were willing to make and interested in making a change. Of course, the change itself was highly non trivial, and caused quite a bit of consternation, but generating a country-wide consensus that it would happen was at least possible. The sorts of inequitable equilibria that are well represented by the Nash demand game are another matter. Every equilibrium in the Nash demand game is *Pareto-efficient*, meaning that for every other possible equilibrium increasing the payoff for one player will decrease it for another. This means that if populations with types are engaged in conventions of this sort, at least one side should resist change to some other possible convention.

In thinking about how actors can create change in situations like this—where there will not be widespread agreement about which convention to adopt—we can employ the evolutionary framework we have been using. As Young (2015) points out, when conventions change, it often happens quickly rather than slowly: "Once a crucial threshold is crossed and a sufficient number of people have made the change, positive feedback reinforces the new way of doing things, and the transition is completed rapidly" (363). Young describes "punctuated equilibria" as a key feature of such dynamics—long periods of stability are interspersed with rapid periods of change (Young, 2001).[7]

Unsurprisingly, this picture fits well with Young's framework for modeling conventions. Forces of social and individual learning, absent other factors, will continue to maintain populations at a coordination

---

[7] For example, during the period when foot binding was the practice in China, women were incentivized to bind their feet in order to marry. Boys were incentivized to marry girls with bound feet because bound feet supposedly promoted fidelity, and were a sign of social success. Despite a number of edicts prohibiting foot binding, it persisted until a campaign convincing individual families to pledge both to not bind girls' feet and to refuse to marry their sons to girls with bound feet. This simultaneously changed expectations on both sides of the interaction, and led to a swift social shift away from the practice. This also echoes insights from Breen and Cooke (2005) who use game theoretic models to understand the persistence of gendered division of labor. They argue that a large proportion of women and men must simultaneously change their behaviors around division of labor.

convention. Populations stay at an equilibrium until a crucial number of individuals simultaneously try non-conventional behavior, owing either to chance deviations or some coordinated effort. This experimentation can move the entire population into the basin of attraction for a new equilibrium, which it then evolves toward and which remains stable until another such random event. We can adopt this framework to help us think about changes in the sorts of conventions we are concerned with— groups are generally kept stable at equilibria by social evolutionary forces, but shocks can lead to change.

This picture means that the size of a basin of attraction around an equilibrium will be very important. An equilibrium with a large zone of attraction around it will be more stable than one with a small buffer. Figure 9.1 illustrates the idea just presented—that social conventions with larger basins of attraction may be harder to change than others. Imagine a population is at the coordination equilibrium represented by the top right corner of the phase diagram. Now suppose that for whatever reason, a number of members of the population switch behaviors, as represented by the white arrow. The population shown in diagram (a) will still be in the basin of attraction for the original equilibrium, which is relatively large. As a result, this change will not be expected to upset the current convention. The population in diagram (b), undergoing the same change, will now be in the basin of attraction for the other equilibrium, and absent other forces should be expected to evolve to it.

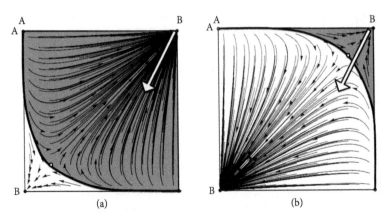

Figure 9.1 Phase diagrams for two populations. In the first, the top right equilibrium is harder to escape

How do such changes occur though? Young's framework suggests that sometimes they are the result of a random shock, and surely some sorts of convention change reflect this. When it comes to inequity, though, shocks are not typically random, but generated by members of social movements who take action to move populations out of a basin of attraction for a coordination equilibrium. Bowles and Naidu (2006) and Hwang et al. (2014), for example, consider models very similar to those explored by Young and collaborators, but where actors' deviations tend towards equilibria that they prefer. They refer to this sort of intentional error, first introduced by Bowles (2004), as "collective action shocks".[8]

### 9.2.1.1 MORAL PREFERENCES

If basins of attraction matter to social change, that means that payoffs matter too. As we have seen throughout Part II of this book, the details of payoffs to actors in a strategic situation will determine the basins of attraction for various equilibria.

One way to change payoffs of others is to change their preferences, for example, by altering their ethical beliefs. Many social justice movements attempt to do something like this by making it clear to more people in a society that certain norms or behaviors are damaging to others. (Haslanger (2017), for example, emphasizes the importance of critiquing cultural ideology in changing oppressive systems.) Because humans do, in fact, have other-regarding preferences, this can change their effective payoffs in a game.[9] Figure 9.2 (a) shows a Nash demand game. In (b) is a similar game, but where actors feel badly taking advantage of others, which drops their payoff when they successfully demand High of an opponent. In this second game, Low vs. High and High vs. Low are not equilibria. Instead, the only pure strategy equilibrium is Med vs. Med.

A population undergoing cultural evolution at an equilibrium that is disrupted in this way will evolve away from that state because it will

---

[8] As they point out, some experimental work has found that players make mistakes in just this self-serving way (Lim and Neary, 2016; Mäs and Nax, 2016).

[9] It is beyond the purview of this book to discuss how such other-regarding preferences evolve. For us, it is enough to observe that they exist in humans. For more on this topic, see work on the indirect evolutionary approach which models the evolution of preferences (Güth, 1995).

(a)

| | | Player 2 | | |
|---|---|---|---|---|
| | | Low | Med | High |
| Player 1 | Low | 3, 3 | 3, 5 | 3, 7 |
| | Med | 5, 3 | 5, 5 | 0, 0 |
| | High | 7, 3 | 0, 0 | 0, 0 |

(b)

| | | Player 2 | | |
|---|---|---|---|---|
| | | Low | Med | High |
| Player 1 | Low | 3, 3 | 3, 5 | 3, 4 |
| | Med | 5, 3 | 5, 5 | 0, 0 |
| | High | 4, 3 | 0, 0 | 0, 0 |

**Figure 9.2** A Nash demand game where actors come to feel badly when making High demands of another player

(a)

| | | Player 2 | | |
|---|---|---|---|---|
| | | Low | Med | High |
| Player 1 | Low | 1, 1 | 1, 5 | 1, 9 |
| | Med | 5, 1 | 5, 5 | 0, 0 |
| | High | 9, 1 | 0, 0 | 0, 0 |

(b)

| | | Player 2 | | |
|---|---|---|---|---|
| | | Low | Med | High |
| Player 1 | Low | 1, 1 | 1, 5 | 1, 6 |
| | Med | 5, 1 | 5, 5 | 0, 0 |
| | High | 6, 1 | 0, 0 | 0, 0 |

**Figure 9.3** A Nash demand game where actors come to feel badly when making High demands of another player, but not enough to disrupt the pure strategy equilibria

no longer constitute a rest point. In this particular case, the population should then move toward the only remaining pure Nash equilibrium—Med vs. Med.

If actors do not have strong other-regarding preferences, then moral arguments may not shift their preferences enough to change the equilibria of the underlying strategic scenario. But even small amounts of moral pressure may decrease the stability of such equilibria. Figure 9.3 demonstrates this. This figure is similar to Figure 9.2, but for a Nash demand game with more disparate demands for High and Low. In this game, the same payoff shift is not enough to disrupt the equilibrium. This shift will make the basins of attraction for the inequitable equilibria smaller, though. A surprising take-away from this observation is that moral education, even if it proceeds slowly, and seems not to be impacting social conventions, is still worthwhile. The stability of a convention can be eroded, setting the stage for future change long before much behavioral change is observed. Under such a scenario, inequitable behavior may be preserved for some stretch of time before a perhaps small population shock moves a group into another basin of attraction and toward equitable behavior.

We should be a bit careful here, though. In this interpretation, actors are still receiving high material payoffs when they demand High against a Low opponent, but do not actually enjoy this outcome. If we assume a dynamics where actors copy group members with material success, this internal preference shift should not make any change. Someone who got rich taking advantage of others might be unhappy because they are a jerk, but others in deciding how to act will see only the success. If we assume, on the other hand, some sort of best response by actors, or individual learning based on their perceived payoffs, the equilibrium *should* be disrupted. In other words, the potential success of moral education in a cultural evolutionary context will strongly depend on how actors are adopting behaviors.

One further thing to note about this sort of shift in preferences is that empirically it is clear that it does not always translate to anything. In particular, this sort of situation is amenable to actors who have stated and conscious preferences for equity, and egalitarian divisions, but who do not necessarily recognize inequitable divisions for what they are.[10] Such actors may hold an internal moral stance, and reap the benefits of external high payoffs without recognizing the hypocrisy in their position.

### 9.2.1.2 PROTEST

Suppose that moral education has decreased the stability of some inequitable equilibrium. How does a population go about escaping it? As mentioned, this requires at least someone to actually change behavior.

---

[10] This is somewhat related to the Marxist idea of false consciousness, where members of one class mislead others as to the level of exploitation they suffer, or, more generally, cases where strategic actors are not aware of the inequitable situation they are in (Eagleton, 1991). In the cases I am interested in, members of both groups may be misled as to what the norms of division are.

Otherwise, the population stays at the equilibrium. Social protest can play this role.

Sometimes actors simply change behaviors in a way that moves one side toward a new convention. For example, one type can start making a higher demand in a situation that is well modeled by a Nash demand game. This means that *everyone* will start to reach the disagreement point, and to receive poor payoffs. However, in the right sort of dynamical situation, this sort of change will move the population out of the basin of attraction of the current convention, and into the basin of attraction for a new one. This means that the forces of social learning and cultural evolution should drive the other side to behaviors that generate more pay-offs for them given their new social environment—ones consistent with a more equitable equilibrium. This is the sort of social movement modeled in Bowles (2004); Bowles and Naidu (2006); Hwang et al. (2014), where actors usually best respond to another population, but sometimes err in the direction of their preferred equilibrium. As Hwang et al. (2014) point out, their models correspond to protests such as sit-ins, employed during the civil rights movement. These involved members of one type simply taking actions that they were normatively barred from, but that consist in making a greater "demand," as regards resource distribution. In the case of the civil rights movement, behavioral shifts by black people led to comple-mentary behavioral shifts by white people including the desegregation of public establishments. Bowles and Naidu (2006) point to a similar pattern in South Africa during the end of apartheid. Widespread strikes meant that both poor black workers and wealthy white business owners were receiving very poor payoffs. This led business owners to capitulate by making lower demands, corresponding to higher wage offerings.

Those involved in social protests can also change payoffs for another type in a way that might shift equilibria by taking actions that deliberately lower others' payoffs, with the implication being that such actions will stop once conventions change. This will involve the same sort of change to payoffs as we saw in Figures 9.2 and 9.3. In other words, protest, like moral education, can disrupt an inequitable equilibrium, or just make the basins of attraction for it smaller. For this type of social protest to work, of course, members of one type have to effectively lower the payoffs of many members of the other type. Good examples of behavior that seem to fit this second scenario are things like the suffragette movement in Britain, where suffragettes planted bombs, destroyed the home of a parliamentarian, and generally disrupted normal social function. In 1957, railway workers in Japan sat on the tracks of over 300 stations, halting the trains.[11] The apartheid South Africa and civil rights movement examples discussed above also fit with this sort of case in that members of the movements engaged in public protests that generally disrupted social function.

### 9.2.1.3 REBOUNDING

In the last two subsections, I analyzed the ways in which typical actions from social movements can be understood in a social dynamical framework. The models from Chapters 5 and 6 tell us something more, though. Suppose that a social movement succeeds in gaining some sort of more equitable arrangement for members of a group. But suppose that this group continues to be disempowered economically, politically, or socially.

Although equity has been won in some arena, or for now, the basin of attraction for the equitable equilibrium should still be relatively small. This is because power, remember, increases the likelihood that inequitable conventions emerge. The powerful group will continue to have higher disagreement points, higher outside options, and higher background payoffs. If there is a minority/majority split, the majority will continue to be in the majority. For these reasons, random shifts can easily carry the population back to inequity. This point complements one made by Tilly (1998), who argues that eradicating racist attitudes or behaviors cannot alone eradicate inequity when social structures support it. Haslanger (2015a) argues that eradicating implicit bias is not expected to create durable change as long as oppressive structures remain in place.

We might also see something like this in a case where there is a more long-term, stabler equitable convention. A political movement could erode the stability of such a convention long before behavioral changes are seen, meaning that once some small set of people decides to move toward a more inequitable arrangement, equity can be unseated relatively easily.

### 9.2.2 *Norms*

To this point in the chapter, I have focused on ways to change coordination conventions. In such cases, when populations move outside the

---

[11] This example is from Schelling (1960).

basins of attraction for an equilibrium, under assumptions of social and individual learning they should move toward another equilibrium. As outlined, there are ways to change the basins of attraction for various equilibria in a coordination situation to make it more likely that this occurs. When conventions gain normative force, though, things can be slightly different.

Norms involve a belief that one *ought* to behave in a certain way.[12] Bicchieri defines a norm as a behavioral rule for a situation where a sufficiently large portion of a population, 1) know the rule and apply it appropriately, and 2) prefer to conform to the rule on the condition that either a) they believe enough others will conform or b) they believe others expect them to conform or b') they believe others may sanction them if they fail to conform (Bicchieri, 2005, 11). The first condition she labels as *contingency*. The second condition she labels as *conditional preference*.

Bicchieri and Mercier (2014) think of norms as self-perpetuating, but there is an important distinction to draw between different sorts of norms. In some cases, norms enforce and promote behavior that is also stabilized by the underlying strategic situation. Conventions of coordination that become normative fall under this heading. If everyone is following a convention, others wish to do so as well because doing so is best for individual payoff. In other cases, norms develop to keep groups of people away from equilibrium behavior in the underlying strategic situation. When it comes to social altruism, for example, norms promote individually costly, but socially beneficial behavior. Bicchieri (2005) points out that in such cases social expectations, and punishment for violators, can transform such situations into coordination games. Because social punishment will result from altruism failures, it comes to be in an actor's best interest to be an altruist. But this does not change the fact that underlying forces do not support the continued normative behavior. In these cases, norms should be easier to erode. If expectations of conformance are removed,

---

[12] These beliefs need not be about behaviors well modeled by equilibria in games, although these are the norms we focus on. They need not correspond to regularly carried-out patterns of behavior. Bicchieri (2005) points out, for example, that many norms concern behaviors not taken, ("do not touch a stranger's hair"), or behaviors that group members will attempt to avoid by avoiding the conditions under which the norm must be met. The Ik of Uganda, she points out, using research from Turnbull (1987), avoid strong norms of reciprocation by patching roofs at night so that no one else who wanders by will offer to help. These observations strengthen the claim that norms and conventions should be untangled, for clearly some norms do not start with behavioral regularities.

actors should revert to equilibrium behavior owing to social evolutionary processes.

Bicchieri and Mercier (2014) discuss methods for changing undesirable norms, such as female genital cutting. They focus on the role of expectations in norm change. Because norms involve both expectations that others will adhere to norms, and expectations that others will likewise expect adherence (and sometimes punish deviance), a tricky, but key, part of such a shift is to change expectations all at once.[13]

How does this framework apply to social movements and attempts to shift conventions of the sort we are interested in here? When inequitable conventions gain normative force, it is the case not just that actors are at an equilibrium, but that they also believe they ought to remain at that equilibrium, and (on Bicchieri's picture) believe that others believe they ought to remain at that equilibrium. In the case of inequity, stated moral norms go against inequitable divisions. However, as I mentioned in the last section, those adhering to inequitable conventions may believe that they are in fact behaving equitably. In a case like this, the key is to change beliefs about what equity consists in, and what people are actually doing. If these beliefs are successfully changed, then norms should actually help push society toward equitable conventions.

•  •  •

While social movements involve actors who must solve public goods games to coordinate their action, it is also important to consider at a higher level what sorts of group actions will be successful in changing inequitable conventions and when. Our cultural evolutionary framework provides a few insights here. First, the fact that many conventions are equilibria means that actual behavioral change will be necessary to unseat them. Someone will have to actually do something different, or else the equilibrium will remain. But, there are ways to make an equilibrium more or less stable with regard to behavior change. Moral education can erode an equilibrium long before change actually happens, as can protest that works to decrease payoff for a certain equilibrium. When it comes to

---

[13] For this reason, these authors emphasize the importance of small-group discussion, including deliberation and argumentation, and then active spread of plans generated in this discussion to simultaneously convince a large portion of a group that a norm change is happening. This sort of discussion, note, falls under the realm of social movement theory at the lower level.

conventions with normative force, more needs to happen. In particular, people need to change their beliefs about what they ought to be doing, rather than just to be in a strategic situation where it benefits them to learn a new pattern of behavior.

Of course, this picture where groups can move from one equilibrium to another is two-sided. While it tells us that there is real possibility of unseating inequitable equilibria, the reverse is also true. If social conditions are such that equitable equilibria have small basins of attraction—as when one group is more powerful, or more numerous—it will be relatively easy to end up in an inequitable arrangement. Even a seemingly stable equitable convention may be eroded by belief and preference changes that make a reversion to inequity possible.

Moreover, modeling results from this book suggest time and again that the conditions needed to generate inequitable conventions and norms are remarkably minimal ones. These are conditions we should expect to hold in our workplaces, academic communities, homes, and societies more broadly. The take-away for those interested in promoting equity is a new way of thinking about what equity and inequity are. Thaddeus Stevens once said, "I know it is easy to protect the interests of the rich and powerful; but it is a great labour to guard the rights of the poor and downtrodden—it is the eternal labour of Sisyphus, forever to be renewed" (Du Bois, 2017, 314). Equity is not something to achieve and be done with. The social processes leading to inequity are too basic, and require preconditions that are too ubiquitous. Instead, equity is a state we must keep seeking in an ever-evolving process that naturally generates inequities.

# 10

# Conclusion

The work I have presented here is not done. This book does not just list modeling results, but also develops a general framework which can be used more broadly to address questions having to do with social categories and inequity. I hope the inquiry here has shown the usefulness of this framework, and that others will find it helpful in further exploring these topics.

This book tells a story about coordination, and ultimately about how the demands of coordination can lead to disadvantage for certain groups of people. As we saw, types can act as a solution for complementary coordination problems, allowing for efficient population-level patterns of behavior unavailable to populations without types. For this reason, types such as gender can emerge spontaneously to solve complementary coordination problems. This process leads to behavioral patterns where gender roles are both conventional (to varying degrees) because they might have been otherwise, and functional in that they facilitate coordination.

The conventions that emerge via this process can be inegalitarian. But once types are established in a population, deeper patterns of inequity can emerge. Despite certain evolutionary pulls toward fairness, there are many reasons why unfairness is actually expected in populations with different social groups. Asymmetries between groups—in material conditions, minority status, etc.—increase the likelihood that inequitable conventions arise. Inequity tends to compound, so that those with more get more. Once such inequities arise, they can have implications for other aspects of social behavior, like who chooses to interact with whom.

There are certain features of this story that I have emphasized. First is the fact that this process proceeds under relatively sparse conditions. Extremely simple actors playing complementary coordination problems and learning can develop types and type-based coordination conventions. Once types are in play, cultural evolution to solve bargaining problems leads to inequitable patterns of division even in the simplest models. As I have argued, these results are robust across changes to modeling assumptions.

This robustness has also led me to emphasize a different way of thinking about inequity and rigid gender norms. These emerge from processes driven by the basic structures of our social situation—structures that are themselves hard to do away with. What this means is that when we take steps to ameliorate the outcomes of these processes, we should expect our fixes to be temporary. The structures driving inequity are still there, and social dynamics can easily carry us back to inequitable patterns of division. The battle for social justice is against a hydra that grows a new head each time any one is cut off.

# Appendix

# The Replicator Dynamics

There are a few forms of the replicator dynamics. One that I use in many of the simulations here is the *discrete time* replicator dynamics. Under these dynamics, a population playing a game changes at time steps. At each time step, the expected payoff for each strategy is calculated given the current population. These expected payoffs are then compared to the average expected payoff for the population. Strategies that beat the average expand and those that do not contract. This dynamics is formulated as

$$x_i' = x_i \left( \frac{f_i(x)}{\sum_{j=1}^{n} f_j(x) x_j)} \right) \tag{A.1}$$

where $x_i$ is the proportion of a population playing strategy $i$, $f_i(x)$ is the fitness of type $i$ in the population state $x$ and $\sum_{j=1}^{n} f_j(x) x_j$ is the average population fitness in this state. It says that $x_i\prime$, the proportion of actors playing $x_i$ in the next time step, is a function of the current proportion $x_i$ multiplied by the ratio of the payoff of those playing $i$ to the average group payoff.

The *continuous time* replicator dynamics can be thought of as the result of taking the limit of the change process modeled by the discrete time version as the length of each time step goes to 0. These dynamics consist of differential equations that model the smooth change of a population undergoing the sort of process already described—increasing relatively good strategies and decreasing poor ones. They are formulated as

$$\dot{x}_i = x_i \left( f_i(x) - \sum_{j=1}^{n} f_j(x) x_j \right) \tag{A.2}$$

I will appeal to both versions of these dynamics throughout the book. While the continuous and discrete time versions of the replicator dynamics vary, they are generally taken as representationally similar, with the continuous time version used for analytic solutions and the discrete time version for simulation solutions.

I will use slightly different versions of these dynamics to represent two-type populations. In perfectly divided populations, actors have two types and each interacts only with the other type. This corresponds well to the standard two-population replicator dynamics where actors exist in two populations and each interacts only with the other population. They then compare strategies with those in their own group and the strategies that are doing better proliferate in each population. The two-population continuous time replicator dynamics are formulated as

$$\dot{x}_i = x_i \left( f_i(y) - \sum_{j=1}^{n} f_j(y)x_j \right) \tag{A.3}$$

$$\dot{y}_i = y_i \left( f_i(x) - \sum_{j=1}^{n} f_j(x)y_j \right) \tag{A.4}$$

where $x$ represents strategies in one population and $y$ represents strategies in the other. Note that the payoff terms in each equation—$f_i(y)$ and $f_i(x)$—depend on the other population state because actors interact with the other population and receive payoffs that way. But strategies expand and contract in comparison to the success of those only in their own population. (The discrete time version involves two update functions like those in (1), but where, again, the payoffs depend on the other population state.)

For two-type mixing populations, actors have types, but also interact with their own type. The evolutionary process for this is best modeled by a version of the replicator dynamics employed by Neary (2012); Bruner and O'Connor (2015); Bruner (2017); O'Connor and Bruner (2017) where actors have two types, but their payoffs are derived from interactions with everyone in the population. These dynamics are formulated as

$$\dot{x}_i = x_i \left( f_i(x,y) - \sum_{j=1}^{n} f_j(x,y)x_j \right) \tag{A.5}$$

$$\dot{y}_i = y_i \left( f_i(x,y) - \sum_{j=1}^{n} f_j(x,y)y_j \right) \tag{A.6}$$

for the continuous time version. The only difference from the standard two-population replicator dynamics is that the fitnesses of the strategies from each population now depend on everybody, $f_i(x, y)$, rather than only the other population, $f_i(y)$ or $f_i(x)$.[1]

---

[1] Models with two types could involve any level of correlation or anti-correlation of interactions between types. Here I have laid out dynamics for complete anti-correlation (perfectly divided) and no correlation at all (two-type mixing). Similar dynamics can be introduced for any other levels of correlation.

In the book, I also look at populations where one type is in the minority. These models employ the two-type mixing replicator dynamics. It is assumed that actors interact with minority population members proportional to their prevalence in the entire population. So the behaviors of minority actors are less significant in determining the payoffs of strategies in either population than the behaviors of the majority members are. The only change, then is to the $f_i(x, y)$ terms of the last equation, where the proportions determine how much fitness is influenced by each group.

# Bibliography

Alesina, A., P. Giuliano, and N. Nunn (2013). On the origins of gender roles: Women and the plough. *The Quarterly Journal of Economics 128*(2), 469–530.

Alexander, J. M. (2000). Evolutionary explanations of distributive justice. *Philosophy of Science 67*(3), 490–516.

Alexander, J. M. (2007). *The structural evolution of morality.* Cambridge: Cambridge University Press.

Alexander, J. M. (2013). Preferential attachment and the search for successful theories. *Philosophy of Science 80*(5), 769–782.

Alexander, J. M. and B. Skyrms (1999). Bargaining with neighbors: Is justice contagious? *The Journal of philosophy, 96*(11), 588–598.

Alkemade, F., D. Van Bragt, and J. A. La Poutré (2005). Stabilization of tag-mediated interaction by sexual reproduction in an evolutionary agent system. *Information Sciences 170*(1), 101–119.

Anderson, E. (2000). Beyond homo economicus: New developments in theories of social norms. *Philosophy & Public Affairs 29*(2), 170–200.

Armelagos, G. J. and M. N. Cohen (1984). *Paleopathology at the Origins of Agriculture.* Cambridge, MA: Academic Press.

Armelagos, G. J., A. H. Goodman, and K. H. Jacobs (1991). The origins of agriculture: Population growth during a period of declining health. *Population and Environment 13*(1), 9–22.

Aumann, R. J. (1974). Subjectivity and correlation in randomized strategies. *Journal of Mathematical Economics 1*(1), 67–96.

Aumann, R. J. (1987). Correlated equilibrium as an expression of Bayesian rationality. *Econometrica: Journal of the Econometric Society*, 1–18.

Axelrod, R. (1997). The dissemination of culture: A model with local convergence and global polarization. *Journal of Conflict Resolution 41*(2), 203–226.

Axtell, R., J. M. Epstein, and H. P. Young (2001). The Emergence of Classes in a Multi-agent Bargaining Model. In S. N. Durlauf and H. P. Young (eds), *Social dynamics*, pp. 191–212. Cambridge, MA: MIT Press.

Axelrod, R. and R. A. Hammond (2003). The evolution of ethnocentric behavior. Midwest Political Science Convention, vol 2.

Ayres, I. and P. Siegelman (1995). Race and gender discrimination in bargaining for a new car. *The American Economic Review, 85*(3), 304–321.

Babcock, L. and S. Laschever (2009). *Women don't ask: Negotiation and the gender divide.* Princeton, NJ: Princeton University Press.

Baker, M. J. and J. P. Jacobsen (2007). Marriage, specialization, and the gender division of labor. *Journal of Labor Economics 25*(4), 763–793.

Bardasi, E. and M. Taylor (2008). Marriage and wages: A test of the specialization hypothesis. *Economica 75*(299), 569–591.

Barjak, F. and S. Robinson (2008). International collaboration, mobility and team diversity in the life sciences: Impact on research performance. *Social Geography 3*(1), 23.

Basow, S. A. (1992). *Gender: Stereotypes and roles*. Pacific Grove, CA: Thomson Brooks/Cole Publishing Co.

Beblo, M. (2001). *Bargaining over time allocation: Economic modeling and econometric investigation of time use within families*. Berlin: Springer Science & Business Media.

Becker, G. S. (1981). *A Treatise on the Family*. Cambridge, MA: Harvard University Press.

Bednar, J. and S. Page (2007). Can game (s) theory explain culture? The emergence of cultural behavior within multiple games. *Rationality and Society 19*(1), 65–97.

Bednar, J., Y. Chen, T. X. Liu, and S. Page (2012). Behavioral spillovers and cognitive load in multiple games: An experimental study. *Games and Economic Behavior 74*(1), 12–31.

Bem, S. L. (1983). Gender schema theory and its implications for child development: Raising gender-aschematic children in a gender-schematic society. *Signs 8*(4), 598–616.

Bergstrom, C. T. and M. Lachmann (2003). The Red King effect: When the slowest runner wins the coevolutionary race. *Proceedings of the National Academy of Sciences 100*(2), 593–598.

Bergstrom, T. C. (1996). Economics in a family way. *Journal of Economic Literature 34*(4), 1903–1934.

Berk, S. F. (2012). *The gender factory: The apportionment of work in American households*. Berlin: Springer Science & Business Media.

Bertrand, M. and S. Mullainathan (2003). Are Emily and Greg more employable than Lakisha and Jamal? A field experiment on labor market discrimination. Technical report, National Bureau of Economic Research.

Betzig, L. (1989). Causes of conjugal dissolution: A cross-cultural study. *Current Anthropology 30*(5), 654–676.

Bianchi, S. M., J. P. Robinson, and M. A. Milke (2006). *The changing rhythms of American family life*. New York, NY: Russell Sage Foundation.

Bicchieri, C. (2005). *The grammar of society: The nature and dynamics of social norms*. Cambridge: Cambridge University Press.

Bicchieri, C. and H. Mercier (2014). Norms and beliefs: How change occurs. In *The Complexity of Social Norms*, pp. 37–54. Cham: Springer.

Binmore, K. (2008). Do conventions need to be common knowledge? *Topoi 27*, 17–27.

Binmore, K., L. Samuelson, and P. Young (2003). Equilibrium selection in bargaining models. *Games and Economic Behavior 45*(2), 296–328.

Bird, R. B. and B. F. Codding (2015). The sexual division of labor. In R. Scott and S. Kosslyn (eds), *Emerging trends in the social and behavioral sciences*, pp. 1–16. Hoboken, NJ: John Wiley and Sons.

Bittman, M., P. England, L. Sayer, N. Folbre, and G. Matheson (2003). When does gender trump money? Bargaining and time in household work. *American Journal of Sociology 109*(1), 186–214.

Blackwood, E. (1984). Sexuality and gender in certain Native American tribes: The case of cross-gender females. *Signs 10*(1), 27–42.

Blood, R. O. and D. M. Wolfe (1960). *Husbands & wives: The dynamics of married living*. New York, NY: Free Press.

Bolton, G. E., E. Katok, and R. Zwick (1998). Dictator game giving: Rules of fairness versus acts of kindness. *International Journal of Game Theory 27*(2), 269–299.

Börgers, T. and R. Sarin (1997). Learning through reinforcement and replicator dynamics. *Journal of Economic Theory 77*(1), 1–14.

Boschini, A. and A. Sjögren (2007). Is team formation gender neutral? evidence from coauthorship patterns. *Journal of Labor Economics 25*(2), 325–365.

Bott, E. and E. B. Spillius (2014). *Family and social network: Roles, norms and external relationships in ordinary urban families*. Abingdon: Routledge.

Botts, T. F., L. K. Bright, M. Cherry, G. Mallarangeng, and Q. Spencer (2014). What is the state of blacks in philosophy? *Critical Philosophy of Race 2*(2), 224–242.

Bowles, H. R., L. Babcock, and L. Lai (2007). Social incentives for gender differences in the propensity to initiate negotiations: Sometimes it does hurt to ask. *Organizational Behavior and Human Decision Processes 103*(1), 84–103.

Bowles, H. R., L. Babcock, and K. L. McGinn (2005). Constraints and triggers: Situational mechanics of gender in negotiation. *Journal of Personality and Social Psychology 89*(6), 951.

Bowles, S. (2004). *Microeconomics: behavior, institutions, and evolution*. Princeton, NJ: Princeton University Press.

Bowles, S. and S. Naidu (2006). Persistent institutions. Technical report, working paper, Santa Fe Institute.

Boyd, R. and P. J. Richerson (2004). *The origin and evolution of cultures*. Oxford: Oxford University Press.

Breen, R. and L. P. Cooke (2005). The persistence of the gendered division of domestic labour. *European Sociological Review 21*(1), 43–57.

Brewer, M. B. (1988). A dual process model of impression formation. In T. K. Srull and R. S. Wyer, Jr. (eds), *Advances in social cognition, Vol. 1. A dual process model of impression formation*, pp. 1–36. Hillsdale, NJ: Lawrence Erlbaum Associates.

Brewer, M. B. (1999). The psychology of prejudice: Ingroup love or outgroup hate? *Journal of Social Issues* 55, 429–444.

Brines, J. (1994). Economic dependency, gender, and the division of labor at home. *American Journal of Sociology*, 652–688.

Brown, G. W. (1951). Iterative solution of games by fictitious play. *Activity Analysis of Production and Allocation* 13(1), 374–376.

Bruner, J. P. (2015). Diversity, tolerance, and the social contract. *Politics, Philosophy & Economics* 14(4), 429–448.

Bruner, J. P. (2017). Minority (dis)advantage in population games. *Synthese*, doi 10.1007/s11229-017-1487-8.

Bruner, J. P. and C. O'Connor (2015). Power, bargaining, and collaboration. In T. Boyer-Kassem, C. Mayo-Wilson, and M. Weisberg (eds), *Scientific Collaboration and Collective Knowledge*, pp. 135–160. Oxford: Oxford University Press.

Buss, D. M. and D. P. Schmitt (2011). Evolutionary psychology and feminism. *Sex Roles* 64(9-10), 768–787.

Butler, J. (1988). Performative acts and gender constitution: An essay in phenomenology and feminist theory. *Theatre Journal* 40(4), 519–531.

Butler, J. (2004). *Undoing gender*. London: Psychology Press.

Butler, J. (2011a). *Bodies that matter: On the discursive limits of sex*. London: Routledge.

Butler, J. (2011b). *Gender trouble: Feminism and the subversion of identity*. London: Routledge.

Camerer, C. (2003). *Behavioral game theory: Experiments in strategic interaction*. Princeton, NJ: Princeton University Press.

Campbell, L. G., S. Mehtani, M. E. Dozier, and J. Rinehart (2013). Gender-heterogeneous working groups produce higher quality science. *PloS one* 8(10), e79147.

Cao, R. (2012). A teleosemantic approach to information in the brain. *Biology & Philosophy* 27(1), 49–71.

Carroll, L. (1917). *Through the looking glass: And what Alice found there*. Chicago, IL: Rand, McNally.

Cartwright, N. (1991). Replicability, reproducibility, and robustness: Comments on Harry Collins. *History of Political Economy* 23(1), 143–155.

Chong, D. (2014). *Collective action and the civil rights movement*. Chicago, IL: Chicago, IL: University of Chicago Press.

Claidière, N. and D. Sperber (2007). The role of attraction in cultural evolution. *Journal of Cognition and Culture* 7(1), 89–111.

Claidière, N., T. C. Scott-Phillips, and D. Sperber (2014). How Darwinian is cultural evolution? *Philosophical Transactions of the Royal Society of London B: Biological Sciences* 369(1642), 20130368.

Clark, J. E. and M. Blake (1994). The power of prestige: Competitive generosity and the emergence of rank societies in lowland mesoamerica. In Elizabeth Brumfiel and John W. Fox (eds), *Factional competition and political development in the New World*, 17–30. Cambridge: Cambridge University Press.

Cochran, C. and C. O'Connor (forthcoming 2019). Inequity and inequality in the emergence of norms. *Politics, Philosophy and Economics.*

Collins, P. H. and V. Chepp (2013). Intersectionality. In J. K. Georgina Waylen, Karen Celis, and S. L. Weldon (eds), The Oxford Handbook of Gender and Politics, Chapter 2, pp. 57–87. Oxford: Oxford University Press.

Coltrane, S. (2000). Research on household labor: Modeling and measuring the social embeddedness of routine family work. *Journal of Marriage and Family* 62(4), 1208–1233.

Cosmides, L., J. Tooby, and R. Kurzban (2003). Perceptions of race. *Trends in Cognitive Sciences* 7(4), 173–179.

Costin, C. L. (2001). Craft production systems. In Gary Feinman and Douglas T. Price (eds), *Archaeology at the millennium*, pp. 273–327. Boston, MA: Springer.

Cross, H. (1990). Employer hiring practices: Differential treatment of Hispanic and Anglo job seekers.

Cudd, A. E. (1994). Oppression by choice. *Journal of Social Philosophy* 25(s1), 22–44.

Cudd, A. E. (2006). *Analyzing oppression.* Oxford: Oxford University Press.

Currarini, S., M. O. Jackson, and P. Pin (2009). An economic model of friendship: Homophily, minorities, and segregation. *Econometrica* 77(4), 1003–1045.

Dahlberg, F. (1981). *Woman the gatherer.* New Haven, CT: Yale University Press.

Danziger, L. and E. Katz (1996). A theory of sex discrimination. *Journal of Economic Behavior & Organization* 31(1), 57–66.

D'Arms, J., R. Batterman, and K. Górny (1998). Game theoretic explanations and the evolution of justice. *Philosophy of Science* 89(1), 76–102.

Davis, S., D. K. Mirick, and R. G. Stevens (2001). Night shift work, light at night, and risk of breast cancer. *Journal of the National Cancer Institute* 93(20), 1557–1562.

de Leeuw, M. B., M. K. Whyte, D. Ho, C. Meza, and A. Karteron (2007). Residential segregation and housing discrimination in the United States. Report. *Poverty & Race Research Action Council. December.*

Del Carmen, A. and R. L. Bing (2000). Academic productivity of African Americans in criminology and criminal justice. *Journal of Criminal Justice Education* 11(2), 237–249.

Denton, N. A. (2006). Segregation and discrimination in housing. In Chester Hartman, Rachel G. Bratt, and Michael Stone (eds), *A right to housing: Foundation for a new social agenda* pp. 61–81. Philadelphia, PA: Temple University Press.

D'Exelle, B., C. Gutekunst, and A. Riedl (2017). Gender and bargaining: Evidence from an artefactual field experiment in rural Uganda. (WIDER Working Paper; Vol. 2017, No. 155). Helsinki. *United Nations University World Institute for Development Economics Research.*

DiPrete, T. A. and G. M. Eirich (2006). Cumulative advantage as a mechanism for inequality: A review of theoretical and empirical developments. *Annual Review of Sociology* 32, 271–297.

Doss, C. R. (1996). Testing among models of intrahousehold resource allocation. *World Development* 24(10), 1597–1609.

Douglas, H. (2000). Inductive risk and values in science. *Philosophy of Science*, 559–579.

Douglas, H. (2009). *Science, policy, and the value-free ideal.* Pittsburgh, PA: University of Pittsburgh Press.

Downes, S. M. (2011). Scientific models. *Philosophy Compass* 6(11), 757–764.

D'souza, D. (1995). *The end of racism: Principles for a multiracial society.* New York, NY: Free Press.

Du Bois, W. E. B. (1906). *The health and physique of the Negro American.* Atlanta, GA: Atlanta University Press.

Du Bois, W. E. B. (2017). *Black reconstruction in America: Toward a history of the part which black folk played in the attempt to reconstruct democracy in America, 1860–1880.* New York, NY: Routledge.

Eagleton, T. (1991). *Ideology: an introduction*, Volume 9. Cambridge: Cambridge University Press.

Eagly, A. H. and W. Wood (1999). The origins of sex differences in human behavior: Evolved dispositions versus social roles. *American Psychologist* 54(6), 408.

Echevarria, C. and A. Merlo (1999). Gender differences in education in a dynamic household bargaining model. *International Economic Review* 40(2), 265–286.

Eckel, C. C. and P. J. Grossman (1998). Are women less selfish than men?: Evidence from dictator experiments. *The Economic Journal* 108(448), 726–735.

Eckel, C. C. and P. J. Grossman (2001). Chivalry and solidarity in ultimatum games. *Economic Inquiry* 39(2), 171–188.

Elliott, K. C. (2011). *Is a little pollution good for you?: Incorporating societal values in environmental research.* Oxford: Oxford University Press.

Epstein, J. M. and R. Axtell (1996). *Growing artificial societies: Social science from the bottom up.* Washington, DC: Brookings Institution Press.

Eswaran, M. (2014). *Why gender matters in economics.* Princeton, NJ: Princeton University Press.

Eswaran, M. and N. Malhotra (2011). Domestic violence and women's autonomy in developing countries: Theory and evidence. *Canadian Journal of Economics/Revue canadienne d'économique* 44, 1222–1263.

Fagot, B. I. (1977). Consequences of moderate cross-gender behavior in preschool children. *Child Development*, 48(3), 902–907.

Falk, A., E. Fehr, and U. Fischbacher (2008). Testing theories of fairness—intentions matter. *Games and Economic Behavior* 62(1), 287–303.

Farley, R., E. L. Fielding, and M. Krysan (1997). The residential preferences of blacks and whites: A four-metropolis analysis. *Housing Policy Debate* 8(4), 763–800.

Fehr, E. and S. Gächter (1999). Cooperation and punishment in public goods experiments. *Institute for Empirical Research in Economics working paper* (10).

Fehr, E. and K. M. Schmidt (1999). A theory of fairness, competition, and cooperation. *The Quarterly Journal of Economics* 114(3), 817–868.

Feldon, D. F., J. Peugh, M. A. Maher, J. Roksa, and C. Tofel-Grehl (2017). Time-to-credit gender inequities of first-year phD students in the biological sciences. *CBE-Life Sciences Education* 16(1), ar4.

Fenstermaker, S. and C. West (2002). *Doing gender, doing difference: Inequality, power, and institutional change*. London: Psychology Press.

Ferber, M. A. and M. Teiman (1980). Are women economists at a disadvantage in publishing journal articles? *Eastern Economic Journal*, 6(3/4) 189–193.

Fiske, A. P. (1992). The four elementary forms of sociality: Framework for a unified theory of social relations. *Psychological Review* 99(4), 689.

Fiske, A. P. (1999). Learning a culture the way informants do: Observing, imitating, and participating. Unpublished manuscript, University of California, Los Angeles.

Foster, D. and P. Young (1990). Stochastic evolutionary game dynamics. *Theoretical Population Biology* 38(2), 219–232.

Francois, P. et al. (1996). *A theory of gender discrimination based on the household*. Institute for Economic Research, Queen's University.

Frank, R. H. (1988). *Passions within reason: The strategic role of the emotions*. New York, NY: W. W. Norton & Co.

Frank, R. H., T. Gilovich, and D. T. Regan (1993). The evolution of one-shot cooperation: An experiment. *Ethology and Sociobiology* 14(4), 247–256.

Freeman, R. B. and W. Huang (2015). Collaborating with people like me: Ethnic coauthorship within the united states. *Journal of Labor Economics* 33(S1), S289–S318.

Frey, B. S. and I. Bohnet (1995). Institutions affect fairness: Experimental investigations. *Journal of Institutional and Theoretical Economics (JITE)/Zeitschrift für die gesamte Staatswissenschaft* 151(2), 286–303.

Fuwa, M. (2004). Macro-level gender inequality and the division of household labor in 22 countries. *American Sociological Review* 69(6), 751–767.

Gale, J., K. Binmore, and L. Samuelson (1995). Learning to be imperfect: The ultimatum game. *Games and Economic Behavior* 8, 56–90.

Gallo, E. (2014). Communication networks in markets. Technical report, Faculty of Economics, University of Cambridge.

Galster, G. and E. Godfrey (2005). By words and deeds: Racial steering by real estate agents in the US in 2000. *Journal of the American Planning Association* 71(3), 251–268.

Gao, L., Y.-T. Li, and R.-W. Wang (2015). The shift between the Red Queen and the Red King effects in mutualisms. *Scientific Reports* 5, 8237.

Garfinkel, H. (1967). *Studies in Ethomethodology*. Englewood Cliffs, NJ: Prentice Hall.

Gates, G. J. (2011). How many people are lesbian, gay, bisexual and transgender? Technical report, Williams Institute, University of California School of Law.

Gibbons, A. (2011). Ancient footprints tell tales of travel. *Science 332*(6029), 534–535.

Gigerenzer, G. and R. Selten (2002). *Bounded rationality: The adaptive toolbox*. Cambridge, MA: MIT Press.

Gilbert, M. (1992). *On social facts*. Princeton, NJ: Princeton University Press.

Gilbert, M. (2006). Rationality in collective action. *Philosophy of the Social Sciences 36*(1), 3–17.

Ginther, D. K. and M. Zavodny (2001). Is the male marriage premium due to selection? The effect of shotgun weddings on the return to marriage. *Journal of Population Economics 14*(2), 313–328.

Gintis, H. (2009). *Game theory evolving: A problem-centered introduction to modeling strategic interaction*. Princeton, NJ: Princeton University Press.

Glick, P. and S. T. Fiske (2001). An ambivalent alliance: Hostile and benevolent sexism as complementary justifications for gender inequality. *American Psychologist 56*(2), 109.

Goffman, E. (1976). Gender display. In his *Gender advertisements*, pp. 1–9. Communications and culture. London: Palgrave.

Gokhale, C. S. and A. Traulsen (2012). Mutualism and evolutionary multiplayer games: Revisiting the Red King. *Proceedings of the Royal Society of London B: Biological Sciences 279*(1747), 4611–4616.

Golub, B. and M. O. Jackson (2012). Network structure and the speed of learning measuring homophily based on its consequences. *Annals of Economics and Statistics/ANNALES D'ÉCONOMIE ET DE STATISTIQUE 107/108*, 33–48.

Goode, W. J. (1971). Force and violence in the family. *Journal of Marriage and the Family*, 624–636.

Goodin, R. E. (1986). *Protecting the vulnerable: A re-analysis of our social responsibilities*. Chicago, IL University of Chicago Press.

Gould, R. V. (2002). The origins of status hierarchies: A formal theory and empirical test1. *American Journal of Sociology 107*(5), 1143–1178.

Greenstein, T. N. (2000). Economic dependence, gender, and the division of labor in the home: A replication and extension. *Journal of Marriage and Family* 62(2), 322–335.

Greenwald, A. G. and M. R. Banaji (1995). Implicit social cognition: attitudes, self-esteem, and stereotypes. *Psychological Review* 102(1), 4.

Gronau, R. (1973). The intrafamily allocation of time: The value of the housewives' time. *The American Economic Review* 63(4), 634–651.

Gronau, R. (1977). Leisure, home production and work–the theory of the allocation of time revisited. *Journal of Political Economy* 85(6); 1099–1123.

Guala, F. (2013). The normativity of Lewis Conventions. Synthese *190*(15), 3107–3122.

Guiso, L. and M. Paiella (2008). Risk aversion, wealth, and background risk. *Journal of the European Economic Association* 6(6), 1109–1150.

Gupta, S. (1999). Gender display? A reassessment of the relationship between men's economic dependence and their housework hours. In *Annual Meeting of the American Sociological Association, Chicago*.

Gupta, S. (2006). Her money, her time: Women's earnings and their housework hours. *Social Science Research* 35(4), 975–999.

Gupta, S. (2007). Autonomy, dependence, or display? The relationship between married women's earnings and housework. *Journal of Marriage and Family* 69(2), 399–417.

Gupta, S. and M. Ash (2008). Whose money, whose time? A nonparametric approach to modeling time spent on housework in the United States. *Feminist Economics* 14(1), 93–120.

Gurven, M., J. Winking, H. Kaplan, C. Von Rueden, and L. McAllister (2009). A bioeconomic approach to marriage and the sexual division of labor. *Human Nature* 20(2), 151–183.

Güth, W. (1995). An evolutionary approach to explaining cooperative behavior by reciprocal incentives. *International Journal of Game Theory* 24(4), 323–344.

Güth, W. and R. Tietz (1990). Ultimatum bargaining behavior: A survey and comparison of experimental results. *Journal of Economic Psychology* 11(3), 417–449.

Güth, W., R. Schmittberger, and B. Schwarze (1982). An experimental analysis of ultimatum bargaining. *Journal of Economic Behavior & Organization* 3(4), 367–388.

Hadfield, G. K. (1999). A coordination model of the sexual division of labor. *Journal of Economic Behavior & Organization* 40(2), 125–153.

Hales, D. (2000). Cooperation without memory or space: Tags, groups and the prisoner's dilemma. In S. Moss and P. Davidsson (eds), *Multi-agent-based simulation*, pp. 157–166. MABS 2000. Lecture notes in computer science. Berling/Hedidelberg: Springer.

Haraway, D. J. (1989). *Primate visions: Gender, race, and nature in the world of modern science.* London: Psychology Press.

Harms, W. (1997). Evolution and ultimatum bargaining. *Theory and Decision* 42(147–175).

Hartshorn, M., A. Kaznatcheev, and T. Shultz (2013). The evolutionary dominance of ethnocentric cooperation. *Journal of Artificial Societies and Social Simulation* 16(3), 7.

Haslam, S. A. (2004). *Psychology in organizations.* Thousand Oaks, CA: Sage.

Haslanger, S. (2000). Gender and race: (What) are they? (What) do we want them to be? *Noûs* 34(1), 31–55.

Haslanger, S. (2015a). Social structure, narrative, and explanation. *Canadian Journal of Philosophy* (10.1080/00455091.2015.1019176).

Haslanger, S. (2015b). Theorizing with purpose: The many kinds of sex. In C. Kendig (ed.), *Natural kinds and classification in scientific practice*, Chapter 8. London: Routledge.

Haslanger, S. (2017). Culture and critique. *Proceedings of the Aristotelian Society Supplementary Volume XCI*, 149–173.

Heesen, R., L. K. Bright, and A. Zucker (2017). Vindicating methodological triangulation. *Synthese* (doi: 10.1007/s11229-016-1294-7).

Hempel, C. G. (1965). Science and human values. In his *Aspects of Scientific Explanation and Other Essays in the Philosophy of Science*, pp. 81–96. New York, NY: The Free Press.

Henrich, J. (2015). *The secret of our success: How culture is driving human evolution, domesticating our species, and making us smarter.* Princeton, NJ: Princeton University Press.

Henrich, J. and R. Boyd (2008). Division of labor, economic specialization, and the evolution of social stratification. *Current Anthropology* 49(4), 715–724.

Henrich, J. and F. J. Gil-White (2001). The evolution of prestige: Freely conferred deference as a mechanism for enhancing the benefits of cultural transmission. *Evolution and Human Behavior* 22(3), 165–196.

Henrich, J. and N. Henrich (2007). *Why humans cooperate: A cultural and evolutionary explanation.* New York, NY: Oxford University Press, USA.

Henrich, J. and R. McElreath (2003). The evolution of cultural evolution. *Evolutionary Anthropology: Issues, News, and Reviews* 12(3), 123–135.

Henrich, J., R. Boyd, S. Bowles, C. Camerer, E. Fehr, H. Gintis, and R. McElreath (2001). In search of homo economicus: Behavioral experiments in 15 small-scale societies. *The American Economic Review* 91(2), 73–78.

Henrich, J., R. McElreath, A. Barr, J. Ensminger, C. Barrett, A. Bolyanatz, J. C. Cardenas, M. Gurven, E. Gwako, N. Henrich, et al. (2006). Costly punishment across Human societies. *Science* 312(5781), 1767–1770.

Herrnstein, R. J. (1970). On the law of effect. *Journal of the Experimental Analysis of Behavior 13* (2), 243–266.

Hewlett, B. S. and M. E. Lamb (2005). *Hunter-gatherer childhoods: Evolutionary, developmental, and cultural perspectives.* Piscataway, NJ: Transaction Publishers.

Hoddinott, J. and L. Haddad (1995). Does female income share influence household expenditures? Evidence from Cote D'ivoire. *Oxford Bulletin of Economics and Statistics 57*(1), 77–96.

Hoffman, E. and M. L. Spitzer (1985). Entitlements, rights, and fairness: An experimental examination of subjects' concepts of distributive justice. *The Journal of Legal Studies 14*(2), 259–297.

Hoffmann, R. (2006). The cognitive origins of social stratification. *Computational Economics 28*(3), 233–249.

Hofmann, W., B. Gawronski, T. Gschwendner, H. Le, and M. Schmitt (2005). A meta-analysis on the correlation between the implicit association test and explicit self-report measures. *Personality and Social Psychology Bulletin 31*(10), 1369–1385.

Holland, J. H. (1995). *Hidden order: How adaptation builds complexity.* New York, NY: Basic Books.

Hopkins, E. (2002). Two competing models of how people learn in games. *Econometrica 70*(6), 2141–2166.

Hopkins, N. (2006). Diversification of a university faculty: Observations on hiring women faculty in the schools of science and engineering at MIT. *MIT Faculty Newsletter 18*(4), 25.

Hume, D. (1739/1978). *A treatise on human nature.* Second Edition. Oxford: Oxford University Press.

Hwang, S.-H., S. Naidu, and S. Bowles (2014). Social conflict and the evolution of unequal conventions. Technical report, working paper.

Jeffers, C. (2013). The cultural theory of race: Yet another look at Du Bois's "the conservation of races". *Ethics 123*(3), 403–426.

Kahneman, D. and A. Tversky (1984). Choices, values, and frames. *American Psychologist 39*(4), 341.

Kaitala, V. and W. M. Getz (1995). Population dynamics and harvesting of semelparous species with phenotypic and genotypic variability in reproductive age. *Journal of Mathematical Biology 33*(5), 521–556.

Kamei, N. (2010). *Little "hunters" in the forest: Ethnography of hunter-gatherer children.* Kyoto: Kyoto University Press.

Kaniewska, P., S. Alon, S. Karako-Lampert, O. Hoegh-Guldberg, and O. Levy (2015). Signaling cascades and the importance of moonlight in coral broadcast mass spawning. *eLife 4*, e09991.

Keller, J. (2005). In genes we trust: the biological component of psychological essentialism and its relationship to mechanisms of motivated social cognition. *Journal of Personality and Social Psychology 88*(4), 686.

Kinzler, K. D., K. Shutts, and J. Correll (2010). Priorities in social categories. *European Journal of Social Psychology 40*(4), 581–592.

Kitcher, P. (1990). The division of cognitive labor. *The Journal of Philosophy 87*(1), 5–22.

Konrad, K. A. and K. E. Lommerud (2000). The bargaining family revisited. *Canadian Journal of Economics/Revue canadienne d'économique 33*(2), 471–487.

LaCroix, T. and C. O'Connor (2017). Power by association. Unpublished.

Lancy, D. F. (1996). *Playing on the mother-ground: Cultural routines for children's development.* New York, NY: Guilford Press.

Lee, C. J. (2016). Revisiting current causes of women's underrepresentation in science. In J. Saul and M. Brownstein (eds), *Implicit Bias and Philosophy Volume 1: Metaphysics and Epistemology*, pp. 265–283. Oxford: Oxford University Press.

Levine, S. S., E. P. Apfelbaum, M. Bernard, V. L. Bartelt, E. J. Zajac, and D. Stark (2014). Ethnic diversity deflates price bubbles. *Proceedings of the National Academy of Sciences 111*(52), 18524–18529.

Levins, R. (1966). The strategy of model building in population biology. *American Scientist 54*(4), 421–431.

Lewis, D. (1969). *Convention: A philosophical study.* Cambridge, MA: Harvard University PRess.

Lichbach, M. I. (1998). *The rebel's dilemma.* Ann Arbor, MI: University of Michigan Press.

Lim, W. and P. R. Neary (2016). An experimental investigation of stochastic adjustment dynamics. *Games and Economic Behavior 100*, 208–219.

Lippa, R. A. (2005). *Gender, nature, and nurture.* New York, NY: Routledge.

Longino, H. E. (1990). *Science as social knowledge: Values and objectivity in scientific inquiry.* Princeton, NJ: Princeton University Press.

López-Paredes, A., C. Hernández, and J. Pajares (2004). Social intelligence or tag reasoning. In *2nd ESSA Conference. http://www.unikoblenz.de/essa/ESSA2004/files/papers/LopezHernandezPajaresESSA04.pdf.*

Lorber, J. (1994). *Paradoxes of gender.* New Haven, CT: Yale University Press.

Losin, E. A. R., M. Iacoboni, A. Martin, and M. Dapretto (2012). Own-gender imitation activates the brain's reward circuitry. *Social Cognitive and Affective Neuroscience 7*(7), 804–810.

Loury, G. C. (1995). *One by one from the inside out: Essays and reviews on race and responsibility in America.* New York, NY: Free Press.

Lundberg, S. (2008). Gender and household decision-making. In Francesca Bettio and Alina Verashchagina (eds), *Frontiers in the Economics of Gender*, pp. 116–134. New York, NY: Routledge.

Lundberg, S. and R. A. Pollak (1993). Separate spheres bargaining and the marriage market. *Journal of Political Economy 101*(6), 988–1010.

Lundberg, S. J., R. A. Pollak, and T. J. Wales (1997). Do husbands and wives pool their resources? Evidence from the United Kingdom Child Benefit. *Journal of Human Resources*, 463–480.

Lynn, F. B., J. M. Podolny, and L. Tao (2009). A sociological (de) construction of the relationship between status and quality. *American Journal of Sociology 115*(3), 755–804.

Manser, M. and M. Brown (1980). Marriage and household decision-making: A bargaining analysis. *International Economic Review 21*(1), 31–44.

Marlowe, F. (2010). *The Hadza: Hunter-gatherers of Tanzania*, Volume 3. Oakland, CA: University of California Press.

Martin, M. K. and B. Voorhies (1975). *Female of the Species*. New York, NY: Columbia University Press.

Marx, K. and F. Engels (1975). *The holy family*. Moscow: Foreign Languages Publishing House.

Mäs, M. and H. H. Nax (2016). A behavioral study of "noise" in coordination games. *Journal of Economic Theory 162*, 195–208.

Maynard-Smith, J. (1982). *Evolution and the Theory of Games*. Cambridge: Cambridge University Press.

Maynard-Smith, J. and G. A. Parker (1976). The logic of asymmetric contests. *Animal Behaviour 24*(1), 159–175.

Maynard-Smith, J. and G. Price (1973). The logic of animal conflict. Nature *246*, 15–18.

McDowell, J. M. and J. K. Smith (1992). The effect of gender-sorting on propensity to coauthor: Implications for academic promotion. *Economic Inquiry 30*(1), 68–82.

McElroy, M. B. (1990). The empirical content of Nash-bargained household behavior. *Journal of Human Resources 25*(4), 559–583.

McElroy, M. B. and M. J. Horney (1981). Nash-bargained household decisions: Toward a generalization of the theory of demand. *International Economic Review*, *22*(2), 333–349.

Mengel, F. (2012). Learning across games. *Games and Economic Behavior 74*(2), 601–619.

Merton, R. K. (1988). The Matthew effect in science, ii: Cumulative advantage and the symbolism of intellectual property. *Isis 79*(4), 606–623.

Merton, R. K. (1968). The Matthew effect in science. *Science 159*(3810), 56–63.

Mesoudi, A., A. Whiten, and K. N. Laland (2006). Towards a unified science of cultural evolution. *Behavioral and Brain Sciences 29*(4), 329–347.

Millikan, R. G. (2005). *Language: A biological model*. New York, NY: Oxford University Press on Demand.

Mohseni, A. (2019). Stochastic stability and disagreements between dynamics. Philosophy of Science. Forthcoming.

Mohseni, A., C. O'Connor, and H. Rubin (2018). On the emergence of minority disadvantage: Testing the cultural Red King. Unpublished.

Money, J. and A. A. Ehrhardt (1972). Man and woman, boy and girl: Differentiation and dimorphism of gender identity from conception to maturity. Oxford: Johns Hopkins University Press.

Money, J., J. G. Hampson, and J. L. Hampson (1955). An examination of some basic sexual concepts: The evidence of human hermaphroditism. *Bulletin of the Johns Hopkins Hospital* 97(4), 301.

Morgan, M. D. (1980). Life history characteristics of two introduced populations of mysis relicta. *Ecology* 61(3), 551–561.

Morton, T. A., T. Postmes, S. A. Haslam, and M. J. Hornsey (2009). Theorizing gender in the face of social change: Is there anything essential about essentialism? *Journal of Personality and Social Psychology* 96(3), 653.

Moss-Racusin, C. A., J. F. Dovidio, V. L. Brescoll, M. J. Graham, and J. Handelsman (2012). Science faculty's subtle gender biases favor male students. *Proceedings of the National Academy of Sciences* 109(41), 16474–16479.

Murdock, G. P. and C. Provost (1973). Factors in the division of labor by sex: A cross-cultural analysis. *Ethnology* 12(2), 203–225.

Nakahashi, W. and M. W. Feldman (2014). Evolution of division of labor: Emergence of different activities among group members. *Journal of Theoretical Biology* 348, 65–79.

Nash, J. (1950). The bargaining problem. *Econometrica: Journal of the Econometric Society* 18(2), 155–162.

Nash, J. (1951). Non-cooperative games. *Annals of Mathematics* 54(2), 286–295.

Nash, J. (1953). Two-person cooperative games. *Econometrica: Journal of the Econometric Society* 21(1), 128–140.

Neary, P. R. (2012). Competing conventions. *Games and Economic Behavior* 76(1), 301–328.

Nersessian, N. J. (1999). Model-based reasoning in conceptual change. In Lorenzo Magnani, Nancy Nersessian, and Paul Thagard (eds), *Model-based reasoning in scientific discovery*, pp. 5–22. New York, NY: Kluwer Academic/Plenum.

Nosaka, H. (2007). Specialization and competition in marriage models. *Journal of Economic Behavior & Organization* 63(1), 104–119.

Nowak, M. A. (2006). Five rules for the evolution of cooperation. *Science* 314(5805), 1560–1563.

Nydegger, R. V. and G. Owen (1974). Two-person bargaining: An experimental test of the Nash axioms. *International Journal of Game Theory* 3(4), 239–249.

Oakley, A. (2015). *Sex, gender and society*. Farnham: Ashgate Publishing, Ltd.

O'Connor, C. (2016). The evolution of guilt: A model-based approach. Philosophy of Science 83(4), 897–908.

O'Connor, C. (2017a). The cultural Red King effect. The Journal of Mathematical Sociology 41(3): 155–171. doi: 10.1080/0022250X.2017.1335723.

O'Connor, C. (2017b). Modeling minimal conditions for inequity. Unpublished.

O'Connor, C. and J. P. Bruner (2017). Dynamics and diversity in epistemic communities. Erkenntnis 84(1), 101–19 doi: 10.1007/s10670-017-9950-y.

O'Connor, C. and J. O. Weatherall (2016). Black holes, black-scholes, and prairie voles: An essay review of simulation and similarity, by Michael Weisberg. Philosophy of Science 83(4), 613–626.

O'Connor, C., L. K. Bright, and J. P. Bruner (2019). The emergence of intersectional disadvantage. Forthcoming in Social Epistemology.

Odenbaugh, J. and A. Alexandrova (2011). Buyer beware: Robustness analyses in economics and biology. Biology & Philosophy 26(5), 757–771.

Ogbu, J. U. (1978). Minority education and caste: The American system in cross-cultural perspective.

Okin, S. M. (1989). Justice, gender, and the family New York, NY: Basic Books.

Okruhlik, K. (1994). Gender and the biological sciences. Canadian Journal of Philosophy 24(sup1), 21–42.

Olson, M. (2009). The logic of collective action Cambridge, MA: Harvard University Press.

Omi, M. and H. Winant (2014). Racial formation in the United States. London: Routledge.

Opp, K.-D. (2009). Theories of political protest and social movements: A multidisciplinary introduction, critique, and synthesis. London: Routledge.

Orzack, S. H. and E. Sober (1993). A critical assessment of Levins's the strategy of model building in population biology (1966). Quarterly Review of Biology, 533–546.

Osborne, M. J. and A. Rubinstein (1994). A course in game theory. Cambridge, MA: MIT Press.

Ott, N. (2012). Intrafamily bargaining and household decisions. Berlin/Heidelberg: Springer.

Page, K. M., M. A. Nowak, and K. Sigmund (2000). The spatial ultimatum game. Proceedings of the Royal Society of London B: Biological Sciences 267(1458), 2177–2182.

Peters, M. and A. Siow (2002). Competing premarital investments. Journal of Political Economy 110(3), 592–608.

Phan, D., S. Galam, and J.-L. Dessalles (2005). Emergence in multi-agent systems: cognitive hierarchy, detection, and complexity reduction Part ii: Axtell, Epstein and Young's model of emergence revisited. CEF 2004, 11th International Conference on Computing in Economics and Finance.

Phillips, K. W., G. B. Northcraft, and M. A. Neale (2006). Surface-level diversity and decision-making in groups: When does deep-level similarity help? *Group Processes & Intergroup Relations* 9(4), 467–482.

Pinch, S. and A. Storey (1992). Who does what, where?: A household survey of the division of domestic labour in Southampton. *Area* 24(1), 5–12.

Potochnik, A. (2007). Optimality modeling and explanatory generality. *Philosophy of Science* 74(5), 680–691.

Poza, D. J., F. A. Villafáñez, J. Pajares, A. López-Paredes, and C. Hernández (2011). New insights on the emergence of classes model. *Discrete Dynamics in Nature and Society 2011* Article ID 915279, 17 pp. https://doi.org/10.1155/2011/915279.

Quattrone, G. A. and E. E. Jones (1980). The perception of variability within in-groups and out-groups: Implications for the law of small numbers. *Journal of Personality and Social Psychology* 38(1), 141.

Rao, V. (1998). Domestic violence and intra-household resource allocation in rural India: an exercise in participatory econometrics. In M. Krishnaraj, R. Sudarshan, and A. Sharif (eds), *Gender, population, and development*, ch. 5. Oxford/Delhi: Oxford University Press.

Richerson, P. et al. (2003). Shared norms and the evolution of ethnic markers. *Current Anthropology* 84(2),(1), 122–130.

Richerson, P. J. and R. Boyd (2008). *Not by genes alone: How culture transformed human evolution*. Chicago, IL: University of Chicago Press.

Ridgeway, C. L. (2011). *Framed by gender: How gender inequality persists in the modern world*. New York, NY: Oxford University Press.

Ridgeway, C. L. and L. Smith-Lovin (1999). The gender system and interaction. *Annual Review of Sociology* 25, 191–216.

Robinson, J. (1951). An iterative method of solving a game. *Annals of Mathematics* 54(2), 296–301.

Roemer, J. (1985). A general theory of exploitation and class. *Critica* 17(49), 71–76.

Rosenstock, S., J. P. Bruner, and C. O'Connor (2017). In epistemic networks, is less really more? *Philosophy of Science* 84(2), 234–252.

Roth, A. E. and I. Erev (1995). Learning in extensive-form games: Experimental data and simple dynamic models in the intermediate term. *Games and Economic Behavior* 8(1), 164–212.

Roth, A. E. and M. W. Malouf (1979). Game-theoretic models and the role of information in bargaining. *Psychological Review* 86(6), 574.

Rousseau, J.-J. (1984, orig. 1754). *A discourse on inequality*. London: Penguin.

Rubin, H. and C. O'Connor (2018). Discrimination and collaboration in science. *Philosophy of Science* 85(3), 380–402.

Rubinstein, A. (1982). Perfect equilibrium in a bargaining model. Econometrica: *Journal of the Econometric Society* 50(1), 97–109.

Sandholm, W. H. (2010). *Population games and evolutionary dynamics*. Cambridge, MA: MIT Press.

Sandholm, W. H., E. Dokumaci, and F. Franchetti (2012). Dynamo: Diagrams for evolutionary game theory. http://www.ssc.wisc.edu/whs/dynamo.

Sarsons, H. (2017). Recognition for group work: Gender differences in academia. *American Economic Review 107*(5), 141–45.

Schelling, T. C. (1960). *The strategy of conflict*. Cambridge, MA: Harvard University Press.

Schelling, T. C. (1971). Dynamic models of segregation. *Journal of Mathematical Sociology 1*(2), 143–186.

Schneider, M., H. Rubin, and C. O'Connor (2019). Promoting diverse collaborations. In G. Ramsey and A. D. Block (eds), *The Dynamics of Science: Computational Frontiers in History and Philosophy of Science*, under contract. Pittsburgh, PA: Pittsburgh University Press.

Schulman, K. A., J. A. Berlin, W. Harless, J. F. Kerner, S. Sistrunk, B. J. Gersh, R. Dube, C. K. Taleghani, J. E. Burke, S. Williams, et al. (1999). The effect of race and sex on physicians' recommendations for cardiac catheterization. *New England Journal of Medicine 340*(8), 618–626.

Sen, A. (1987). *Gender and cooperative conflicts*. Helsinki: World Institute for Development Economics Research.

Shannon, C. E. (2001). A mathematical theory of communication. *ACM SIGMOBILE Mobile Computing and Communications Review 5*(1), 3–55.

Sigmund, K., C. Hauert, and M. A. Nowak (2001). Reward and punishment. *Proceedings of the National Academy of Sciences 98*(19), 10757–10762.

Simons, M. and K. Zollman (2018). Natural conventions and the conventional/inferential divide. Unpublished manuscript.

Sinervo, B., C. M. Lively, et al. (1996). The rock-paper-scissors game and the evolution of alternative male strategies. *Nature 380*(6571), 240–243.

Skyrms, B. (1994). Sex and justice. *The Journal of Philosophy 91*(6), 305–320.

Skyrms, B. (1996). *Evolution of the Social Contract*. Cambridge: Cambridge University Press.

Skyrms, B. (2004). *The stag hunt and the evolution of social structure*. Cambridge: Cambridge University Press.

Skyrms, B. (2010). *Signals: Evolution, learning, and information*. New York, NY: Oxford University Press.

Skyrms, B. (2014). *Evolution of the social contract*. Cambridge: Cambridge University Press.

Skyrms, B. and K. J. Zollman (2010). Evolutionary considerations in the framing of social norms. *Politics, Philosophy & Economics 9*(3), 265–273.

Smith, E. A. and J.-K. Choi (2007). The emergence of inequality in small-scale societies: simple scenarios and agent-based simulations. In Timothy A. Kohler and Sander E. van der Leeuw (eds), *The model-based archaeology of socionatural systems*, 105–20. Santa Fe, NM: SAR Press.

Smith, V. L. (1994). Economics in the laboratory. *The Journal of Economic Perspectives 8*(1), 113–131.

Solnick, S. J. (2001). Gender differences in the ultimatum game. *Economic Inquiry 39*(2), 189.

Solomon, M. (2001). *Social empiricism*. Cambridge: Cambridge University Press.

Sommers, S. R. (2006). On racial diversity and group decision making: Identifying multiple effects of racial composition on jury deliberations. *Journal of Personality and Social Psychology 90*(4), 597.

Sperber, D. and D. Sperber (1996). *Explaining culture*. Oxford: Blackwell Publishers.

Steckel, R. H. and J. C. Rose (2002). *The backbone of history: Health an d nutrition in the Western hemisphere*, Volume 2. Cambridge: Cambridge University Press.

Steinpreis, R. E., K. A. Anders, and D. Ritzke (1999). The impact of gender on the review of the curricula vitae of job applicants and tenure candidates: A national empirical study. *Sex roles 41*(7-8), 509–528.

Stevenson, B. and J. Wolfers (2006). Bargaining in the shadow of the law: Divorce laws and family distress. *The Quarterly Journal of Economics 121*(1), 267–288.

Stewart, Q. T. (2010). Big bad racists, subtle prejudice and minority victims: An agent-based analysis of the dynamics of racial inequality. In *Annual Meeting of the Population Association of America*.

Strevens, M. (2003). The role of the priority rule in science. *The Journal of Philosophy 100*(2), 55–79.

Sugden, R. (1986). *The economics of cooperation, rights and welfare*. New York, NY: Blackwell.

Sugden, R. (2000). The motivating power of expectations. In Julian Nida-Rümelin and Wolfgang Spohn (eds), *Rationality, rules, and structure*, pp. 103–129. Berlin/Heidelberg: Springer.

Sugimoto, C. R. (2013). Global gender disparities in science. published by *Nature News*, https://www.nature.com/news/bibliometrics-global-gender-disparities-in-science-1.14321

Sullivan, O. (2011). An end to gender display through the performance of housework? A review and reassessment of the quantitative literature using insights from the qualitative literature. *Journal of Family Theory & Review3*(1), 1–13.

Tajfel, H. (1970). Experiments in intergroup discrimination. *Scientific American 223*(5), 96–102.

Tajfel, H. (1978). Interindividual behaviour and intergroup behaviour. In H. Tajfel (ed.), *Differentiation between social groups: Studies in the social psychology of intergroup relations*, 27–60. Cambridge, MA: Academic Press.

Thoma, J. M. (2015). The epistemic division of labor revisited. *Philosophy of Science 82*(3), 454–472.

Thomas, D. (1990). Intra-household resource allocation: An inferential approach. *Journal of Human Resources*, 635–664.

Thomas, D. (1993). The distribution of income and expenditure within the household. *Annales d'Economie et de Statistique* 25(1), 109–135.

Thomas, D. (1994). Like father, like son; like mother, like daughter: Parental resources and child height. *Journal of Human Resources* 25(4), 950–988.

Thomas, W. et al. (1997). Navajo cultural constructions of gender and sexuality. In Sue-Ellen Jacobs, Wesley Thomas, and Sabine Lang (eds), Two-spirit people: Native American gender identity, sexuality, and spirituality, 156–73. Urbana, IL and Chicago, IL: University of Illinois Press.

Thorndike, E. L. (1898). Animal intelligence: An experimental study of the associative processes in animals. *The Psychological Review: Monograph Supplements* 2(4), i.

Thrall, C. A. (1978). Who does what: Role stereotypy, children's work, and continuity between generations in the household division of labor. *Human Relations* 31(3), 249–265.

Tilcsik, A. (2011). Pride and prejudice: Employment discrimination against openly gay men in the United States. *American Journal of Sociology* 117(2), 586–626.

Tilly, C. (1998). *Durable inequality*. Berkeley, CA: University of California Press.

Tinsley, C. H., S. I. Cheldelin, A. K. Schneider, and E. T. Amanatullah (2009). Women at the bargaining table: Pitfalls and prospects. *Negotiation Journal* 25(2), 233–248.

Treas, J. and S. Drobnic (2010). *Dividing the domestic: Men, women, and household work in cross-national perspective*. Stanford, CA: Stanford University Press.

Turnbull, C. (1987). *Mountain People*. New York, NY: Simon and Schuster.

Udry, C. (1996). Gender, agricultural production, and the theory of the household. *Journal of Political Economy* 104(5), 1010–1046.

Van Huyck, J. B., R. C. Battalio, and F. W. Rankin (1997). On the origin of convention: Evidence from coordination games*. *The Economic Journal* 107(442), 576–596.

Van Valen, L. (1973). A new evolutionary law. *Evolutionary Theory* 1, 1–30.

Vanderschraaf, P. (1995). Endogenous correlated equilibria in noncooperative games. *Theory and Decision* 38(1), 61–84.

Wagner, E. O. (2012). Evolving to divide the fruits of cooperation*. *Philosophy of Science* 79(1), 81–94.

Watts, A. (2001). A dynamic model of network formation. *Games and Economic Behavior* 34(2), 331–341.

Weber, M. (2009). *The theory of social and economic organization*. New York, NY: Simon and Schuster.

Weibull, J. W. (1997). *Evolutionary game theory*. Cambridge, MA: MIT Press.

Weisberg, M. (2006). Robustness analysis. *Philosophy of Science* 73(5), 730–742.

Weisberg, M. (2007). Three kinds of idealization. *The Journal of Philosophy* 104(12), 639–659.

Weisberg, M. (2012). *Simulation and similarity: Using models to understand the world*. New York, NY: Oxford University Press.

Weisberg, M. and R. Muldoon (2009). Epistemic landscapes and the division of cognitive labor. *Philosophy of Science* 76(2), 225–252.

West, C. and D. H. Zimmerman (1987). Doing gender. *Gender & Society* 1(2), 125–151.

West, J. D., J. Jacquet, M. King, S. Correll, and C. Bergstrom (2013). The role of gender in scholarly authorship. *PLoS ONE* 8(7).

Williams, W. L. (1992). *The spirit and the flesh: Sexual diversity in American Indian culture*. Boston, MA: Beacon Press.

Wimsatt, W. C. (2012). Robustness, reliability, and overdetermination (1981). In Lena Soler, Emiliano Trizio, Thomas Nickles, and William Wimsatt (eds), *Characterizing the Robustness of Science*, pp. 61–87. Berlin/Heidelberg: Springer.

Wood, W. and A. H. Eagly (2002). A cross-cultural analysis of the behavior of women and men: Implications for the origins of sex differences. *Psychological Bulletin* 128(5), 699.

Wood, W. and A. H. Eagly (2012). Biosocial construction of sex differences and similarities in behavior. *Advances in Experimental Social Psychology* 46(1), 55–123.

Yaari, M. E. and M. Bar-Hillel (1984). On dividing justly. *Social Choice and Welfare* 1(1), 1–24.

Yinger, J. (1986). Measuring racial discrimination with fair housing audits: Caught in the act. *The American Economic Review* 76(5), 881–893.

Young, H. P. (1993a). The evolution of conventions. *Econometrica: Journal of the Econometric Society* 61(1), 57–84.

Young, H. P. (1993b). An evolutionary model of bargaining. *Journal of Economic Theory* 59(1), 145–168.

Young, H. P. (2001). *Individual strategy and social structure: An evolutionary theory of institutions*. Princeton, NJ: Princeton University Press.

Young, H. P. (2015). The evolution of social norms. *Annual Review of Economics* 7, 359–387.

Zollman, K. J. (2007). The communication structure of epistemic communities. *Philosophy of Science* 74(5), 574–587.

# Index